Industrial Subcontracting in the UK and Japan

JOHN T. THOBURN
University of East Anglia

MAKOTO TAKASHIMA
University of Nagasaki

Avebury

Aldershot · Brookfield USA · Hong Kong · Singapore · Sydney

© J.T. Thoburn 1992 [except chapter 7];
M. Takashima 1992 [chapter 7]

Published by
Avebury
Ashgate Publishing Limited
Gower House
Croft Road
Aldershot
Hants GU11 3HR
England

Ashgate Publishing Company
Old Post Road
Brookfield
Vermont 05036
USA

A CIP catalogue record for this book is available from the British Library and the US Library of Congress

ISBN 1 85628 347 X

Printed in Great Britain by
Billing & Sons Ltd, Worcester

Contents

Preface

This monograph is based on a research project "Industrial subcontracting: a comparative study of the United Kingdom and Japan", financed by the Economic and Social Research Council (UK) under research grant R000232650, which is gratefully acknowledged. The project was carried out in parallel with, though independently of, another project at the University of East Anglia's Economic Research Centre, "Subcontracting and the Small Business", which was financed under the ESRC's Small Business Initiative, and conducted by P.M. Townroe, B.R. Lyons and S.W. Davies. I should like to thank Peter Townroe for his encouragement of my suggestion to establish a related project. I am also grateful to Bruce Lyons for making various findings of the parallel project available at an early stage, and to Susan Bailey and Janet Anderson of the Economics Research Centre for research assistance - while absolving them all, and the ESRC, of responsibility for the final product.

The present project was conceived at a time when increased subcontracting was starting to attract attention in British industry as a means of improving international competitiveness. Such attention has been focused by the Partnership Sourcing Initiative of the Confederation of British Industry, and the work of the Department of Trade and Industry on partnership purchasing under its "Managing into the 90s" programme. Japan, it seemed, might have lessons to offer based on its long experience of subcontracting relations, and a widespread belief that these were part of the explanation of its export successes. The main thesis of this book will be that, although the underlying economic and technological reasons for subcontracting have changed to some extent, sheer competitive pressure has pushed British firms towards the use of already existing but hitherto unexploited opportunities to use subcontractors. This has prompted a search for more effective means of organizing subcontracting relations. Here there is the most to learn from the Japanese, while recognising that some of Japanese practice depends on unique social and cultural characteristics.

The core of the research was an interviewing programme of companies in Japan and the UK, both principals and subcontractors. The Japanese interviewing programme was largely organized by Makoto Takashima, then of Tsukuba University near Tokyo, who had been an academic visitor at UEA for the 1989-90 academic year. It was carried out while I was an academic visitor at Tsukuba in the autumn term of 1990. Shigeru Fujita of Showa Ota & Company in Tokyo also deserves thanks for arranging some extremely useful interviews. In addition, I am grateful to Hiro Odagiri of Tsukuba for discussions on subcontracting, and to Yoshio and Fumi Inoue for their kind hospitality. I am also grateful to May Wong of Hong Kong City Polytechnic for interpreting for me in Japanese in an interview in Hong Kong. The British interviews were done by myself over the period August 1990 to September 1991, and Makoto Takashima did some additional interviewing in Japan in 1991. We should like to thank all our interviewees, both companies and officials, who gave generously of their time. Also, I should like to thank Mari Sako of the London School of Economics for useful discussion, and for giving me permission to cite material from her doctoral thesis on subcontracting in electronics (Sako, 1990; forthcoming as Sako, 1992).

The approach of the book is essentially qualitative, although it has been conducted against the "large numbers" background provided for the UK by the parallel UEA project, and for Japan by the extensive published statistics of the Small and Medium Enterprise Agency of the Japanese Ministry of International Trade and Industry. Qualitative research is more often pursued in areas of the social sciences other than economics. I would argue that economists would gain a deeper understanding of many economic processes by using qualitative approaches to precede and supplement their more usual quantitative methods. Chapters 1, 2 and 3 cover theories and empirical evidence on subcontracting, and introduce material on the three industries chosen for study. Chapters 4, 5, and 6 use the interview material to examine issues related to decisions about subcontracting, how it is organized and monitored, and how it works for the subcontractors themselves. Chapter 8 provides conclusions.

Originally, the intention was that Professor Takashima and I would work jointly on the whole project. This thoroughgoing cooperation was prevented by a serious and prolonged illness on Takashima's part. Happily, he now has recovered sufficiently to contribute a piece setting out a Japanese view of the essentials of the subcontracting relationship. This is included as chapter 7, and it also will form part of a longer work on subcontracting which he plans to publish in Japanese. He takes full responsibility for chapter 7, and I for the rest of the book.

I am grateful to Kyoshi Shiratori for translating material for me from Japanese, and to Kurumi Shiratori for introducing me to the Japanese language. I should like to thank Danielle Barwick for typing part of the manuscript, and Sue Rowell for preparing the book as camera-ready copy. Finally, and subject to the usual disclaimer, I should like to thank for comments on parts of the manuscript: Chris Edwards, Shaun Hargreaves Heap, Serap Kayatekin, Judith Mehta and Chris Starmer, all of UEA; Peter Townroe, now with Sheffield Polytechnic, and Nigel Halliday of Norwich.

J.T.T.
UEA, Norwich
May 1992

1 Introduction

Industrial subcontracting is the provision, by one firm to another, of relatively specialized inputs, which are then incorporated into the final product of the buying firm. These inputs are distinguished from inputs of a standard kind, such as raw materials or electric power, which can be purchased on the open market (1). It has the implication of a continuing (though not necessarily continuous) relation between the buying firm (or 'principal') and the subcontractor, which may be backed by legal contract, or trust, or both. Often, though not always, the supplying firm may be small in relation to the principal, and issues of differential power relations can arise. Industries comprising several tiers of firms are an established feature of most Western economies, the first tier consisting of large firms making or assembling the final product, with lower tiers supplying components and services. While Britain, and other industrial countries, have faced increasing difficulties in international competition, Japan has established a leading position as an exporter of products such as motor cars and consumer electronics. Attention has focused on Japan's system of subcontracting as one source of its competitiveness, especially in the motor industry, where it has been associated with new management techniques such as 'just in time' supply of components. The high degree of trust and commitment between principal and subcontractor in Japan also has been seen as promoting innovation within a secure relationship.

Section 1 looks at how the issue of subcontracting has arisen as part of a more general debate on changes in industrial societies and the international economy since the 1970s. Section 2 considers subcontracting from the viewpoint of economic analysis, with particular reference to transactions costs, while section 3 asks how external pressures on firms may alter the underlying determinants of subcontracting identified by transactions cost theory.

1.1 Subcontracting, flexible specialization, and Britain's international competitiveness

Subcontracting has come to the attention of a wide academic audience

1

through the debates on 'flexible specialization' in the so-called 'post-Fordist' era, following the work of Piore and Sabel (1984). Piore and Sabel argue that a 'crisis of mass production' has been associated with major changes in the world economic environment - the end of the post-war boom following the 1970s oil crises, the restrictionist macro-economic policy at the end of that decade and in the early 1980s, and the apparent failure of Keynesian demand management. Also important have been the growth of competition from newly industrializing countries to established industrial producers, the growing volatility and differentiation of consumer good markets, and accelerated technical change, especially in electronics technology.

Mass production (or 'Fordism'), 'the manufacture of standardized products in high volumes using special-purpose machinery and predominantly unskilled labour' is contrasted with craft production, or flexible specialization (Hirst and Zeitlin, 1991, p.2). According to Piore and Sabel, a craft tradition continued alongside mass production methods as they became became dominant in the twentieth century. Small firms could exist alongside mass production in a dualistic economic structure, taking up the slack of demand fluctuations for the larger firms, in subordinate fashion. The craft tradition, however, was based on innovative firms, often small but not necessarily so, producing non-standardized products. An essential dimension was the development of cooperative relations between firms, such as existed in industrial districts like Lyon, in France, in the 19th century (and until the 1960s) with its silk industry. Sometimes these cooperative relations would be in the form of networks of highly specialized small firms, others might involve a larger firm organizing production in association with smaller firms. Subcontracting relations within this system depended on verbal contracts and trust (Piore and Sabel, 1984, ch.2). Piore and Sabel see the renewed development of the craft tradition, in the form of flexible specialization, as a means by which industrial countries can regenerate their industries, coping with volatile consumer demand, and reducing the threat of low-cost Third World competition in standard manufactures. It is also an alternative to the relocation of Western industry to less developed countries under the 'new international division of labour' (2). Piore and Sabel stress the role of flexible specialization in the success of regions like Emilia-Romagna in the Third Italy (3). The Italian garment and footwear industries are examples where activities, which might seem to lend themselves to labour-intensive Third World production, have competed by being closely attuned to fashion changes and by the development of highly flexible machinery (Piore and Sabel, 1984, pp.226-9). It must also be said, though, that success in these industries in some cases also has been due to the ability of subcontracting to tap into the informal economy of lower cost (and non-unionised) labour employed in small firms or as outworkers, the Spanish footwear industry being an example. In Emilia-Romagna too, the process of decentralization to small firms was partly to escape union power in the 1960s (Portes et al, 1989, pp.23-5).

Flexible specialization has generated a large literature and many criticisms (4). Based on networks of firms in industrial districts, it represents something of an ideal type, and it is not always clear how actual practice conforms to it. Much Japanese production, for example of machine tools, is mass production based on high volumes, and may seem hard to claim as an example of flexible specialization, as Piore and Sabel do. However, it is highly vertically disintegrated, and the supplier firms do seem to conform to flexible specialization notions

2

(Friedman, 1988, ch.4). Interesting, too, is that the expansion of that industry from the late 1970s was based on staking out a new market among smaller firms (such as those which act as subcontractors in the Japanese economy) for relatively cheap, computer-numerically-controlled ('CNC') machine tools, which could cope with frequent changes in product specification (see chapter 3; and Piore and Sabel, 1984, pp.216-220). However, it is not the aim of this monograph to contribute to the flexible specialization debate more generally, but to consider the growth of subcontracting as part of an industrial strategy to cope with difficult times for British industry.

In the introduction to a widely-quoted set of essays, Reversing Industrial Decline?, Hirst and Zeitlin (1989) chronicle the decline in British international competitiveness, particularly since the early 1970s, and the start of virtual 'deindustrialization'. This decline is seen in terms of poor product development, failure to see the importance of non-price competition, and failure to utilize new technology effectively. Also important, they argue (p.7), has been the tendency of British management to think in terms of efficiency gains from competition to the exclusion of the value of collaboration and mutual assistance between firms. British firms have tended to stress cut-throat competition, and firms have been isolated from others except for purely market relations.

Changes in attitudes in British industry, particularly dating from the recession of the early 1980s, and now again during the current recession (1990-2), have been apparent, however. In a report commissioned by the National Economic Development Office and the Ministry of Employment, Atkinson and Meager (1986) discuss the need for firms to increase their 'flexibility' in the face of the sorts of pressures identified in the flexible specialization debate. Though primarily concerned with employment policy, the report has wider implications. Changing labour practices are seen as necessary to allow firms to generate productivity gains in the face of increased international competition, to allow for a more effective response to markets which are more volatile, and to adapt to (and facilitate the introduction of) new technology in circumstances where technical change has accelerated. Among their concerns are methods of increasing flexibility in the number of workers, and in the tasks they perform, but also alternatives to flexibility within the firm, such as the use of subcontracting arrangements. Atkinson and Meager write of a 'flexible firm' consisting of a core group of workers surrounded by peripheral groups who may not be employees, but employed by subcontractors. They find, in an investigation of four sectors (5), that over 70% of firms surveyed had increased their use of 'distancing strategies', of which subcontracting was the most important. Of this 70%, over half had increased their subcontracting beyond the putting out of ancillary services (catering, cleaning, etc) to non-ancillary areas like component manufacture. This raises the fundamental issue of what indeed should be the core of a firm, to which the next section turns.

1.2 Subcontracting and the economics of transactions costs

While flexible specialization issues have caught the imagination of a wide variety of social scientists, economists have tended to conconcentrate on what constitutes the efficient (vertical) boundary of the firm (6), using the transactions cost framework pioneered by Coase

(7), and developed by Oliver Williamson (8). Increased interest by companies in exploring possibilities for expanding subcontracting can be seen in these terms as a concern with how better to delimit their core business.

Subcontracting represents an intermediate position between using the market and organizing all stages of production within the firm (i.e. complete vertical integration). A classic paper by Richardson (1972) explains why firms are not all vertically integrated, and why the market mechanism is not the only alternative to vertical integration (9). A firm derives its competitive strength from its comparative advantage in performing particular activities. These capabilities may involve knowledge and experience of using a technology, but they could also consist of knowledge of (or reputation in) a particular market (such as that of Marks and Spencer in the retail trade). A firm's growth might also be mapped out by such capabilities, which may be relatively narrow in scope (and difficult for other firms to replicate) (Nelson and Winter, 1982, pp.134, 119). Different stages of a production process may involve activities which, though complementary, are not similar (i.e. they involve different capabilities). Building houses gives a firm no particular skill at making bricks. The problem is further complicated if different stages are subject to economies of scale to different extents. These problems, which work against vertical integration, may simply be solved by using the market if the products produced upstream in the production chain are fairly standard, like bricks, with the producer of the intermediate product selling to a range of customer firms. If they are specific to the customer firm's requirements to any significant extent, a closer form of association may be suitable, in which obligations about future custom are given, to assure the supplier. This is especially so if the supplier must invest in narrowly specialized skills or equipment to meet the customer's needs. (Richardson, 1972, pp.885-7).

However justified subcontracting may be (compared to vertical integration) in terms of the reduction of production costs, Williamsonian transactions cost economics suggest there may be other influences, which limit it. Economic actors are assumed to behave with opportunism, exploiting advantages over their partners, and breaking promises, if they think they can get away with it. Firms are limited in their knowledge, and can therefore only act rationally the limits of that knowledge (bounded rationality). The information a principal has, for example, on a subcontractor's costs, may be less than the subcontractor herself possesses. A principal may hesitate, therefore, to be dependent on a subcontractor for a vital input even if in-house production costs are higher; a subcontractor may hesitate to make a highly specific investment, fearing the principal may try to extract unreasonable terms once the investment has been made. Legal contracts do not in themselves solve the problem. With uncertainty, contracts cannot specify all contingent events. There is a problem of post-contractual opportunism, where a contract may be worth breaking, and a contracting party's bad faith may be hard to prove in court (Klein et al, 1978). Societies where there can be more reliance on trust - and which have effective social sanctions against bad behaviour - may therefore be more conducive to subcontracting than those which rely on legal sanctions. Thus Williamson (1985, pp.122-3) argues that subcontracting in Japan, though dependent on the same transactions cost considerations as elsewhere, is more extensive because of such social checks, and he notes the much lower propensity in Japan to litigate, at least compared to the

4

United States.

Given that the principal has less information than the subcontractor about the latter's costs and performance, there is a problem for the principal in monitoring the behaviour of the subcontractor (who can be regarded as acting as the principal's agent), for example with regard to the care the subcontractor takes over quality control or in really striving for cost reduction. This means that there are control costs for the principal in using a subcontractor, to be set against the saving in production cost (Lewis and Sappington, 1991, pp.888-890) (10). These monitoring problems could be lessened by an investment of time and effort by the principal in the careful selection and training of subcontractors. Japanese inward investors in the UK have acquired a reputation for such selection, for instance (NEDC, 1991a; NEDC, 1991b; Trevor and Christie, 1988). Monitoring subcontractors routinely may also be facilitated by geographical proximity. Internal provision of the activity by the principal, of course, would also have costs in the form of the 'incentive and bureaucratic disabilities' of internal organization (Williamson, 1985, p.163).

The Williamsonian approach would hypothesise that, if the necessary capital assets are sufficiently specific to render open market transactions unsuitable (11), subcontracting then would be less likely, the more specific are the assets required, subject to the problem of economies of scale. In general, economies of scale will push a principal towards using subcontracting, while asset specificity pushes towards in-house production. If scale economies are large, a principal producing in-house might have to consider entering the market as a component supplier; this would be more difficult the more specific were the product to the principal's needs and the more specific the equipment for producing it (12). If such sale to other customers is possible, subcontracting might be preferred. These issues arises in the motor industry (see chapter 5); some components, such as gear boxes, are sold by some manufacturers to rivals in a highly oligopolistic industry, but there are also specialist suppliers of components who are very large companies, both in the UK and Japan. Where capital assets are highly specific, but the production of the component is not subject to significant scale economies, in-house production is likely to be preferred by the principal, although the decision could be modified if skills and experience are required to operate the equipment which the principal may not possess (13).

However, there appears to be a contradiction in the Williamsonian analyis in that, while economies of scale (with respect to assets of medium to low specificity) push a company towards subcontracting, subcontracting is widely associated with small and medium firms. This can be resolved to some extent by realizing that a capital-intensive small firm producing, say, a highly specialized engineering component, may reap economies of scale at an output beyond the needs of most principals. Also, small firms which gain subcontracting business on the basis of specialized expertise may be strengthened if technical change brings advanced-technology capital equipment within their reach. Thus technical change associated with a reduction in economies of scale might have ambiguous implications for subcontracting (Bollard, 1983, especially pp.46-8).

The efficient boundary of the firm can be viewed as delimiting its strategic core (14). Only transactions where there is high asset specificity and uncertainty should be governed within the core, to economise on transactions costs. These core assets consist not only of capital assets and human capital, but also locational advantages and 'dedicated assets', such as investment made to meet the needs of particular customer. Outside the core, the market should normally be used unless contractual difficulties make more specialized governance (i.e. organizational) structures necessary. Where the firm requires skills complementary to its core activities and these skills are of medium asset specificity, enough to make market relations unsuitable, there is a role for strategic alliances with other firms (15), including subcontracting relations with suppliers. Effective vertical positioning of the firm with respect to suppliers (and customers) can also increase its market power, as well as increasing efficiency in terms of transactions and production costs.

Firms need to give thought on how to protect and develop their core skills in a changing environment. Clearly one important aspect of the development of the strategic core is the maintenance of in-house innovative capacity with regard to a firm's core technology. This may sometimes be in conflict with considerations of short-term cost reduction (for example, as will be shown later, where computer companies have to choose between buying-in cheaper semiconductors or keeping their own capacity in order to be up to date with technology). Where innovation is required in several stages of the production process, and the technological capabilities required differ, in-house innovation by the principal may be less effective without coordination with other firms in the chain (Richardson, 1972, pp.892-5). Here formal legal contracts between the firms are likely to be insufficient to bring about the openness of cooperation required, and the constant contact. More 'relational contracting' (16) is needed for cooperative innovation, contracting of the sort commonly associated with Japan (17). Also, technological advances by the principal may require technology transfer to suppliers in order for them to meet the principal's requirements, again which are easier in a closer relationship expected to continue. In general, well-organized vertical relations may help solve problems associated with the appropriability of the gains from innovation; and more so than vertical integration, which loses the benefits of competition, and of the economies of scale in input production which allow the gains from input innovation to be reaped through sales (Geroski, 1992). Porter's work too, on the international competitiveness of nations, identifies the importance of related and supporting industries in enhancing comparative advantage in particular fields, and he stresses the role such industries play in innovation and the interchange of information between principals and suppliers (Porter, 1990, pp.100-107). MITI, the Japanese Ministry of International Trade and Industry, is quoted to the effect that 'Japanese manufacturing industry owes it competitive advantage and strength to its subcontracting structure' (cited Kawasaki and McMillan, 1987, pp.327-8)

1.3 How do external pressures on firms lead to more subcontracting?

The flexible specialization debate has suggested that pressures in the world economy have led to a resurgence of craft-type production, often though not necessarily based on small firms, and in which subcontracting and other types of inter-firm relations are important. It is plausible that some such pressures may favour regions or countries with a strong craft tradition based on networks of firms, say in reponding to a shifting market dominated by niches in which fashion is important.

However, what of an individual firm, say in Britain, perhaps quite vertically integrated with regard to its purchases of intermediate products? It may wish to change its behaviour, but will this include increased subcontracting?

Nelson and Winter's work on evolutionary economic change has made familiar the notion that 'a changing environment can force firms to risk their very survival on attempts to modify their routines', where 'routines' refer to the firm's ways of doing things and ways of determining what to do (Nelson and Winter, 1982, p.400) (18). Atkinson and Meager's (1986) study, cited above, has made familiar the fact that British firms have increased their use of subcontractors in attempts to become more 'flexible' (19). However, in principle, if we believe that subcontracting can be analysed most effectively in transaction cost terms, it would be reassuring to be able to trace any increase in subcontracting in Britain to changes in those underlying determinants. In other words, if rational decisions have already been made on in British industry on the efficient vertical boundary of the firm (i.e. make/buy decisions), how have the 'pressures for change' highlighted in the flexible specialization literature changed the relative transaction costs of the alternative organizational forms? What we should be looking for includes:
- has technical change changed economies of scale?
- has technical change affected differentially the production costs of principals and prospective subcontractors, for example by producing sophisticated equipment at a price within the range of small firms? (20)
- has technical change, by making capital assets more flexible, also made them less specific? This would also lessen the standard transactions cost problem that subcontractors might underinvest in specific assets and/or choose assets which were less specific but had higher production costs (21).
- has increased international competition taken the form of an accelerated product life cycle, with implications that firms need to compete by innovation in new product development? This may change subcontracting relations. It also highlights the fact that some firms may be initiating change in the world economy and others may be reponding to it in more of a passive fashion .

In general, the extreme pressures faced by British companies in the recession of the early 1980s and the current recession (1990-92), have put them into a position where decisions about changing their organization are not marginal ones in search of extra profit, but decisions about survival. Japanese companies also faced pressures after 1970s oil shocks, and again after the appreciation of the yen exchange rate from the mid 1980s. It will be argued later on the basis of the interviews, that there is evidence that it is not only that underlying factors like asset specificity and economies of scale have changed, but also that the severe pressures from overseas competition and domestic deflation (admittedly in the context of rapid technical change) have forced British firms to look at already-existing opportunities to reduce costs by subcontracting, which hitherto has been unexploited because of lack of trust between companies. The very recent interest on the part on bodies such as the Confederation of British Industry, the Department of Trade and Industry, and the National Economic Development Council in improved supply chain management, partnership sourcing, and similar areas, all point to a recognition of the possibilities for improved British competitiveness if interfirm relations could be improved (e.g. CBI, 1991; DTI, 1990a, 1991b; NEDC, 1990a) (22). This applies both to

7

industries with a long history of outsourcing, such as motor vehicles, and to industries which have increased their outsourcing recently, such as machine tools.

NOTES

1. The term 'subcontracting' is used by some companies in Britain to refer to the handing over of the complete product to another firm to produce, when the first firm has insufficient capacity to deal with a temporarily high volume of orders. This is 'overflow' subcontracting, and it is discussed further in chapter 2. Sometimes, too, companies use 'subcontracting' to refer exclusively to a situation where the principal supplies, and maintains ownership, of the materials the subcontractor uses. This 'free-issuing' of materials indeed is the basis for the measure of subcontracting used in the UK Census of Production (see chapter 3). **The term supplier, unless otherwise made clear, is used in this study to include all suppliers of inputs, standard or not (i.e. as a generic term, including subcontractors).** We also use the term **outsourcing** to refer to the buying-in of inputs from suppliers. In Japan, there is sometimes a splitting into three: suppliers of standard items; subcontractors who are large and technologically independent enough to have considerable bargaining power in relation to the purchasing company (who are then referred to as 'suppliers', and in whom the purchasing company may hold some equity - see Aoki, 1988, pp.208-210); and 'subcontractors' proper (shitauke, in Japanese). This three-way split, though possibly confusing for readers, will appear in chapters 4, 5, and 6, as it is used by various interviewees.

2. The standard work on the new international division of labour is Frobel et al (1980). Relocation takes place in order to access low labour costs, often in particularly labour-intensive stages of a production process, rather than the whole product. Generous investment incentives provided by Third World countries, often in the form of free-trade-zones, have also influenced relocation to some extent. For an up-to-date, and sceptical, assessment of the prospects for NIDL investment, see Kaplinsky (1991).

3. The Third Italy refers to the villages and small cities of the central and north-east part of the country, for example around Bologna. The contrast is with the established industrial regions (centered on Milan and Turin, and Genoa), and the Italian south (Schmitz, 1989, p.7).

4. Sayer (1989) gives one of the most useful discussions of what flexibility and flexible specialization mean in practice, and also whether Japan can be fitted into these moulds. A very detailed survey is provided by Hirst and Zeitlin (1991), who stress distinctions between several schools of 'post-Fordist' literature and the literature on flexible specialization. They contrast both to a 'regulationist' literature which looks at long-term trends in capitalism and tries to combine flexible specialization with 'the systemmatic nature of capitalism as a mode of production and the centrality of class struggle in its development'(p.18). One of

their criticisms is the tendency of some writers to see flexible specialization as a passive reaction to the collapse of mass markets and to technical change and increased, and to underestimate the ability of producers using flexible specialization stategies to influence their environment. For some other discussions of flexible specialization, see Schmitz (1989) and Meegan (1988). Schmitz also discusses the relevance of flexible specialization to the Third World.

5.   Engineering, food and drink, retail distribution, and financial services.

6.   The horizontal boundary of the firm would involve considerations of, for example, horizontal merger to increase market power, or diversification into unrelated activities to spread risk or as a channel of growth.

7.   Coase (1937) had explained the existence of firms by the advantages they offered in terms of economising on transactions costs.   To take the example of Adam Smith's pin makers, the existence of pin-making firms would avoid the need for each final consumer of pins to transact through the market with each individual worker of the pin-making process. The firm in this sense acts to replace a product market (selling the output of each individual worker in the process) with a factor market (for the workers' services) (Cheung, 1983, p.3). The size of the firm reached a limit where the extra cost of organizing a transaction within the firm became equal to that of organizing it through the market mechanism.

8.   See Williamson (1975) for a basic analysis of transactions cost economics. Williamson (1985) incorporates a wide range of his subsequent papers. Williamson's introduction to Aoki et al (1990; pp.1-25) gives a useful literature review.

9.   Although Williamson rightly is given most of the credit for developing transactions cost economics from the basis of Coase's original (and now Nobel prize-winning) contribution, I am struck on rereading Richardson's paper after a twenty years gap, by how far Richardson's work anticipates most of the later economic analysis of subcontracting, except for the latter's stress on the likelihood of opportunistic behaviour by the parties involved. Richardson notes the importance of subcontracting, and other forms of cooperation, in facilitating innovation in dissimilar but complementary areas (discussed further above). He also notes that inter-firm relationships based on mutual obligation can be found in circumstances where specific assets are not involved - a point on which Williamson has been criticised by Dore (1983, pp.179-80), who notes that 'obligational relational contracting' is found in Japan with respect to highly standard commodities like steel.

10.   Note, though, that the interesting test of transactions cost theory in relation to the US motor industry by Walker and Weber (1984), found that the relative production costs of subcontracting vs in-house production tended to be better at explaining make/buy decisions about components than were variables proxying

transactions costs (p.387).The latter included indicators of technological uncertainty, and the experience of the motor company with the equipment a subcontractor would need to make the component. However, the components studied were all relatively simple ones.

11. There is a continuum from purely market transactions to increasingly close forms of cooperation. A purely market transaction would be one which gave no consideration given to any similar transactions in the future. We move along the continuum as expectations are raised and obligations incurred about subsequent transactions (Richardson, 1972, p.887). The Williamsonian account also mentions <u>frequency</u> as an important dimension of transactions (along with asset specificity and uncertainty) - in the sense that only recurrent transactions will support a specialized governance structure (Williamson, 1985, pp.72-3).

12. Clearly, some highly specific products could be produced by equipment (and human skills) which could be turned easily to other uses. Equipment and skills apparently specific to a principal's needs might be usable, with modification and time, for other customers. If the equipment and skills really were totally specific, the subcontractor would not be able to reap any economies of scale by supplying to other customers! In this case, only vertically integrated production would make sense.

13. An example in advance from the company interviews in Britain can serve to illustrate this point (see also chapter 4). An engineering subcontractor received an order to produce a key (and totally specific) part for a fountain pen, and had to purchase equipment to do it for which it could see no alternative use. The subcontractor was willing to make the investment because the pen work would be only a small part of its turnover, and because it thought it would take the principal some months to work up another subcontractor who would fully meet requirements. The subcontractor also tolerated not having any form of long-term contract in these circumstances (and the principal's decision at the beginning to opt for single-sourcing could be regarded as a form of <u>credible commitment</u> - see Williamson, 1985, ch.7) The principal had subcontracted in order to use the subcontractor's engineering capabilities, and the physical assets though specific were not expensive or subject to economies of scale. However, the principal appeared to be showing some signs of worry on being dependent on the one supplier for a vital part, and was making approaches to buy an equity stake in the subcontractor - an example very near the margin of vertical integration, and one where human assets had been decisive.

14. This paragraph depends heavily on Reve (1990), who tries to integrate transactions cost economics with the business strategy literature, in his analysis of the strategic core of a firm.

15. Reve's analysis is wider than the vertical boundary of the firm, and he also considers alliances involving horizontal and diversified relations.

16. Williamson (in Aoki et al, 1990, pp.3-4) argues that the term 'contract' as employed by economists to cover a wide range of undertakings and relations between firms (and other economic actors), should be replaced by the term 'treaty', which does not have the same legal overtones.

17. However, it is worth noting in advance that, while the Japanese firms interviewed tended to have contracts which were to a large extent very general and ritualistic, contracts were sometimes highly specific with regard to the secrecy of technology revealed to subcontractors during the relationship. Indeed, the very first Japanese company interviewed had been in process of litigation over technology ownership! [For further discussion of this case, see chapter 7, by Makoto Takashima].

18. Nelson and Winter's work is primarily concerned with technological rather than organizational change, but they note, in relation to a brief discussion of Williamsonian transactions costs, that '.. in principle, an evolutionary theory can treat organizational innovation just as it treats technical innovation' (pp.36-38).

19. See also the study by Pinch et al (1991), which notes increases in subcontracting, while also commenting that increases in functional flexiblility (increased ability to redeploy workers between tasks, and to new techniques) has led some firms (e.g. in electronics) to bring some tasks back in-house which previously were subcontracted (pp.212-4)

20. Technical change which affects principal and subcontractor equally is likely to lead to more in-house production, by lessening the absolute production cost differential between principal and subcontractor (Lewis and Sappington, 1991).

21. Capital goods which are apparently more flexible do not necessarily generate more flexibility for the subcontractor. Indeed, they may make the subcontractor more dependent on seeking large volume-work. This point was made to me by several small, but apparently successful British engineering subcontractors, who commented that firms who had gone over heavily to CNC equipment in the early 1980s had found themselves less flexible in the face of demand fluctuations. Highly cost-effective production, they claimed, could be achieved with specially modified, more traditional machines. Sayer (1989) makes some similar comments.

22. Note that this interest is fairly recent, however. For example, the study by the NEDC in the mid-1980s of the financial aspects of industrial restructuring had virtually nothing to say on these issues (NEDC, 1986).

2 Subcontracting in the United Kingdom and Japan

2.1 Subcontracting in the UK

The increase in subcontracting in British industry found by Atkinson and Meager's (1986) survey has been mentioned in the previous chapter. There is some evidence that the extent of industrial subcontracting already may have been greater in Western industrial countries generally than first suspected before the current wave of interest (UNIDO, 1974, ch.4). There is also a wide range of fragmentary but accumulating published evidence that there have been increases over the last twenty years (1).

Substantial recent increases in subcontracting in British industry have been found by the survey conducted by the parallel research project at the University of East Anglia, 'Subcontracting and the Small Business'. This covered engineering, broadly defined to include mechanical and electrical engineering, and transport equipment, which accounts for about a third of UK manufacturing GDP (CSO, 1991c) (2). It was found that 50% of principals had increased the proportion of inputs put out to subcontractors in the last five years (by an average of 47%), 32% recorded no change, and only 18% recorded decreases (which averaged 26%) (3)

The survey also yielded some interesting information on the extent to which transactions cost variables can explain why firms (as our interviews will show) are interested in increasing subcontracting. According to Lyons (1991b, p.6), 33% of the significant inputs mentioned by principals as being produced in-house, compared to 62% of the inputs chosen as examples of significant subcontracted inputs, are subject to economies of scale [actual economies of scale in the case of the subcontracted input, and potential economies of scale if the in-house input's production were to be doubled]. Of course, some of these in-house inputs subject to economies of scale may be produced in-house because they require specific assets. However, Lyons writes (p.10): 'only [sic] 56% of in-house inputs with non-specific technologies exhibited economies of scale, compared to 80% of those with a specific technology'. While this difference certainly is reassuring from the point of view of transactions cost economics (i.e. in explaining which

12

inputs are more likely to be subcontracted), the fact that over half of the in-house inputs with non-specific technologies had economies of scale suggests that there is considerable scope for further outsourcing if monitoring arrangements could be improved.

One key factor in deciding to subcontract, as suggested in the previous chapter, is the degree of trust between companies (4). In a study of British and French engineering companies, Lorenz (1989) (5) notes the much closer relations between French companies and their subcontractors, and the much greater sense or responsibility felt by French principals. In contrast, British subcontractors in Lorenz's study said they had been encouraged by large principals to invest, and then had not been given sufficient orders.

It has been argued by various commentators (e.g. by UNIDO, 1974, p.6) that a distinction should be made between different types of subcontracting:
-economic, or cost-saving, subcontracting,
-capacity, or overflow, subcontracting,
-specialized subcontracting.
Whilst 'economic' subcontracting can be defined (as it was by UNIDO) to include cases of subcontracting to reap economies of scale, a more useful definition is narrower and centres on subcontracting as a way of taking advantage of segmented labour markets, and perhaps itself contributing to that segmentation in an attempt to bypass trade unions. Specialized subcontracting essentially is the sort with which the previous chapter has been concerned. Overflow subcontracting to some extent, like 'economic' subcontracting, tends to imply a subordinate status for the subcontractor.

In its survey of subcontracting in industrial countries in the late 1960s, UNIDO noted that, while subcontracting in the USA is considered important:

> In the United Kingdom, on the other hand, the pattern of industry is generally firmly established, and subcontracting has little influence on the country's industrialization. Subcontracting is generally of the capacity type, to make up for insufficient capacity in the large companies and especially to absorb production overloads.(UNIDO, 1974,p.58)

There must be some doubt about this finding, given that the UK motor industry, at least, has had a long history of specialized outsourcing (see chapters 3 and 5). In any case, it does seem that the increase in subcontracting has taken the form of speciality subcontracting, at least in the broadly defined engineering industry covered in the University of East Anglia survey, and from the evidence of the interviews to be presented. Lyons and Bailey (1991) report that special expertise and technology received the largest number of mentions when British subcontractors were asked what they considered to be the major sources of their competitive advantage over in-house production by principals.

Nor does cheap labour appear to be a major factor in the reasons for British engineering subcontracting. Only a third of British subcontractors in the UEA survey thought they had access to cheaper labour (with reasons equally split between a lower degree of unionization,lower overheads, and being in a geographically low-wage area). None of the subcontractors thought low-cost labour was their most important advantage (Lyons and Bailey, 1991). As the next section will show, this is often argued to be an important difference between the UK

13

and Japan.

The apparent absence of subcontracting based on cheap labour is important in view of the long-running debate as to whether the small-firm sector represents a dualistic aspect of the economy, based particularly on segmented labour markets. Industrial subcontracting with small, peripheral firms, often has been considered by both mainstream and Marxist writers to be an anachronistic feature of industrial societies, associated with outworking, and the use of marginalized labour, and which would disappear during the process of economic development (6). However, Galbraith (e.g.1977, ch.2) has highlighted the continuing difference between the large firm and small firm sector in the United States, arguing that the large firms can control their environment to some extent, whereas the small firms are subject to market forces and are much more constrained in their opportunities.

Dualism, too, can vary within a country, both in the sense of there being some industries which are more prone to the use of cheap labour than others, and in the sense that the variation in wages between firms within an industry may be greater for some industries than others (7). Of the industries identified as 'traditional subcontracting sectors' (e.g.automobiles, mechanical engineering, electrical and electronic engineering, shipbuilding) (UNIDO, 1974, p.61) (8), highly labour-intensive sectors like textiles and clothing (and in some countries, footwear) seem prone to dualism, in both senses. Thus, while the textile and clothing industries have seen a resurgence in Europe based apparently on the 'flexible specialization' techniques of such companies as Benetton (Murray, 1985, p.30), it also seems as if the clothing industry depends in part at least on tapping into low-cost female labour from ethnic minorities in Britain (Mitter, 1986). Lloyd's (1988) study of textiles in the West Midlands also regards the industry as having growing dualism, with innovation in certain aspects making for further differentiation between firms. Even the retail clothing (and food) chain, Marks and Spencer, the most famous and most apparently successful British example of the use of subcontracting (Tse, 1985), has been criticised. Rainnie (1984, p.149) notes the importance of small firms in the British garments industry, and argues that Marks and Spencer's suppliers are tightly squeezed on their profits, and have to accept an extreme degree of control in exchange for no more than batch-to-batch contracts (9).

Labour market segmentation is often, though not necessarily, associated with the existence of a substantial sector of small firms within an economy (10). Britain in the 1960s had one of the smallest sectors of small firms (establishments employing less than 100 workers) (11) in the industrialized world, according to the findings of the 1971 Bolton Committee of Enquiry on Small Firms (Marsden, 1990, p.226). Since then the size of the sector has grown considerably - a trend common to most industrial countries, but especially pronounced in Britain (Sengenberger et al, 1990, p.11). By the early 1980s, the share of small businesses (enterprises of under 100 workers) in total manufacturing employment in the UK was larger than in the US or Germany, though still well below the Japanese and Italian figures (Sengenberger et al, 1990, pp.12-13). Table 2.1 presents a comparison between the UK and Japan for 1988.

Although there is some evidence of labour market segmentation in the UK, as in other industrial countries (McNabb and Ryan, 1990), the growth of the small firm sector in the UK seems to have been accompanied by a reduction in wage differentials for comparable workers by size of firm

14

(see Marsden, 1990, pp.232-4 - who uses evidence from engineering) (12).
How much of the development of the small firm sector can be traced to
subcontracting is uncertain. Much of the evidence dates from the early
1970s, and indicated that small firms generally were independent
(Marsden, 1990, p.228-9). Also, where small firms started by being
dependent on a few, larger customer-firms, this dependence tended
quickly to lessen over time (Mason, 1987, p.137). Nevertheless, the
situation appears to have changed since the 1970s. Significant evidence
of increased use, by large firms, of small firms as subcontractors has
already been cited, Other factors may be important too in the growth of
the British small firm sector, such as self-employment growth during
recessions and technical change improving small firm competitiveness.
The UK appears to lack the networks of small firms found in Italian-
style flexible-specialization production (Sengenberger et al, 1990,
ch.1; Szarka, 1990). The 'dualism' issue of whether small firms are
exploited by larger firms, or are more independent innovative entities,
has been discussed more for Japan than for the UK. Evidence for the UK
suggests that it has been mainly small firms (in this case, under 500
workers), and very large ones (10,000+) who have been most active in
technical innovation, and that the performance of small firms in this
regard has improved since the 1950s (Marsden, 1990, p.251) .
  Note too that the labour market segmentation hypothesis only implies
that peripheral workers are exploited - their employers could do well -
but there is often an implication (especially for Japan), that the
peripheral employers are also at a disadvantage.

Table 2.1
Shares of Small and Medium Firms in Manufacturing Employment and
Output, UK and Japan, 1988

	Percentage of Total Employment	Percentage of Total Gross Output
UK		
1-99 employees	28.2	21.2
1-299 employees	47.9	39.2
Japan		
5-99 employees	52.2	33.6
5-299 employees	72.9	52.4

Sources: CSO (1989a, PA1002), SMEA (1990b)
Notes: The totals, on which the Japanese percentages are based, do not
include firms of 1-4 employees either. According to MITI (1990, p.170)
such firms employed 13.9% of the total Japanese manufacturing workforce
in 1986-7. The British output shares are given in gross output terms to
facilitate comparison with the Japanese statistics, but the differences
between the British gross and net output shares are minimal.

2.2 Subcontracting in Japan

Discussions of subcontracting in Japan are usually linked to an interest in the small firm sector, whose growth has been closely associated with the dualistic development pattern of the economy in the past. Among major industrial countries only Italy has a small firm sector of comparable relative size, and no country's small firms have attracted so much domestic academic and political attention as Japan's (13).

Broadbridge (1966, p.9) has argued that the forced pace of Japanese industrial development after the country was opened to Western contact in the second half of the 19th century made the growth of dualism almost inevitable. Fearing that it might suffer the same dismemberment as China as the hands of the Western powers, Meiji Japan resolved to build 'a rich country, a strong army'. Sales of state businesses to the private sector in the 1880s facilitated the development of Japan's great business combines, the zaibatsu. Scarce capital resources were concentrated on big business through the banking mechanism, closely tied to the zaibatsu, and encouraged by government. Meanwhile, a secondary sector of small firms developed to cater for the consumption needs of the population, whose surprisingly substantial savings were channeled through the financial system to large companies. The small firm sector also served to take up labour leaving agriculture. From about the time of the First World War, wage differentials grew up between small and large firms, especially as a result of labour militancy in the latter, and the large firms also introduced a seniority wage system to try to limit labour turnover (Paine, 1971, pp.115-7), a system which was the forerunner of the highly structured internal labour markets of large Japanese firms today (Aoki, 1990). Subcontracting relations between large and small firms seem to have developed in the 1930s, as the economy moved on to a war footing. During the Second World War, extensive subcontracting developed, especially in machinery production, as large firms looked to small firms to make good shortfalls in capacity (Friedman, 1988, ch.2).

The pattern of large firm domination of the economy was such that, prior to the Allies' attempt to break them up after 1945, the four largest zaibatsu (Mitsui, Mitsubishi, Sumitomo, and Yasuda) accounted for a quarter of all Japanese paid-up industrial capital (Broadbridge, 1966, p.37). The labour surplus after the war, the capital shortage, and a stress on rapid industrialization, combined to continue industrial dualism. To a significant extent the old zaibatsu reemerged in new guise, though joined in positions of economic power by large independent companies such as Hitachi, Matsushita, Nissan and Toyota. Such independent groupings, were the main company heads a vertical group of suppliers and subcontractors, are known as keiretsu, although of course the individual companies in the large, horizontal groups equally may form their own keiretsu's with vertically organized suppliers (14). Vertical grouping often involve formal assocations of suppliers, but long term relations may be maintained with suppliers who are not part of the keiretsu (Orru et al, 1989, p.555).

The fortunes of the small firm sector have been a major political issue in Japan. Popular with the military in the 1930s, who saw them as a source of support and a bastion of traditional values, they were encouraged before the Second World War to strengthen themselves by mergers. A dual structure was very clear by the 1950s, with large wage

16

differentials by size of firm. In 1957, for example, the economy was officially described as dualistic, and small firms as belonging to the 'pre-modern' sector (Koshiro, 1990, p.173). According to Friedman (1988, p. 166), 'the abuse by large firms of their subcontractors was one of the most significant political issues of the 1950s'.

The Small and Medium Enterprise Agency was established in 1957, to administer programmes for small business (15). The 1963 Basic Law for Small and Medium-Sized Enterprises established a legal definition of small and medium enterprises (SMEs) as firms of below 300 workers or Y50 million (later Y100 million) capital, and provided for various measures to help SMEs upgrade (Friedman, 1988, p.167). It also gave subcontractors a legal status, along with the SME size definition (Aoki, 1988, p.209).

Whether the dual economy persists has been the subject of much controversy. Friedman (1988) argues that the end of the labour surplus by the early 1960s caused wage differentials to be reduced between large firms and SMEs. He also believes that regional groupings of firms were important in enforcing better behaviour on principals, and there are strong regional concentrations of manufacturing with supporting institutions and services around them (McCormick, 1988). What does seem clear is that major changes occured in subcontracting in the 1960s. Broadbridge (1966) and Paine (1971) date these to the effects of monetary restrictions following balance of payments problems in 1963, when large firms, themselves squeezed, squeezed their subcontractors and started to rationalize their subcontractor networks. The less efficient subcontractors tended to be dropped and the remaining ones were expected to become more technologically independent. Paine notes the importance of the lending and sale of second-hand capital equipment by principals to subcontractors, encouraged by laws permitting accelerated depreciation, which resulted in considerable technical upgrading, though Watanabe (1970) argues this was declining by the late 1960s. Rationalization of supply chains to save on transactions costs, so that upper-tier subcontractors were encouraged to administer lower-tier ones was an important feature of this period. In the motor industry, in some cases, principals encouraged supplier firms to seek business with other principals in order to achieve economies of scale. From about 1960, motor parts manufacturers moved towards the use of new rather than second-hand equipment, pushed their capital-intensity further than their principals, and achieved substantial cost reductions (Odaka et al, 1988, pp.50-1, 78-9). Small firms were also helped in their development as more independent innovative firms after the 1950s by greatly improved channels for financial resources. Legislation was also introduced in the 1960s to prevent principals excessively delaying payment to subcontractors.

There is certainly evidence of continuing wage differentials between large firms and SMEs in Japanese manufacturing, more so than in Britain. Time series of indices for monthly wages and hourly total earnings (which include bonuses and overtime payments) for 1965-84 and 1970-84 (respectively) both show large and growing differentials, which are greater, the smaller the firm. The picture changes somewhat when these figures are corrected for age and education level, and what appears to emerge is that differentials are minimal for young male workers, but increase with a worker's age (Koshiro, 1990, pp.209,212-3; Aoki, 1988, p.220; Watanabe, 1970, pp.548-550). Since workers in SMEs may, with experience, leave to set up their own businesses, and thereby raise their incomes (16), this lessens the apparent inequality. Of course, the growth of differentials by age is consistent with the labour market segmentation hypotheses discussed in the previous section, and springs from large firms operating a structured internal labour market, rewarding length of service, whereas SMEs do not.

Subcontracting is still of major importance in the Japanese economy, although its importance seems to have lessened since a peak in the early 1980s. In 1987 55.9% of SMEs were engaged in subcontracting (17) At the 1981 peak, when 65.5% of SMEs acted as subcontractors, 54% of all SMEs depended on subcontracting for more than 80% of their business (Koshiro, 1990, p.183).

To what extent has subcontracting in Japan developed away from its past dependence on sourcing cheaper labour, and its use as an overflow mechanism, towards more speciality subcontracting? Clark (1979, ch.2) refers to the Japanese company typically as being narrowly specialized. Manufacturing companies tend to keep their activities within their industry, and expand along related lines. Subsidiaries may be formed to work in new areas, but are likely to be independently run (18). Indeed, the grouping of companies expresses this specialization, with group members not trespassing on each others' territory (19). The specialization is vertical too, argues Clark, and the extensive use of subcontractors represents a division of labour between them and the principal. Aoki (1987) argues that an important motive for what he calls this 'quasi disintegration' (i.e vertically disintegrated production, with close relations retained among the parties) is to keep employees in the principal as homogeneous as possible, in terms of career prospects and conditions, so as to facilitate human resource management. Such structured internal labour markets within the principals might seem evidence of dualism, of course, but Aoki (1984, p.28) has argued that the internalization of the employment structure is also now to be found in SMEs to some extent. He also argues (1984, p.30) that, besides more standard reasons like differing mininimum efficient sizes between activities, a quasi-disintegrated structure generates better quality control, with each unit taking responsibility for its part of the process. Quality control, indeed, is regarded in Japanese manufacturing industry as a major source of competitive strength, with the Deming prize for QC being greatly sought after.

In the 1987 survey of Japanese SMEs, 41.7% of principals were said to use subcontractors in order to cut costs, 30.4% because the subcontractor had a technology which the principal did not have, and 28.7% to cope with demand fluctuations. However, for the perceived future the access to technology became the most single important, followed at a distance of about 10% points, almost equally, by cost reduction and coping with fluctuations (20).

Much emphasis has been laid in the literature (e.g.Dore, 1983) about the difference in relations between subcontractors and principals in Japan compared to the UK or other Western countries. Sako (1990, to be published as Sako, 1992) describes the difference between the obligational relational contracting of Japan and the arms length contractual relations of the UK or US, as contrasting polar types. She provides a most interesting case study of the electronics industries of the UK and Japan, trying to assess quantitatively, using a variety of criteria, the extent to which 'OCR' or 'ACR' apply. She finds a continuum in each country, but with the Japanese slanted more to the OCR type. OCR relies less on detailed legal contracts, and more on the trust built up during a long relation, especially goodwill trust (see note 4). Under ACR, principals are willing to switch suppliers for short term cost advantage, whereas in OCR principals try to help subcontractors develop appropriate capabilities, including long-term cost reduction. The ACR type of arrangement, in its search for the lowest short-term cost, tends to see subcontracting in terms of allocative efficiency, whereas the OCR arrrangement is concerned more with Leibenstein-style X-efficiency, the achieving of higher output from given inputs (21).

In understanding the subcontracting relationship in Japan, there is some danger of confusing myth and reality, in a society where surface appearance (_tatemae_) is politely presented first, while the real state of affairs (_honne_) is often concealed (22). Odagiri (1992, pp.151-161) attacks two myths about subcontracting. One is that subcontracting is a means whereby SMEs and their workers are exploited by large companies; this is the dualism hypothesis, which has already been discussed (and hardly a tatemae!). The other, though, is that SMEs are protected from competition within a paternalistic relation with the principal. Odagiri's argument is that reputation-effects will prevent subcontractors submitting false claims about cost levels, that the (often) superior expertise and long experience of the principal will give it a good sense of what costs to expect, and that there will be a willingness to shift orders towards other suppliers if one is too high-cost. Past experience too suggests that principals can be ruthless, as when Hitachi dropped over 70% of its subcontractors during the reorganizations of the 1960s! (Koshiro, p.203) Also, it seems that relations were harsher in declining industries like shipbuilding.

The relative power of the subcontractor and principal varies with the subcontractors position in the vertical hierarchy. Firms in the first tier of subcontractors tend to be the larger ones (sometimes too large to be classified as SMEs), often with independent designing capacity, and serving a range of customers. Firms in lower tiers, who are subcontractors to the subcontractors in the tier above, tend to be smaller and more dependent, both in the sense of having less technological capability, and fewer customers. Chalmers (1989) in her major study of the Japanese peripheral workforce, argues that there is a continuum from larger to smaller SMEs, and that the dualism hypothesis holds more strongly on the outer periphery of firms; there is a peripheral continuum as imbalances of power increase. Asanuma (1989a) distinguishes between firms in the motor industry and in electrical machinery who have designs supplied by the principal, and those who supply their own designs for the principal's approval. The latter type of supplier earns the higher profit, and only the former type of supplier is truly regarded as a subcontractor (_shitauke_). In fact, the term shitauke has overtones of inferiority and exploitation; according to a newspaper report of a survey by Tokyo's Chamber of Commerce and Industry, nearly 90% of SME respondents thought the term should be dropped. The reason was confidence in their own technology, with 80% saying they had their own technology and products (_Nihon Keizai Shinbun_, 9.11.90) (23). However, according to the 1987 survey by the SMEA (1990a) over 70% of subcontractors worked with designs supplied by principals, and under 40% had their own design sections. In terms of equipment, there were not great differences between subcontractors and principals in whether they owned NC machine tools (more than 70% of each did), machining centres, or robots, but CAD (computer-assisted-design) was far more the province of principals. Only a quarter of subcontractors had products of their own, not produced to customer special order. Perceptions of their bargaining power among subcontractors were that

19

about two-thirds thought it was as strong as their principals'; only 19% of ordinary subcontractors thought the principals' bargaining power was stronger, and only 14% of what the SMEA refers to as 'superior' subcontractors. However, the Subcontractors Association in Tokyo (interview, 28.11.90) mentioned continuing complaints by small companies, whose position is weak, who often has no contract document, and on whom severe conditions were imposed. In spite of the much-quoted prevalence of 'trust' in Japanese subcontracting relations, the Association was pressing for more use of a standardized contract document.

Aoki (1988, ch.6) argues that first-tier suppliers (leaving aside the suppliers of standard items) have sufficient bargaining power, on the basis of their technological knowledge, to take a substantial share of the 'relational quasi-rent' (24) which arises from the savings in transactions costs ('the unique informational efficiency') generated by a subcontracting grouping. Smaller subcontractors cannot bargain so effectively. Nevertheless, it seems that (risk-averse) subcontractors may be insulated by the principal from fluctuations in business, contrary to the 'dualism' view, as Kawasaki and McMillan (1987) have shown in their interesting attempt to model principal-agent relations in Japanese subcontracting. Also, firms can move in the hierarchy, and particularly progressive subcontractors may move to higher tiers as their technological level improves. Asanuma (1985), writing of the motor industry, stresses that the subcontracting relationship, though there is constant pressure on suppliers to reduce costs, does retain some incentives to innovation by allowing original prices to be maintained for a period.

Independence also is likely to increase with a subcontractor's range of customers, and complete dependence is not widespread. In 1987, almost 70% of subcontractors received orders from companies other than their main customer (SMEA, 1990a). There is, though, clear evidence that the number of customer-companies increases with the size of subcontractor, ranging in 1982 from an average of 3 in total manufacturing (and 4 in general machinery) for firms of 1-3 workers, to 11 (12 in the case of general machinery) for firms of 200-299 workers. Interestingly, larger subcontractors are more likely to receive help from principals - in the 1-20 employee group, only 5% of firms received capital help and 2.9% personnel assistance in 1982, while the respective figures for firms of 101-300 employess were 35.4% and 37.8%. Firms of more than 300 workers, though, received even more help from clients - 56% and 58%, respectively (Friedman, 1988, pp.149,151). The larger flow of capital and personnel from principal to supplier in the case of the larger (and generally) higher tier subcontractors almost certainly reflects their participation in product development and technological innovation, a crucial benefit of the Japanese subcontracting relationship.

The high yen (endaka) crisis, following the appreciation of the yen in 1985, appears to have caused an upheavel in subcontracting relations (Glasmeier and Sugiura, 1991, pp.397-8), with the loss of international competitiveness having to be made up by improved domestic efficiency (or relocation offshore). MITI's SMEA survey show many changes in attitude. The proportion of principals expected to choose subcontractors on the basis of a past long relationship falls from 85% before endaka to 41% for the expected future, but the importance of cost as a criterion for subcontractor choice falls considerably in relation to quality and technology on the part of the subcontractor. There was a fall in the number of subcontractors who felt their bargaining power would be the same as their principals, but a quarter of 'superior' subcontractors thought they would have a position stronger than their principals'. These changes seem to reflect the growing importance of technical change in relation to the simple cheap-labour advantages of subcontracting. The SMEA (1990a) stresses that when consumers demand higher quality, and firms must produce small quantities of many varieties with short product cycles, the use of subcontractors in essential, and high technical capacity is required of the subcontractor. The SMEA also stresses the impact of labour shortage in Japan, and 60% of subcontractors cite this as a difficulty, while only a quarter (each) cite as problems the cost reduction required by principals, the need to diversify production, and the shortness of required delivery dates. The labour shortages, as our interviews will show, are also a factor in principals' decisions to subcontract, both in terms of their own difficulty in recruiting labour for in-house expansion, and of using subcontractors to access labour (such as housewives willing to work part-time) which they would not recruit for their core labour force.

Finally, how far are the differences in subcontracting behaviour reflected in the degree of vertical (dis)integration in industries in Japan and Britain? Table 2.2 shows that materials purchases as a percentage of gross output tend to be higher, industry for industry, for Japan than the UK. While, within a country, interindustry variation in the ratio cannot be taken as an indication of differences in subcontracting behaviour, because of obvious differences in the amount of standard materials purchased by different industries (25), comparing an industry between countries, assuming similarity in raw material use, gives a very rough first approximation. For mechanical engineering in the UK and general machinery in Japan the difference appears to be greater than in the case of motor vehicles (and the Japanese figure may be lowered by the inclusion of other transport equipment), perhaps relecting the long history of outsourcing in the British motor industry (see ch.3). Table 2.2's coverage includes the industries which chapter 3 will show are suitable candidates in which to study subcontracting.

Table 2.2
Materials Purchases as Percentages of Gross Output, UK and Japan,
1988

UK		
31	Metal manufacturing	48.3%
32	Mechanical engineering	47.8%
33	Office machinery and data processing equipment	56.2%
34	Electrical and electronic engineering	49.1%
35	Motor vehicles and parts	65.5%
36	Other transport equipment	43.0%
3	Metal goods, engineering and vehicle industries	51.5%
2-4	All manufacturing	53.5%
Japan		
28	Fabricated metal products	54.2%
29	General machinery	56.8%
30	Electrical machinery, equipment and supplies	59.3%
31	Transportion equipment	67.9%
32	Precision instruments and machinery	55.6%
F	All manufacturing	57.5%

Sources: CSO (1989a, PA 1002), MITI (1990)
Notes: The codes are those of the British Standard Industrial Classification (1980), and the Standard Industrial Classification for Japan (1984)

1.	A comprehensive survey of work on this area, much of it done by economic geographers, is given by Holmes (1986). See also the survey by Imrie (1986). UNIDO (1974) is a useful source too, and has assembled a mass of information on subcontracting in developed countries with a view to examining its relevance for industrial development in the Third World. UNCTC (1981) is conducted with similar aims, but with special reference to the motor industry. Other international agency material on subcontracting has tended to focus on its international aspects (e.g. Germidis, 1980).

2.	This was a postal survey, organized by Bruce Lyons and Susan Bailey. Questionnaires were answered (usably) by 102 principals and 91 subcontractors. Questionnaires returned by subcontractors who produced only standard products (.i.e. products not customized to the requirements of specific principals) were excluded, and not all respondents answered all questions. In addition, about 20 interviews were made, by Janet Anderson of the UEA Economics Research Centre, to back up the questionnaire and clarify the meaning of the quantitative answers. For analysis of these results see Lyons (1991a, 1991b), and Lyons and Bailey (1991). These mainly concern the role of transactions costs in explaining the pattern of UK subcontracting, and will be published in due course; only selected points of direct relevance to the _increase_ in subcontracting in the UK are extracted here.

3.	As far as I can judge, no sectoral pattern within engineering emerged with respect to which firms increased, decreased, or held constant their degree of subcontracting, however.

4.	For a good discussion of the meaning of trust see Sako (1991). She stresses the distinction between _competence trust_ (that the other party can do what it says), _contractual trust_ (that contracts, once entered into, will be adhered to), and _goodwill trust_ (which goes beyond the others into a relationship where each side takes positive initiatives to help the other). For a discussion of the importance of trust in Japanese subcontracting relationships, see our chapter 7.

5.	All the companies were producing high precision machinery. The British companies were mainly machine tool companies.

6.	Holmes (1986, p.101, n.1) describes various academic debates on these points, including whether such activities in the mid-Victorian UK economy represent 'pre-industrial survivals' [see also Piore and Sabel (1984, pp.26-8) on 'industrial dualism', as noted in our section 1.1]. In their recent survey of labour market segmentation, McNabb and Ryan (1990) argue that the term 'dualism' should be reserved for situations exhibiting extreme segmentation, in the sense of bimodality in the distribution of job rewards, rather than just a spread of earnings for people of comparable ability. However, since most of the literature follows the practice of using the two terms interchangeably, so shall we.

7.   In a pioneering study of labour market segmentation in Britain, Bosanquet and Doeringer (1973, p.426) stress the generally low-wage nature of certain industries, such as clothing, although they note that within clothing there are some high wage firms (and within engineering some low-wage firms). Also, see Phillimore (1988) for further discussion as to whether there are sectoral dimensions in whether subcontracting firms are marginalized or not.

8.   See chapter 3 for a discussion about which are the appropriate industries in which to study subcontracting.

9.   Of course, the textile and clothing industries have been subject to heavy import competition, squeezing principals as well as subcontractors. In some areas, such as knitwear, there has been a strong response from British firms based on rapid reaction to consumer fashion needs (NEDC, 1987). Some interviews in the present project were conducted with knitwear firms (see chapter 3).

10.   In principle, even a large firm has a choice of adopting a cheap labour policy if it feels that 'enterprise-specific skills' are not required, and it can hire workers on the open market and perhaps tolerate high labour turnover. A firm which requires such skills will wish to train its own workers, and operate a structured internal labour market to reward and promote them sufficiently to retain them. In practice, this choice will be constrained by market and technological conditions to some extent, and low wage employment is more likely to be found where there are low skill requirements, low capital-intensity and a high degree of product market competition (Bosanquet and Doeringer, 1973, p.425). These conditions can coexist in an industry if a periphery of firms take up the fluctuations in demand, for example, while core firms cater to the stable component. Such peripheral firms are likely to be small, as evidence shows (McNabb and Ryan, 1970, p.165). Firms on the periphery thus represent a 'secondary' labour market, where disadvantaged workers (such as ethnic minorities) are likely to be concentrated, but the key feature is that earnings differentials are larger than can be explained in terms of differences in workers' attributes. The importance of structured internal labour markets in large firms is a very strong feature of the Japanese scene (Aoki, 1990).

11.   The most commonly used definition of small firms is that of the OECD, which refers to an establishment of under 100 workers. The Bolton Committee of 1971 used a definition of 200 workers, but there is no institutional definition in the UK. For small firms, the distinction between an 'establishment' (plant) and an 'enterprise' (the company) is not of great significance, since few small firms operate more than one plant, and large firms tend not to operate plants of under 100 workers. The average number of establishments per enterprise in the UK has remained constant at about 1.2 since the 1970s. The major change has been that the 100 largest companies which, though retaining their share of total output at about 40% since the 1970s, have increased the number of plants per enterprise, as the average size of plant has fallen.

Prior to the 1960s, the share of establishments employing up to 200 workers fell from 44% in 1935 to 31% in 1963 (Marsden, 1990). From 1986, the UK Census of Production has changed its basic reporting unit from the 'establishment' to the 'business'. However, where a business operates at several addresses, information is sought separately for each address. In Japan, a small/medium enterprise ('SME') is one of up to 300 workers, or with paid-in capital of up to Y100,000 -see subsection 2.2

12.   In general, the British Census of Production statistics giving wage levels by size group of company do not strongly support the idea of dualism for manufacturing as a whole - operatives in companies employing 1-99 workers, 100-199 workers, and 200-299 workers, received (respectively) 91.8%, 92.6%, and 95.7% of the average operative wage payment, without correction for skill levels (CSO, 1989a, PA1002). In mechanical engineering (SIC 32) differentials by company size are slight, and in metal working machine tools operatives in companies of under 100 employees earn almost exactly the average wage in the group (CSO, 1989a, PA 322). In the manufacture of office machinery and data processing (SIC 33) equipment, however, there are quite some substantial increases in wage payments by size of company. In motor vehicles and parts (SIC 35) there are also some differentials. In electrical and electronic engineering (SIC 34)   the differences are little more than for manufacturing as a whole -   SIC 34 has payments to operatives in firms of under 100 workers equal to 90% of average payments; but 82% in SIC 35, and 80% for SIC 33. Interestingly, for footwear and clothing (SIC 45), in spite of the case study evidence to the contrary, there is minimal difference in operative pay by size group, although the group 1-99 workers is not disaggregated in PA1002.   [For more discussion of these sectors, see chapter 3. The SIC categories are those of the 1980 UK Standard Industrial Classification]

13.   A very useful survey of the Japanese literature on the country's small firm sector is included in Koshiro (1990), and a good, older account is Watanabe (1970). Friedman (1988, ch.4)   also uses Japanese material to give an exceptionally interesting account of the relation between subcontracting, politics, and the small firm sector. [For comments on more general books on Japan, see note 22]

14.   See Odagiri (1992, Chs. 6 and 7), who stresses that the present day horizontal groups (kigyo-shudan) are looser groupings than the old zaibatsu. Clark (1979, pp.77-80) also distinguishes, as a third type of grouping, 'bank groups' such as Sanwa, where a large bank lends to perhaps a dozen companies in which it holds shares.

15.   It also has been publishing an annual report on small and medium industry, since 1963. At present there is a full-length version (e.g. SMEA, 1990a), and a shorter version which is also published in English translation (e.g.SMEA, 1990b). These reports, or 'white papers', have a wealth of useful statistical information, including surveys of attitudes.

16.   Friedman (1988, p.142-3) quotes evidence from Japanese studies that as many as 50% of blue-collar workers in SMEs may leave to

set up their own firms, and that the profitability in SMEs is higher than large ones.

17.   Approximately three-quarters of all enterprises in Japan were SMEs - the subcontracting figures for subcontractors of 300 workers or more are not given in the SMEA White Paper. The SME subcontracting figures for earlier years were: 1981:65.5%, 1976:60.7%, 1971:58.7% (SMEA, 1990a, p.157)

18.   Aoki (1987, p.284) provides evidence of a substantially growing proportion of share capital held in the form of subsidiaries over the period 1965 to 1984, both in industry in general, and in the auto and electronics industries in particular.

19.   And interlocking shareholdings between group members, and with major suppliers, tend to protect companies from hostile takeovers, and reduce their reliance on short-term profitability. However, banks, which provide substantial amounts of capital to Japanese industry, provide a check on the company being run without sufficient reference to profits (Aoki, 1990)

20.   The source of all these statistics is SMEA (1990a). The percentages sum to somewhat more than a 100% because several reasons could be chosen. The percentages refer to the number of respondents citing a particular reason.

21.   For his more recent thoughts on efficiency, see Leibenstein (1987, especially chs.13 and 14, which discuss the Japanese system).

22.   See Woronoff (1990, pp.17-27). Woronoff's provocative book, written as an antidote to what he sees as the rosy view presented by Vogel's, Japan as Number One (1980), is sometimes useful in dispelling some of the more blatant Western misconceptions about Japan. I have also found helpful Reischauer (1988), though it presents a rather rosy view too; and Horsley and Buckley (1990), especially ch.5, which gives a sobering account of Japanese methods of competition with the West.

23.   I am very grateful to Hiro Odagiri for bringing this article to my attention.

24.   A quasi-rent is normally defined as a return to an asset over and above that in its best alternative use. For further discussion, and especially on how such rents can be appropriated, see Klein et al (1978).

25.   The normal measure of vertical integration is the ratio of value-added to sales, more or less the obverse of that used in Table 2.2. This measure has various disadvantages, such as indicating lower vertical integration for industries producing final goods than for industries making intermediate products. See Davies and Morris (1991).

3 The industries and firms

This chapter discusses, in section 1, the basis on which the choice of industries to study subcontracting in Britain and Japan was made, and how the sample of firms was selected. Section 2 then provides an introduction to the three industries chosen.

3.1 The choice of industries and firms

3.1.1 The choice of industries

The accumulation of observations that subcontracting has been growing in importance in British industry, in response to pressures from increasing international competition, faster technical change and consumer market volatility, has been discussed in the previous two chapters. This has also indicated some industries where subcontracting has been especially important, such as the motor industry. To draw lessons from Japan it would be desirable to choose industries where subcontracting was important in Japan and which had produced good performance, in exports for example. It would also be desirable to choose industries in Britain which had found themselves under pressure. In fact, almost all sectors of British industry have been under pressure since the late 1970s! Even relatively protected areas like defence electronics and telecommunications are encountering difficulties (as a result of the demise of the military threat of the Soviet Union, and from changes in government procurement, respectively). Japanese export industries too have been under pressure, from the high yen crisis of the late 1980s (see Steven, 1990, chs.1 and 2), and previously following the oil crises in the 1970s.

Those industries which use subcontracting the most intensively in Japan will not necessarily be the same as those in Britain. Some industries are likely to be highly vertically integrated for basically technological reasons; these are mainly industries like fertilizer production, where production takes the form of producing a final product from raw materials by means of, say, a chemical process. Such process industries differ from many engineering industries, where the individual products are highly divisible. However, where the technology permits greater choice about the degree of vertical integration, this could differ between countries, according to differences in the transactions costs of using external supply in different societies. In extreme cases, one even could imagine a situation, analagous to that of factor intensity reversals in international trade (1), where an industry which was highly outsourced (i.e. highly using of subcontracting) in one country was relatively vertically integrated in another country. Such a situation could arise if conditions in one country made external supply hazardous, because for example of a lack of trust between firms or a legal system which was ineffective in enforcing contracts (2), given that some industries would have much more choice about their degree of vertical integration than others.

The UK indeed does seem to be a country where there is a lack of trust between companies, compared to Japan (see, e.g. Dore, 1983) or to continental European countries such as Germany (Parkinson, 1984, p.101) or France (Lorenz, 1989). However, the industries using subcontracting the most intensively do, in fact,seem to be quite similar, at least in so far as the data allow an accurate picture. Some data on subcontracting by industry are available from official sources for the UK, and there is more detailed information for the Japanese economy.

British data on subcontracting are given in the Census of Production (3). This lists information on 'work done and industrial services rendered' (as an indication of industries acting as subcontractors) and 'cost of industrial services received' (as an indication of use of subcontractors), disaggregated down to the level of Activities (the 4-digit level in the British 1980 Standard Industrial Classification) (4). These show that the average 'cost of industrial services received' in British manufacturing was 3.2% of the gross value of output in 1987, a slight but fairly steady rise over the figure for 1974 (the earliest year available) of 2.7%

4-digit level activities were identified which either used or rendered industrial services in excess of 3% of the value of gross output, approximately the average figure for all manufacturing over the 1980s. Use of these data identified a concentration of work done as subcontractors in a wide variety of 4-digit level activities within engineering broadly defined (Standard Industrial Classification Division 3, i.e. SIC Classes 31,32,33,34,35,36,37 - metal goods manufacture, mechanical engineering, office and data processing equipment, electrical and electronic engineering, motor vehicle and other transport manufacture, and instrument engineering), with the heaviest concentration in mechanical engineeering. Use of subcontracting (i.e.cost of industrial services received) was also most in evidence in engineering, though it was not as widely spread (i.e. only in classes 31,32,34, and 36 were there activities with proportions above 3%). The narrower spread of the use of subcontracting, rather than the rendering of subcontracting services, reflects the fact that many engineering subcontractors work for firms outside engineering. There was a secondary concentration of subcontracting services (both given and received) in textiles and clothing.

A summary at the 2-digit level for the UK for 1988, using the services-used definition, is given in Table 3.1, for comparison with the 2-digit level data available for Japan in Table 3.2. The relatively high figure for mechanical engineering is clear. However, the limitations of the data suggest considerable caution in their use. There are two problems. First, the 'services' include repairs, and thus are too widely defined. Second, the services are defined as being those performed on materials remaining in the ownership of the customer firm. While, to judge by the interviews to come, much subcontracting in the UK is done on the basis of the 'free-issue' (to use the term normally used by the companies) of materials to the subcontractor, even more is not. Moreover, the tendency which the interviews will show for larger companies to try to devolve management of the supply chain to the subcontractors themselves, not only involves larger subcontractors in arranging supplies of components from smaller ones (i.e. the sub-subcontractors), but also increasingly in handling raw material purchases. While, abstracting from repairs problems, activities identified by the Census of Production definitions are indeed involved in subcontracting, other industries involved in subcontracting may not be identified.

Similar data on work done on materials owned by the customer-firm from Japanese sources, at the two-digit level for 1984, are shown in Table 3.2. Given the problems associated with this measure, the fact that there is some congruence between the industries picked out by the Japanese data and the British is reassuring. However, the much higher figures for Japan may indicate greater use of free-issued materials as well as more subcontracting in general.

Table 3.1
Industrial Services Received, by Sector, UK, 1988
(percentages of gross output)

Textiles	3.1%
Footwear and clothing	2.9%
(Clothing	3.3%)
Metal products	3.5%
Mechanical engineering	4.1%
(Metal working machine tools	3.2%)
Office machinery and data processing equipment	2.3%
Electrical and electronic engineering	2.3%
Motor vehicles and parts	1.6%
Other transport equipment	7.8%
Instrument engineering	2.5%
All manufacturing	3.2%

Source: CSO (1988a, PA1002)

Table 3.2
Sales Revenue from Work on Customers' Materials
Japan, 1984
(as percentages of total sales)

Textiles	12.9%
Apparel	21.0%
Mechanical engineering	12.6%
Electrical and electronic engineering	9.0%
Transport equipment	5.9%
All manufacturing	6.4%

Source: Sako (1990, p.30)

Other data are available for Japan, and are shown in Table 3.3. These
indicate the proportion of small and medium enterprises (defined in
manufacturing, it will be remembered, as firms employing under 300
workers) which engage in subcontracting, in the sense of work under
subcontract to larger companies; and also the proportion of firms which
employ subcontractors. Since over three quarters of employment in
Japanese manufacturing is in SMEs (see Table 2.1) the importance of
subcontracting for SMEs reflects its importance for industry as a whole.
The importance of subcontracting for SMEs in engineering is clear from
the table, and also in textiles and clothing, although subcontracting
clearly is widely practiced over most parts of Japanese industry, except
for food, wood products, oil and chemicals. The well above average
figures for SME involvement in subcontracting in the engineering
industries are also supported by the evidence of the relatively high
proportion of companies which use subcontractors, whereas in textiles,
and to some extent clothing, the evidence diverges.

Given the evident importance of subcontracting, relative to other
industries, in both Japanese and British engineering, it was decided to
draw companies for interview from engineeering broadly defined, and to
take mechanical engineering, the motor industry and electronics as
covering a representative spectrum of activities (5). Mechanical
engineering, as a producer of capital goods, has a crucial role in
diffusing technical change through the economy, and in recent years much
technical change, both in capital goods and consumer goods, has come
from electronics (Rosenberg, 1982, pp.21, 72). The decision to
concentrate within the mechanical engineering sector on machine tools,
and within the electronics sector on computers, was in part influenced
by the wish to examine areas important to technical change and
(therefore) to international competitiveness. The choice was also
influenced by the access gained to companies, as was the decision to
choose passenger cars. Cars are also one of the goods most clearly
affected by consumer market volatility, and where the pattern of
international competition has changed considerably in the last twenty
years. Some further discussion of the choice of machine tools and
computers is given in section 2 of this chapter.

Table 3.3
Subcontracting in Japanese Manufacturing

	Percentage of SMEs engaged in subcontracting 1981	Percentage of SMEs engaged in subcontracting 1987	Percentage of firms using subcontractors 1981
Total manufacturing	65.5	55.9	37.0
Foodstuffs	17.5	8.6	5.5
Textiles	84.9	80.1	26.5
Clothing	86.5	79.3	40.9
Wood products	48.0	21.5	20.3
Furniture	51.6	38.3	34.9
Pulp and paper	51.6	41.8	42.9
Publishing and printing	59.0	42.5	65.7
Chemicals	38.5	22.9	27.1
Oil and coal products	38.9	16.9	17.1
Plastics	na	69.0	na
Rubber products	71.8	66.2	40.2
Leather products	68.8	65.7	31.4
Ceramics	36.6	36.3	24.5
Steel	72.0	53.8	41.6
Non-ferrous metals	73.6	62.8	47.4
Metal products	78,6	71.1	44.5
General machinery	84.2	75.0	55.7
Electric machinery	85.3	80.5	57.9
Transportation equipment	87.7	81.2	48.8
Precision equipment	80.9	71.1	54.4
Other manufacturing	62.2	43.5	37.7

Sources: 1981 figures from Sako (1988, p.72), 1987 total from SMEA (1990a, p.157),
and other 1987 figures from SMEA (1989a, p.102)
Notes: Figures for SMEs engaged in subcontracting distinguish between those dependent for more than,
and less than, 50% of their sales on subcontracting. For 1987, for almost all the industries where
subcontracting was important, the overwhelming majority of firms engaged in subcontracting at all got
more than 50% of their business from it.

3.1.2 The company interviewing programme

The Japanese companies were interviewed during a fieldtrip to Japan in October and November 1990. A small number of British companies were interviewed in the summer of 1990, and the rest from spring to autumn 1991.

The interviews in Japan were:
-Engineering industry: three principals, four subcontractors
-Motor industry: one principal and five subcontractors
-Electronics industry: two principals and two subcontractors
-and: Textile industry: one principal [over 20 textile companies were approached but the reponse rate was minimal]
-also: the Japanese associate of an international firm of accountants (who arranged some interviews); the Union of Japanese Scientists and Engineers, who administer quality control awards; the head office of the Subcontractors Association in Tokyo).

The British interviews were:
-Mechanical engineering: four principals and two subcontractors
-Motor industry: two principals, three subcontractors (who also did work for mechanical engineering)
-Electronics industry: five principals and three subcontractors
-and: Textiles: three principals and three subcontractors
(including three pilot, pre-project interviews)
-also: Confederation of British Industry Partnership Sourcing Initiative organizer; Department of Trade and Industry enterprise initiative division, and Japan Electronics Business Association; National Economic Development Office; Association of Contract Electronics Manufacturers and Electronic Components Industry Federation.

In Japan, companies were chosen for interview from mechanical engineering, electronics and the motor industry (and textiles -see note 5), with names taken from company handbooks (6). The responses to some extent conditioned the choice of subsector - for example two of the Japanese earliest interviews were with a machine tool manufacturer and a company with computers as an important product, who introduced their major subcontractors. Other interviewees gave information about other companies, either their subcontractors or their principals, which often led to further interviews. In sum, although the choice of subsector was made on the basis of criteria about its economic interest, there also was an arbitrary element. For example, if there had been a widespread response from Japanese consumer electronics firms, a decision would have had to be made whether to maintain an interest in computers or to switch. Once the Japanese interviews had been made, British interviewees were chosen broadly to match the Japanese ones. At an early stage in the research it was undecided whether to include the motor industry, since much secondary source material already existed (see subsection 3.2.2), but a positive response from a Japanese motor manufacturer, and its offer to introduce five of its subcontractors, seemed an opportunity to gain first hand knowledge not to be missed.
    In each industry some firms were included besides those in the chosen subsector, partly to seize interview opportunities in Japan, where access to companies is not easy, but more to give a broader view of each industry.
    For the British interviews, initially companies were selected from

company handbooks (7), and the sample was rounded out as interviewees gave information about other firms in their industries.

In Japan, all firms interviewed were indigenous Japanese. In the UK, there is substantial foreign investment in many activities, with 45% of output controlled by foreign multinationals in the motor industry, 37% in office machinery and data processing equipment, 20% in mechanical engineering, and 17% in electrical engineering, compared to an average of approximately 18% for manufacturing as a whole (Crum and Davies, 1991, p.61). As a result, some foreign-owned companies of long-standing in the UK were included in the sample.

The interviews were semi-structured. There was a checklist of questions asked to all interviewees, to elicit basic information about the company's operations and its reasons for involvement in subcontracting; but the interviews were allowed to take their own course so that leads into areas of interest to the interviewee's operation could be followed through. This qualitative approach reflects the fact that, although economic theory (particularly the economics of transactions costs) gives many pointers, it yet may miss significant issues, including ones about which economists might subsequently wish to theorize. This indeed is the notion of theory which is 'grounded' in prior qualitative investigation, and which has gained wide acceptance in other social sciences (8). Additionally, the parallel University of East Anglia project, 'Subcontracting and the Small Business', has generated a data base (mainly with a view to testing transactions cost theory), which forms a 'large numbers' background on subcontracting in British engineering.

3.2 Introduction to the industries

This section introduces the three industries chosen for study:
-mechanical engineering (with special reference to machine tools),
-the motor industry (with special reference to passenger cars), and
-electronics (with special relevance to computers).
The first subsection discusses mechanical engineering and machine tools in the context of engineering in general (which includes all three industries) (9). The second and third subsections then focus more narrowly on the motor industry and electronics.

3.2.1 Engineering

Pressures for change: reporting on the performance and position of the British engineering industry at the start of the 1990s, the chairman of the National Economic Development Council's engineering industry sector group comments that much of its findings make sombre reading:

> The industry is no longer one of the great strengths of our economy. Trade deficits, declining employment, a poor investment record and major training gaps have become almost commonplace. Its performance is perhaps symptomatic of the wider problems of our economy. (NEDC, 1990c, p.iii)

The NEDC report refers to engineering on the broadest possible definition (i.e. classes 31 to 37 in the UK Standard Industrial

33

Classification, 1980) which, as set out in Table 3.4, experienced a fall of approximately a million in its workforce during the 1980s (10). From 1978 to 1987, the (again, broadly defined) engineering trade balance as a proportion of GDP had fallen from 2.3% to -0.8%, while the proportionate trade surpluses of Germany and Japan had risen. Of the major exporters, only the USA showed comparably poor trade and employment performance. (NEDC, 1990c, pp.14,16).

Much, but by no means all, of this decline has resulted from the performance of motor industry, which has had the largest employment fall of all the engineering sectors. The motor industry also has been responsible for much of the poor trade results. Its 1990 trade deficit was almost as large as that for the whole of engineering (although there was a surplus in other transport equipment)(11).

In output terms, however, the decline is less apparent, and the employment falls reflect to a large extent the employment shakeout during recession. In spite of the trough during the early and mid-1980s (see Table 3.5), a substantial increase in UK motor vehicle output was recorded by the end of the 1980s, albeit influenced by Japanese direct investment into the UK (see subsection 3.2.2). Of all the engineering sectors in the UK shown in Table 3.5, only mechanical engineering failed significantly to increase its output over the 1980s as a whole.

Electronics and related sectors grew substantially, though, like motor vehicles, foreign investment played a major role in the increase.

Though output has increased in most engineering sectors, and the decline in employment in the 1980s largely reflects increased labour productivity (12), there has been pressure on British engineering in the form of worsening export performance and increased import penetration. While the trade deficit is mainly made up of the motor vehicle deficit, a marked and more general secular deterioration in UK engineering trade performance is clear. A 1979 surplus equivalent to 24% of engineering exports (excluding motor vehicles) had turned to a substantial deficit by the late 1980s. In terms of world exports of machinery (13), the UK retained its fourth place over the 1980s, although its share fell, while Japan rose ahead of the USA and Germany to become the largest exporter (14)(15). Over the period 1980-89, too, Taiwan and South Korea's exports rose markedly, together accounting for almost as much as those of Britain by 1989 (GATT, 1990)

Besides increased international competition, engineering has experienced also the pressures from increased market volatility and accelerated technical change. These have most obviously affected the electronics industry and motor vehicle production, and this is discussed in later subsections. For mechanical engineering, consumer market volatility has mainly been felt indirectly in the form of the magnified effects of the business cycle traditionally suffered by capital goods industries. The sharp falls in output in the UK from the early to the mid 1980s are clear from Table 3.5.

Japanese engineering also has experienced sharp cyclical fluctuations in demand, both as a result of falls in domestic demand in the post-1973 oil crisis, as a result of export problems in the early 1980s from recession in the USA and Europe, because of trade frictions, and the high Yen exchange rate from the mid 1980s. Thus, the annual growth rate in sales of the industrial machinery sector fell from 27.6% in 1970 to -12.4% in 1975. In 1980 it was up to 17%, but 0.3% in 1983. In 1984 it was 9.6% (KSK, 1986). Table 3.6 shows that by 1989 engineering in general had resumed rapid growth, although the rises were greater in electical (and electronics) engineering than in most other sectors. The

34

Table 3.4
UK Engineering Employment, 1973-89

('000)		1973	1980	1989	Percentage Change 1980-89
SIC 31	Metal goods, not elsewhere specified	556	483	333	-31.1%
32	Mechanical engineering	1048	1005	763	-24.1%
33,34,37	Office machinery, electrical engineering and instruments	1008	938	733	-21.9%
35	Motor vehicles and parts	512	434	262	-39.6%
36	Other transport equipment	397	365	228	-37.5%
Total 31-37		3521	3225	2319	-28.1%
2-4	All manufacturing	7,673	6,808	5,101	-25.1%

Source: DE (November 1991)

Table 3.5
Engineering in UK Manufacturing, 1980 and 1989

GDP at factor cost, by industry	1980 (£mil)	1989 (£mil)	1980 (index)	1989 (index)
Metal goods, not elsewhere specified	3,291 (6.1%)	5,512 (5.5%)	101.4	113.5
Mechanical engineering	7,719 (14.4%)	11,774 (11.7%)	108.3	109.7
Electrical and instrument engineering	6,849 (12.8%)	13,334 (13.2%)	77.8	126.2
Motor vehicles and parts	3,084 (5.8%)	6,198 (6.1%)	113.3	125.3
Aerospace	1,641 (3.1%)	4,285 (4.2%)	[109.5]	[127.7]
Other transport equipment excluding aerospace	1,153 (2.1%)	1,454 (1.4%)	[109.5]	[127.7]
Total manufacturing	53,588 (100%)	101,015 (100%)	96.8	118.9

Source: CSO (1991c)
Notes: Indices for aerospace and other transport equipment excluding aerospace are only given jointly. The industries listed above accounted for 44.3% of manufacturing GDP in 1980, and 42.1% in 1989. Production values are at current factor cost, and the constant factor cost indices take **1985 = 100**.

Table 3.6
Engineering in Japanese Manufacturing, 1985-9

	Share of 1985 industrial value-added	1989 production (1885 = 100)
Mining and manufacturing	100%	119.8
Manufacturing	99.50%	120.0
Machinery and equipment	43.93%	128.5
general machinery	12.92%	121.9
metal cutting machinery	1.29%	106.1
Electrical machinery	17.94%	141.9
integrated circuits	2.74%	157.8
electronic computers	2.51%	159.2
Transportation equipment	11.43%	116.0
passenger cars	4.71%	123.3
motor vehicle parts	1.27%	141.4

Source: MITI (1990)
Notes: Shares of industrial production are the value-added weights cited in the source.

Table 3.7
Japanese Engineering Employment Indices, 1981-88

(1985 = 100)	1981	1988
General machinery	91.1	100.5
Electrical machinery	74.5	102.1
Transportation machinery	95.5	94.6
All manufacturing	94.1	100.3
All industries	94.0	103.5

Source: MITI (1990)

fact that this growth in engineering output in Japan, especially since the mid 1980s, has been accompanied by very little growth in employment (see Table 3.7), reflects a growing labour shortage in Japan, rather than the unemployment which has accompanied such output growth as there has been in the UK.

Pressures from technical change vary somewhat between mechanical engineering, motor vehicles and electronics. They are best considered separately for each; and discussion of technical change in the motor industry and electronics is postponed until the next two subsections.In mechanical engineering the crucial technical development has been in the application of electronics technology, particularly the substitution of electronic control for electrical-mechanical control devices over a wide range of machinery (Chudnovsky et al, 1983, p.22). The late 1970s saw a rapid spread of computer-numerical-controlled ('CNC') machine tools (16). CNC equipment can also be used more generally as part of automation systems, incorporating robotics, and computer-aided design and manufacture; this can include flexible manufacturing systems, which combine highly automated production with scope for many variations in product (Cross, 1991). Electronics technology has accelerated both process innovation (i.e. has made engineering production more technically efficient) and product innovation (see Freeman, 1985, ch.1)

The machine tool industry well illustrates the combination of technical change and competitive pressure, and the rise of Japan as the major producer of CNC lathes (17). Over the period 1975 to 1981 Japan increased its share of world CNC lathe production from 15% to 45%, capturing half of the non-Japanese market. The competitive strategy of the Japanese producers involved the development of smaller, lower performance, but substantially cheaper machines. This allowed them to compete against western firms on price, and against producers from newly industrializing countries on technology. CNC equipment has been available since the 1950s, but the development of a small, relatively cheap CNC unit based on a low cost microprocessor by Fujitsu Fanuc, the largest producer of CNC units in Japan, facilitated the production of CNC lathes on a larger scale and to a wider range of customers. Small and medium firms who had not previously used CNC equipment especially were targetted. Interestingly, this success followed a period of relatively poor performance by the Japanese machine tool industry, where import penetration in the domestic market reached a peak of 57% of domestic production, and was still 20% in 1965 (Friedman, 1988, pp.100, 118). The Fanuc operation had been started by the electronics giant, Fujitsu, in cooperation with an engineering company, with heavy use of imported numerical control technology. Friedman argues that success in machine tools owed little to the activities of MITI, whose efforts were mainly directed, unsuccessfully, at forcing consolidation on a reluctant industry.

Reactions to this challenge by firms from (then West) Germany, the world's largest producer of machine tools in the late 1970s, and by UK firms, are instructive (18). While German firms attempted to remain ahead by concentrating on high cost, very high performance lathes, UK firms had seen their advantage in terms of price competitiveness. UK firms tended to lose market share both to Third World exporters, who (eventually) moved from simpler low-cost lathes to CNC ones, and to Japanese, German and other European producers (19) (20). However, recent evidence suggests that the Japanese are now also attacking the high-quality niche markets, and that German firms are having difficulty

37

keeping up with computer-aided machining technology, while, as medium size companies (see note 19), being unable to finance the investment required for mass production of standard equipment (The Economist, 16.11.91).

Subcontracting and change in engineering: because of the high degree of divisibility of most machinery, and the differences in minimum efficient size in the production of different parts, there traditionally has been scope for vertically disintegrated production in mechanical engineering (Chudnovsky et al, 1983, pp.14-17; Freeman, 1985, p.13; Thoburn ,1973). There has also been scope for the division of labour between firms to increase during the course of economic growth as the market for individual components grew large enough to support specialized production (Stigler, 1951) (21). Jacobsson's study of CNC lathe production suggests that as much as 75% of the cost of a CNC lathe (and 40% for a conventional lathe) may be accounted for by externally purchased components (22). He clearly does not see scope for cost reduction by increasing this already high proportion, and comments that some larger producers of lathes have started integrating backwards into CNC units. This has been both in order to escape monopsonistic exploitation by the large suppliers (Fanuc, for example, is said to operate highly differential pricing between customers, although by 1983-4 its market share was down to 50%) and to get synergy between the electronics and the mechanical aspects of machine tool innovation.

The expansion of Japanese machine tool exports in the late 1970s and early 1980s was based on large volume production by a small number of producers. By 1981, the five largest producers of CNC lathes accounted for 76% of Japanese output (Chudnovsky et al, 1983, p.190). However, machine tool production in Japan was highly outsourced (Piore and Sabel, 1984, pp.219-220). Economies of scale consisted more of spreading organizational, R&D, and marketing costs over a large output, than in actual in-house manufacture, since most equipment was highly divisible. Indeed, by providing small and medium firms with the opportunity to equip with CNC machines, previously unavailable, the Japanese machine tool industry contributed to the efficiency of the subcontracting system in manufacturing more generally (23).

In Britain, in the 1980s there was evidence of increases in subcontracting as a reaction to intensified competitive pressure. Thus the work on British industry by Atkinson and Meager (1986) (24) found three quarters of the firms it studied in engineering had increased their use of 'distancing stategies' since 1980 (e.g. subcontracting of ancillary services and of inputs, increased use of self-employed workers), and two-thirds of these (i.e. over half the total engineering sample) had increased subcontracting (excluding services). By the beginning of the 1990s, as chapter 1 has indicated, official attention was turning to subcontracting, and the management of subcontracting relations, as a means of increasing British competitiveness in engineering and other industries (25) (26).

3.2.2 The motor industry (27)

Motor manufacturing exemplifies the case of an industry undergoing a process of increased market differentiation and volatility, and intensified international competition. There also has been considerable technical change, both in the final product and in manufacturing methods. Outsourcing has long been a feature of the British motor industry, but there is some evidence of recent further increases. Subcontracting in the motor industry in Japan is widely regarded abroad as one of the industry's most distinctive features. The present research has concentrated on passenger cars, rather than commercial vehicles, because the pressures on British car manufacturers have been so clear.

Pressures for change: in the late 1960s, the world motor industry appeared to have become a 'mature' industry, with well-established technology and low but steady demand growth (28). Very little technical change, for example, had taken place in the USA, then the world's largest producer, since the early 1950s. National markets in industrial countries tended to be distinct and served by national producers. By the early 1970s, and even before the 1973-4 oil shock, there was a slowing of economic growth and the development of overcapacity, with increasing competition taking the form of cross-penetration of national markets. Japanese car production was less than 0.2% of world production in 1955; even in the early 1960s the industry was not competitive, and survived through import protection. After reorganization, and major cost-reducing investment by component suppliers (Odaka et al, 1988, ch.2), the Japanese motor industry's share of world production grew to 14% in 1970, and had reached almost 25% by the mid 1980s (Carr, 1990, pp.61 and 67). It had overtaken the USA as the world's largest motor vehicle producer by 1980 (MVMA, 1989, pp.11,13). Based initially on a small domestic market, Japanese manufacturers moved away from the prevalent 'Fordist' method of production (which produced a standardized product, and used unskilled labour, and dedicated equipment subject to great economies of scale), and developed more flexible, smaller scale manufacturing methods, with extensive use of subcontracting networks. Japanese advances effectively 'dematured' the industry, and laid the basis for more highly differentiated products catering to a growing variety of market niches. During this process, the British motor industry saw its output of vehicles halve from 1973 to 1979 (Carr, 1990, p.191), with a major rise in import penetration unmatched by increased exports.

There is also a long-established presence of foreign, predominantly American, multinationals in the UK, and a decreasing presence of indigenous UK companies, as smaller manufacturers like Jaguar have been bought by overseas interests. At the beginning of the 1990s, only the Rover Group remained as an indigenous British volume manufacture, and even Rover has close links with Honda; while other Japanese manufacturers have entered as direct investors.

In Britain, motor components suppliers have had pressures of their own, over and above those caused by the decline of British domestic car production. Carr (1990, p.81, quoting an unpublished 1985 paper by D.T. Jones) notes that in 1984 the volume of UK components supplied to car assemblers in the UK was only a third that of 1972. From 1972 to 1979 this could be traced to falls in British car production, but from then to 1984 half of the decline was due to import penetration. The component manufacturers were hit by the high sterling exchange rate during the 1979-82 depression, and by the tendency for the motor manufacturers to go global in their component sourcing policies. This was particularly the case with the American owned companies operating in the UK, while Rover remained a much higher degree of UK sourcing. More generally, a consequence of multinational presence in the UK has been that the UK content even of apparently British cars has fallen sharply, both with tied imports of complete cars and overseas sourcing of components - from 90% in 1969 to 34% in 1984 (HoC, 1987, p.xiii). The UK components manufacturers themselves exported only about 10% of their output, and in 1986 the UK experienced its first net deficit in trade in motor vehicle parts and accessories (HoC, 1987, p.x).

Despite growth in demand in the late 1980s and apparent moves back towards a 'mature' world motor industry, there have been structural problems of a fragmented production base and overcapacity following increased investment (DTI, 1990b, p.21). The 1990-92 recession has, for the moment, severely affected the motor industry, and this period has seen the start of a serious attempt by the Japanese to penetrate the luxury car market too. However, in the UK, production is forecast to increase during the 1990s with the inflow and expanded production of Japanese foreign investors (see for example NEDC, 1991a), and this may solve the 1980s problem for UK components suppliers of lack of local motor vehicle production (DTI, 1990b, pp.25-6)

Subcontracting and change in the motor industry: in this situation of flux, the role of outsourcing is an important aspect of the organizational and technological change which Western motor manufacturers have considered in order to survive (29).

The long history of outsourcing in the UK has already been mentioned. In the 1960s, Turner (1964, p. 49) records that Ford UK, often seen as a relatively vertically integrated producer, outsourced some 65% of the costs of its cars, while the then British Motor Corporation (later to become British Leyland) had over 4000 different suppliers (30). Of 600,000 employed in the UK motor industry in the mid-1980s, approximately 450,000 were in the production of components (and supply of material and services for vehicle production), and only 150,000 in vehicle manufacture itself (HoC, 1987, p.x).

This history of outsourcing appears to derive from Britain's long-established engineering industry being available to service the motor industry from its early development. In contrast, car production in the United States was more vertically integrated (31). So, in the British motor industry recently, issues of supply chain management have been as important as the question of the sheer volume outsourced, though outsourcing decisions have been also subject to review.

A distinctive feature of the motor industry, especially in Britain, is that the first-tier suppliers are often very large, and in the 1970s ten firms (including household names such as Lucas and GKN) accounted for 50% of the bought-out component value of British cars (Rhys, in Bhaskar, 1979, pp.304 and 309 - who notes that European suppliers are typically smaller). The House of Commons trade and industry report on motor components cited figures to the effect that, although in the mid-80s there were some 2,000 component manufacturers, 100 accounted for 80% of output, and 20 accounted for 40% of the value of vehicle company purchases (HoC, 1987, p.xiv). The relation between the large suppliers and the motor vehicle manufacturers has been one of bilateral monopoly, where bargaining power has shifted over time, and where such shifts sometimes have been exploited to the detriment of good relations. Also, some large component manufacturers have themselves a long history of outsourcing. Lucas, for example, in 1960-61 spent an amount equivalent to almost 38% of its turnover on outsourced components (Turner, 1964, pp.51 and 58). [Hence the inclusion in chapter 5 of two large motor industry suppliers as principals.]

Although the reviews of outsourcing conducted by the car assemblers (32) have been mainly in terms of the location of supply, the number of suppliers, and relations with suppliers, there is some evidence too that the proportion outsourced has increased. It also has varied considerably between motor companies in the UK, as well as between countries. According to the DTI report on automotive castings (DTI, 1990b, p.23), total outsourcing averages in Japan about 70% of the value of the car [so the Japanese motor manufacturer in chapter 5, MOT-J-P1, is exactly in this respect], compared to 58% in Europe, and 50% in Ford USA. Some car manufacturers in Britain were claiming that they were now outsourcing 80% of the value of the car, higher than in the Japanese motor industry, in order to concentrate on their core business. For example, all major motor manufacturers in Britain, 'have, under pressure of international competition, outsourced more castings work, closed or sold tied [casting] operations and sought lowest total global costs for sourcing' (DTI, 1990b, p.29).

Relations between motor manufacturers and suppliers: since 70% or more of a car's value in the UK or Japan may be made by external suppliers, relations with these suppliers assume crucial importance, not only in terms of ensuring efficient supply lines but also of developing technical change and cost reduction to stay competitive.

The Japanese system will be well illustrated by the examples of the sample companies in chapter 5, and although minor complaints surface, basically the system appears to work harmoniously. The British system of motor supply, in contrast, has a history of unsatisfactory relations, especially in the changing power balance between suppliers and motor manufactures. Attempts by existing manufacturers to improve relations with suppliers have to operate against this background. Attempts by new arrivals, namely Japanese inward investors such as Toyota and Nissan, to operate less adversarial supply chain management are instructive (see NEDC, 1991a).

The changing balance of power between the manufacturers and the large component suppliers has been carefully documented in the case of the Austin Rover Group of British Leyland by Bessant et al (1984), and more generally by Carr (1990). In the West Midlands, the centre of the component sector, a strong and stable position has developed for the automotive suppliers by the early 1970s; the motor manufacturers had enjoyed a steadily rising market and there was a strong and confident supplier base (33). Over the 1970s, the largest 66 components companies in the UK earned a rate of return on capital employed of 18% on average, double that of the average of the motor manufacturers (Carr,1990, pp.190-1, 199).

Difficulties faced by the car-makers in the later 1970s caused a new and harder attitude on the part of car-makers, as import penetration rapidly eroded their share of the UK car market. Ironically, Austin Rover introduced many practices, now praised as part of the Japanese system, such as target price reductions, and requiring suppliers to open their books. Suppliers were squeezed between these requirments and rising prices for energy and raw material inputs from suppliers against whom the automotive suppliers had little market power. Automotive suppliers generally suffered losses during the 1979-82 recession, and their trading activities were hard hit by the rising real exchange rate. 'Suicidal' pricing in the early 1980s reduced the ability of many suppliers to finance R&D and investment out of retained profits (although the major suppliers had debt-equity ratios sufficiently low to allow them to borrow for expansion if necessary - Bessant et al, 1984, p.78).

By 1983, in spite of Austin Rover moving towards 2-3 year contracts with suppliers, a previously rare arrangement for the group, many suppliers interviewed by Bessant et al (1984, p.67) still felt badly towards Austin Rover. This was despite claims by the group that it had subsidized suppliers in the form of higher prices than necessary (i.e. with respect to import supply prices). Only Ford among the well-established car makers in Britain appeared to have moved to better relations. The newer, less friendly attitude which had developed among the suppliers by the early 1980s appears to have persisted; it includes an unwillingness to collaborate on research, and also in many cases an explicit policy to reduce dependence on the motor industry (DTI,1990b, p.49).

3.2.3 The electronics industry (34)

No industry has experienced as rapid technological change as electronics. Changes in electronics technology also have been fundamental in changes in manufacturing methods in other industries, and in their final products; this is certainly true for our other two industries, engineering and motor manufacture. Changes in technology also have led consumer demand, with new consumer electronics products such as video recorders and CD players. There have been enormous increases in computing power, associated with developments in semiconductor technology. This has resulted in drastically shortened product life cycles, as desktop personal computer use expanded during the 1980s, to be followed rapidly by the use of portable computers, reduced to notebook size by the early 1990s. These changes have been accompanied by the rise of Japan as a leading competitor to challenge the United States; by the growth of technological capacity in East Asian countries, especially South Korea; and by the globalization of the industry, with growing foreign investment in industrial countries. Europe, and especially Britain, have tended to fall behind in all but telecommunications and defence.

Pressures for change in the world economy: experience has varied between different sectors in electronics. There seems little agreement between most commentators on electronics as to what precisely the sectoral division should be (35), but a division into at least five sectors is useful for our purposes:

--semiconductors,
--consumer electronics,
--computers and information technology,
--defence, aerospace, and telecommunications,
--(other) electronic components.

Developments in semiconductors underlie most changes in the electronics industry (36). Developed in the United States over forty years ago, semiconductor technology was make widely available by generous licencing arrangements offered by Bell Laboratories, and spread rapidly not only to independent manufacturers in the US, but also to Japan and other countries in East Asia. The availability of this new electronics technology, was crucial to the development of exports of transistor radios from Japan, pioneered by Sony. This export boom became the basis of the growth of the consumer electronics industry in Asia (37). Production of radios was largely ceded to the Japanese, and American and European manufacturers shifted to television production. While radios later were subcontracted to Hong Kong, subsequently followed by Taiwan, and then Korea, Singapore and Malaysia, orders for semiconductors and passive components were sourced back to Japan, further stimulating Japanese technological capacity. Competition, and the development of a labour shortage in Japan (and Hong Kong) in the late 1960s led to investment offshore in Taiwan, Korea and Singapore, both by Japanese (38) and American television manufacturers. However, in the 1970s, when Japanese colour televisions began making serious inroads into the American market and American manfacturers started to move their production offshore as they had done with monochrome TVs, Japanese manufacturers moved to more automated production, and to large-scale integrated circuitry based on their capabilities in semiconductor design. In this way the Japanese proved able to compete against production based on low labour costs, and the pattern was repeated for semiconductor manufacture itself (Gregory, 1982, pp.48-9).

In semiconductor production, European firms had lost ground to American competition after the late 1960s, as integrated circuits, developed by US firms, replaced discrete components like transistors. European producers retreated into more specialized ICs, leaving standard ICs to the Americans. Only a handful of European firms, especially Siemens and Philips, were able to match American research expenditure. American direct investment in Europe, to source cheaper technical labour and to circumvent the EEC external tariff on semiconductors, has left US companies accounting for a substantial proportion of European semiconductor production (Morgan and Sayer, 1988, pp.48-51).

The stimulus to semiconductor developments in the United States had come first from defence and the space programme, and then from the computer industry (which required not only very advanced chips but large volumes of standard ones). Japan's semiconductor development was centred on consumer electronics firms, with encouragement and aid from the Ministry of International Trade and Industry, and has derived far more of its demand from innovative developments in consumer products (Morgan and Sayer, 1988, pp.55-59). Indeed. much of Japanese competitive stategy in consumer electronic products has been based on an interaction of innovations in semiconductor technology and product development, which has seen Japanese companies establishing a dominant position. Other East Asian countries have tried to emulate Japan, especially South Korea, whose heavy R&D expenditure in semiconductors and other areas may help it displace Britain for fourth place (after the USA, Japan, and West Germany) in world electronics production (FEER, 31.10.91).

Changes in Britain: the McKinsey report on electronics, produced for the National Economic Development Office (NEDC,1988), argues that at first sight, developments in Britain over the 1970s and 1980s have looked quite promising. Over the decade 1976-86 the size of the electronics market in the UK rose by 9.4% annually (in real terms), above the average for the six major industrial countries surveyed, and second only to Japan. UK electronics production rose by exactly the average (8.4% p.a.), again, second only to Japan's performance. However, this masks a considerable penetration of the British industry by foreign investors (including most main Japanese consumer electronics companies) and relatively poor performance by indigenous British firms. The eight major British companies surveyed for the report (39) had seen their share of the UK market fall from 48% to 31%, and their share of consumer electronics products had fallen to 1%, a virtually complete exit in the face of Japanese and other Asian competition. At the same time, their dependence on defence and aerospace, and telecommunications, had risen from 47% to 56% (of which about two-thirds was defence and aerospace). Since these markets were relatively protected over that period and are likely to decline in future with the collapse of the Soviet Union and the liberalization of procurement in the UK, the prospects for British companies are less than encouraging (40).

Subcontracting and change in electronics: the McKinley report's recommendations for change to improve British performance in electronics were:

--British companies should concentrate on fewer areas of business and **think out more carefully what should be the core areas they chose**.
--that they should **work with suppliers to create a better components infrastructure**.
--that they should change their structure to gain greater synergies between different parts of the business.
--that they should communicate their long-term strategy to the financial markets in order to combat 'short-termism'.
--that they should pay attention to human resources and develop world class skills (NEDC,1988, p.3).

Thus, within these proposed reorganizations, issues associated with subcontracting play an important part. Later official reports have concentrated on opportunities for developing the components industry, particularly with respect to the requirements of Japanese inward investors (since much of the consumer electronics market has been lost to them anyway!) (see DTI, 1990a,1990c, 1991a, 1991b); and the National Economic Development Council has tried to persuade British electronics companies of the benefits of collaborative sourcing (NEDC, 1991b), as also does the DTI (1991b)
   The work of Sako (especially 1990, Ch.6), Ikeda (1979), and the case study material to be presented in chapter 6, shows Japanese electronics production, in consumer electonics and computing for example, to be highly outsourced. Outsourcing in electronics, however, presents particular problems about what should be the core technology to be kept in-house. In semiconductor production in particular, short-term cost gains from buying chips from merchant producers who can reap large economies of scale may be at the expense of long-term technological dependence. Major computing companies like IBM, and the large Japanese consumer electronics companies, maintain considerable in-house technological capability in this area. Morgan and Sayer (1988, p. 51) warn of the dangers to British companies of lacking this capability. Other items, however, can be outsourced more logically. Some 45% of the market for printed circuit boards is 'captive' (i.e. generated by in-house production). While this is to be expected for high technology (multilayed) PCBs (where the in-house proportion is much higher), simpler boards could be outsourced more cheaply from specialist producers (DTI, 1990c, p.36). The adoption of surface-mount technology for PCB assembly, subject to greater economies of scale than the older (through-hole) method (which itself had been automated), has seen the growth of contract assemblers in the UK (ACeM, 1991), who serve a variety of electronics sectors (41).
   According to the NEDC (1991b, p.3), many major British electronics companies are now buying amounts equivalent to about 50-70% of their turnover. However, components tend to be globally sourced, and a study

of component purchasing by Japanese foreign investors showed that only 15% of their component requirements were sourced in the UK, while 20-30% were sourced in-house (including purchases from affiliates in Japan). Roughly double the British proportions were each sourced in continental Europe and Asia (DTI, 1991a,p.ii).

Computers as a sector for study: in chapter 6, computers have been chosen as the sector from which most of the electronics interviewees have been chosen. Unlike consumer electronics, this is an area where indigeous British companies still have some presence (42), although the main British computer company, ICL, was taken over in 1990 by the largest Japanese manufacturer of mainframes, Fujitsu, on whom it had become overwhelmingly dependent for supplies of chips. Europe in general, not only the UK, has lagged behind the United States in computer technology. Following initiatives from MITI in the 1970s (Morgan and Sayer, 1988, p.87), there has been Japanese competition against the United States in mainframe computers by Fujitsu, NEC and Hitachi. Other Japanese companies, Mitsubishi Electric, Oki and Toshiba eventually withdrew from mainframes, but have been active in micro computers and in peripheral equipment such as printers. The expansion of micro computers in the early 1980s has greatly changed the computer market, moving it towards mass-marketing, mass-production and also to considerable new entry, as new companies such as Apple challenged IBM's dominant position (43), as also have a variety of entrants from East Asia. Consumer electronics companies in Japan, such as Sharp and Toshiba, have become formidable competitors in the production of notebook computers, and there are new British companies such as Viglen.
The European computer industry has been severely affected by the 1990-2 recession. Germany's largest computer manufacturer, has lost money on its computer business, as has Bull, the main French manufacturer (The Economist, 20.4.91). Semiconductor manufacture too has had problems, with losses for most chipmakers, including Philips, Europe's largest electronics company (FT, 29-4-91). IBM has recently (November 1991) announced job cuts of 20,000 from its 300,000 world-wide work force, including job losses in the UK, and in February 1992 its first ever losses were announced (Guardian, 18.1.91). Recession in overseas markets also has adversely affected the electronics industry in Japan (FEER, 28.2.91).
Thus, there are many pressures for change in the computing industry, and chapter 6 will try to locate the role of subcontracting decisions among them. The interviewing is not exclusively confined to the computing sector of electronics, since many suppliers (e.g. printed circuit board manufacturers and assemblers) service several sectors, and because it is of interest to see some contrasts between computing and other aspects of electronics.

NOTES

1. A factor intensity reversal is said to occur when an industry which uses relatively highly capital-intensive methods in one country ('relatively', that is, to some other industry) uses relatively less capital-intensive methods in another country; in other words, where the ranking of industries by the ratio of capital to labour use differs between countries. Such reversals can occur because industries differ in the extent to which they

can substitute capital for labour in production. Thus an industry with a relatively high elasticity of substitution between capital and labour can use relatively labour-intensive methods in countries where labour is cheap, and relatively capital-intensive methods in countries where labour costs are high. If technology in the industry also differs between countries, further complications can arise.

2.   An example of a country where the legal framework governing intercompany transactions is ineffective to an extent that could inhibit subcontracting is mainland China (see Leung et al, 1991, Thoburn et al, 1990, p.154, and Thoburn et al, 1991). A case where an industry which is highly vertically integrated in one country (South Korea) and highly outsourced in another (Taiwan) is provided by Levy (1991) in his study of footwear. Levy argues the difference can be traced to transactions costs differences, such as the longer experience of commercial transactions in Taiwan. It will be shown later in the present chapter that the motor industry in the United States developed in a far more vertically integrated fashion than in the UK.

3.   The analysis of British Census of Production data (for 1987) was done in a working paper by Susan Bailey, research associate on the parallel University of East Anglia subcontracting project 'Subcontracting and the Small Business'. Mrs Bailey very kindly has made her working paper available to me.

4.   Data in the Census of Production on the share of materials purchases in gross output is not useful for present purposes. It gives an indication of vertical integration but, since it includes raw materials as well as manufactured inputs, variations between industries need not reflect interindustry differences in the use of subcontracting. Comparisons of a particular industry across countries may be instructive, however (see ch.2).

5.   During the early stages of the research some textile companies were interviewed in Britain, and originally the intention was also to include textiles, since subcontracting appeared to be important in that industry. However, it proved possible to secure only one interview with a textile company in Japan, after approaches had been made to many others. Although some further British textile companies were interviewed in 1991, it was decided eventually that the lack of a comparison with Japan would prove a compelling drawback. Also, the parallel University of East Anglia subcontracting project was not able to include textile companies in its quantitative data base. Where material collected on textiles is relevant to the discussion, it will be introduced into the text, and could be the subject of more research at a later date, with more interviewing.

6.   The initial identification of companies from Japanese-language sources, the practical arrangement of most interviews, and translation during most interviews, was carried out by Makoto Takashima. Other interviews were arranged by Shigeru Fujita of Showa Ota Company, Tokyo. See also chapter 7 for some further comments on the interviewing programme in Japan arranged by

Professor Takashima.

7. The earlier interviewees were companies identified during the course of a pilot postal questionnaire used by the parallel University of East Anglia project. Janet Anderson of the UEA Economics Research Centre made the practical arrangements for these interviews.

8. See Walker (1985). For some further discussion about qualitative research applied to the study of firms, see Thoburn et al (1990, pp.4-7). Note too that many studies of technical change in economics have focussed on change at the level of individual firms and have adopted a basically qualitative approach -see for example Katz (1987). The organizational change represented by the growth of subcontracting lends itself to a similar approach.

9. Besides being a convenient way to introduce engineering, this also reflects the fact that the motor industry and electronics have more of a literature of their own. Mechanical engineering is often discussed as part of a more general framework, which presents data on the industry only in the wider context. Useful material on engineering is found in a series of National Economic Development Council reports (NEDC, 1990a, 1990b, 1990c), and in Atkinson and Meager (1986). See also Freeman (1985) on technical change. Chudnovsky et al (1983) and Pack (1981) discuss the development of capital goods production in the Third World, which is relevant to growing competition, especially in machine tools, from newly industrializing countries like Taiwan. For a study of the development of machine tool production in Taiwan, and the role of government intervention in that development, see Amsden (1977). Chudnovsky et al (1983, Ch.1) also give a useful introduction to the industrial economics of engineering in the world economy, and (ch.5 - by S. Jacobsson) a study of technology in the machine tool industry (with special reference to computer-numerically-controlled lathes). For a discussion of the British machine tool industry, which compares it to that of West Germany, see Parkinson (1984). For Japan, Friedman (1988) is excellent. There is much material in the annual English-language survey by KSK, the Japan Society for the Promotion of (the) Machine Industry (see KSK, 1986 - according to the librarian of the KSK Library in Tokyo in November 1990, the 1986 edition was the last issue published of this survey). KSK also conducted a large-scale survey of principals and subcontractors in Japanese engineering in 1981 (KSK,1982). The KSK material includes electrical engineering and the motor industry, as well as 'industrial machinery' (the nearest Japanese equivalent to mechanical engineering).

10. The NEDC report (1990c, p.16) cites employment figures from the Engineering Employers Federation. These figures in general differ only slightly from those of the Department of Employment used in Table 3.7; except for mechanical engineering, where the difference is quite marked - a 39% fall from 1979 to 1989, compared to a fall of 24% on Department of Employment data.

11. In 1990,in the UK, Standard International Trade Classification division 78 (road vehicles) accounted for £5.298 billion of the

total deficit of £5.310 billion for SITC section 7 (machinery and transport equipment). Division 79 (other transport equipment) had a surplus of £0.886 billion (CSO, 1990b).

12.   Of course, this labour shakeout, though it raises labour productivity in an individual sector, has not been accompanied by increased labour absorption from growth elsewhere in the economy, hence growing unemployment in the UK. Freeman (1985, p.124) is pessimistic about reversing the long-term decline in mechanical engineering employment, given the possibilities for technical change, in the absence of a major expansion of demand for British engineering products.

13.   SITC section 7 (machinery and transport equipment), excluding divisions 78 and 79 (road vehicles, and other transport equipment).

14.   The UK's share of world exports of all machinery and transport equipment fell from 7.5% in 1980 to 5.5% in 1989, and from 6% to 4% for automotive products alone. The rises for Japan were, respectively, 14.5% to 18%, and 20% to 22% (GATT, 1990).

15.   Engineering in both the UK and Japan is highly export-orientated. This is especially so in Japan, with over 44% of output exported, and nearly 49% in industrial machinery (KSK, 1986, p.4). In the UK, engineering on the broadest definition exported (at least) 32% of its output in 1989 (the figure rises by half a percentage point if motor vehicles and other transport equipment are excluded). For mechanical engineering alone the figure is (at most) 43%, and for machine tools 33%. [Production figures for engineering in general are those from the UK Census of Production, SIC division 3, compared to export figures for SITC section 7. For mechanical engineering, exports are taken as SITC 71-74, and output is that of SIC class 32. However, SITC 74 appears to include some products of SIC 31 (manufacture of metal goods, not elsewhere specified); while some products of SIC 31 may be included in SITC 69. Machine tools are taken as SITC 73 and SIC 322.]

16.   Another technological development in machine tools has been that of physico-chemical devices such as electro-chemical machining, which shapes metal by erosion (Parkinson, 1984, pp.108-9).

17.   This account draws heavily on the case study by Jacobsson of CNC machine tools (in Chudnovsky et al, 1983, ch.5), and Friedman (1988, ch.3) on Japanese machine tool policy. Jacobsson's case study is made with special reference to lathes, which he says account for about a quarter of all investment in machine tools.

18.   Germany moved from no.1 to no.3 world producer of machine tools from 1977 to 1981, with the USA becoming no.1 and Japan no.2 (Parkinson, 1984, p.111). In terms of exports of machine tools, however, (West) Germany remained the largest, though its share of world exports dropped from 31% in 1970 to 24% in 1990, while Japan's share rose from 3% to 18% over the same period, overtaking the USA (The Economist, 16 November 1991).

19.   Parkinson's (1984) comparison of the British and West German
      machine tool industries starts with the assumption that new
      product development is essential to competitive advantage for
      Western producers, as Third World producers will have lower
      manufacturing costs for standard products. He regards this as true
      for most manufacturing industry, but especially for mechanical
      engineering. He traces the better performance in new product
      development and technological innovation in German machine tool
      production to a better interaction between machine tool producers
      and domestic customers, and to other factors such as the greater
      use of engineers in German management, and more and better use of
      applied research in engineering in universities and research
      institutes. The greater independence of the German machine tool
      companies, which usually are medium size and independent also
      allows more innovation, he argues. The British ones are more
      typically part of groups and less able to make independent
      decisions, yet do not pool resources within the   group for
      innovation. Parkinson's account, though interesting and worthwhile
      on its own terms, has little to say about Japanese competition.
      That competition changed the rules-of-the-game and made the
      difference between British and German stategies more of a marginal
      choice, more relevant to meeting Third World competition;
      meanwhile the Japanese captured the market by dramatic product
      change. Note too that according to Freeman (1985, pp.66,68) there
      were great differences between British best-practice and the
      average level of labour productivity in British engineering
      companies; especially since the mid-1970s and more so than for
      example in electronics.

20.   Piore and Sabel (1984, Chs.6 and 8), explain German historical
      dominance in machine tools in terms of the importance of craft
      production. The machine tool industry kept the craft tradtion
      alive in Germany, and helped German engineering retain its
      competitive position in the face of American mass production by
      building on technical virtuosity (p.144). Piore and Sabel see
      Japanese success in machine tool production as depending on
      developing mass production of the machine tools, while aiming at
      the small/medium firm market which was based on more flexible,
      craft-style production (pp.216-220).

21.   Of course, this abstracts from the transactions-cost-economics
      problem discussed in chapter 1 that individual suppliers may
      hesitate to undertake highly specific investment and become
      dependent on a small number of customers even though they can
      produce more cheaply than their customers can do in-house, and
      buyers may hesitate to depend on external supply for a vital input
      even if the external supply is cheaper.

22.   But note that his figures are for a firm in a 'developing country
      in Asia' (Chudnovsky et al, 1983, pp.198-9). The interviews in
      Ch.4 will suggest that in the early 1980s British machine tool
      production was more vertically integrated. International trade in
      engineering   components   has   given   developing   countries
      opportunities for starting in a limited way with engineering items
      which were suitable for local production, while importing the rest
      - see Thoburn (1973). The reason for the higher proportion of

components outsourced in CNC compared to conventional lathe production almost certainly lies in the relatively high cost of the CNC unit.

23. However, note that according to the 1981 survey by the Japan Society for Promotion of [the] Machine Industry, a combination of rapid technical change and intensified competition in engineering more generally, was forcing changes in subcontracting, although less in the amount of outsourcing than with regard to the relations between principal and subcontractor, which were becoming harsher (KSK,1982,pp.1-5). Indeed, there were some expectations that the already high degree of subcontracting might be somewhat diminished in the process of rationalization (KSK,1982, pp.9-10).

24. Their work included a study of 19 engineering companies, covering mechanical engineering, office machinery and data processing equipment, electrical/electronic, and instrument engineering (i.e. 1980 SIC groups 32,33,34,37).

25. For example, a report by the National Economic Development Council on success factors in British engineering (NEDC, 1990b), based on interviews with ten 'highly successful' companies covering a wide spectrum of the engineering industry, identified six key factors in their performance:
   -i.a committed,long-term management philosophy
   -ii.emphasis on the product and its quality (including considerable emphasis on design for manufacture)
   -iii.continuous improvement in production processes (including better stock control, though rarely explicit just-in-time supply. The report [p.5] seemed to regard j-i-t as slightly gimmicky, though it later [p.9] mentions its use by large firms in their supply chain management)
   -iv.**close relations with suppliers** (with a stress on trust <u>and</u> contracts [sic])
   -v.valuing people
   -vi.financial strength - this especially was with regard to the ability to restructure, though no details were given in the report of what restructuring had been done. Subsidiaries of foreign companies were held to have an advantage in this respect.

26. This contrasts with the Parkinson (1984) study of British machine tools in the early 1980s, which did not make a single comment on machine tool companies' relations with their own suppliers, either in relation to new product development or any other aspect of performance. Jacobsson (in Chudnovsky et al. 1983, p.191) notes that the largest Japanese maker of CNC units had been in close contact with the machine tool manufacturers, and this cooperation had been crucial in the development of low cost CNC units. What Parkinson does comment on, however (p.100), is the importance (for innovation) of what he calls 'organizational interdependence' between machine tool manufacturers and selected customers in Germany, which replaced the traditional (British) pattern of buyer-seller transactions around specific purchases or sales. The reason why British machine tool companies did not cooperate with customers on development work on new machines was partly that they doubted their customers interest in new

technological developments and their ability to make a contribution to them, but also a lack of trust. It is easy to draw the inference that the machine tool companies' relations with their own suppliers may have suffered from a similar lack of trust, which would have inhibited the use of subcontracting.

27. For the motor industry there is a vast range of literature, and no attempt will be made here to survey it. On Britain: I have found Carr (1990) a very useful source of information on this literature, both with regard to motor manufacturers and to component makers. Bessant et al (1984) give a full and perceptive account of the relation between one major motor manufacturer (the Austin-Rover Group of British Leyland) and its suppliers in the West Midlands, still the area with the largest concentration of automobile components manufacture in Britain. There is also the compendium of information submitted in evidence to Parliament on the motor industry (HoC, 1987), much of which has been effectively mined by Carr. The survey of automotive castings manufacture, commissioned by the Department of Trade and Industry (DTI, 1990b), contains much on the motor manufacturer's policies [and I am grateful to the DTI for permission to quote from this report, and to one of my interviewees for bringing it to my attention]. Garel Rhys' chapter on automotive components in Bhaskar (1979) is a good picture of the components sector prior to major upheavel, though rather optimistic in the light of subsequent events; and Turner (1964) yielded some useful pieces of information. D.T. Jones (ch.2 in Freeman, 1985) discusses motor industry technology. On Japan: Odaka et al (1988) is a very full account of the institutional details of the Japanese motor industry and its subcontracting, and there is also the well-known work of Asanuma (1985 and 1989a), mentioned in chapter 2.
On the motor industry in a global context, Tolliday and Zeitlin (1986) is helpful, and I have also found useful the United Nations Commission for Transnational Corporations case studies of motor industry subcontracting in selected Third World countries (India, Peru and Morocco) (UNCTC, 1981).

28. The material in this paragraph derives heavily from the introductory chapter of Tolliday and Zeitlin (1986).

29. For discussion of other aspects of reorganization, such as changing employment practices, see Tolliday and Zeitlin (1986).

30. Of course, some of these suppliers will have been supplying standard items, and are not subcontractors in our sense. Issues on the size of the supplier base are taken up in chapter 5. The record for the total number of suppliers may be held by Toyota. Aoki (1988, pp.204-5) notes that in 1977 an unnamed motor company in Japan, believed to be Toyota, was found in a survey by MITI's Small and Medium Enterprise Agency to have direct relations with 122 first tier suppliers, and indirect relations with 5,437 second tier and 41,703 third tier suppliers. After allowing for double-counting, Toyota was thought to stand at the apex of a stratified group with a membership of 35,768 suppliers. [This is discussed further by Makoto Takashima in chapter 7 - see Figure 7.2]
Bessant et al (1984, Ch.7) estimated that in the West Midlands,

for each of Austin Rover's first tier suppliers (38 of whom constituted 80% of Austin Rover's supply), there were a further 200 second tier suppliers with an average of 70 workers each. Against a total Austin Rover West Midlands workforce of 17,600, there were some 21,000 workers in first tier, and some 20-47,000 in second tier firms, engaged on work for Austin Rover. This a highly 'outsourced' workforce, even compared to that of the Japanese motor manufacturer of chapter 5, MOT-J-P1.

31. For example, Ford's famous Baton Rouge plant in the USA, built at the end of the First World War, was vertically integrated from steel making to final assembly, with its own railways, docks and power plant (Tolliday and Zeitlin, 1986, pp.2-3).

32. Both Ford and British Leyland in the early 1980s carried out detailed international surveys of component costs, and found that almost all parts were produced in Japan 10-35% more cheaply than in Europe (Carr, 1990,pp.80-81). Of course, this was before the large rise in the Yen exchange rate.

33. Note that car and component manufacture in the UK had had tariff protection up to 1960 (Carr,1990,p.79), subsequently eroded by international trade negotiations and the freeing of trade within the European Community.
   By 1979, nominal tariff protection (i.e. protection on gross output value) on motor vehicles and parts was down to 1.8%, and the effective rate of protection (i.e. on value-added) was 3.3%. Effective rates of protection for our other industries of interest were: metal working machine tools 2.3%; electronic components and subassemblies 2.3%, electronic consumer goods 21.9%; and domestic electrical appliances 7.7% (Greenaway, 1988)

34. The most useful reference I have found on the electronics industry is Morgan and Sayer (1988). OECD (1985) gives a good introduction to semiconductor technology, and Soete (1985) discusses electronics technology more generally. Gregory (1982) traces the development of electronics in Asia in a global context. Developments in Britain are traced in the McKinsey report (NEDC, 1988), and much information on Britain is also given in various reports for the DTI (1990a, 1990c, 1991a, 1991b). On Japan, Ikeda (1979) discusses subcontracting in electronics, and the work of Sako (1988, 1990, 1991, 1992) is extremely useful.

35. For example, Morgan and Sayer (1988, pp.41-2) divide the industry into four sectors (semiconductors, consumer electronics, computer systems, and telecommunications), and argue that finer detail is likely to be of limited and transitory interest. The McKinsey report (NEDC,1988, p.5) writes of seven sectors (defence and aerospace, computers and automation, electronic components, software, consumer electronics, telecommunications equipment, and instruments), and Gregory (1982) stresses the diversity of experience between three sectors (consumer electronics, semiconductors, and industrial electronics).

36. A semiconductor is an active component, i.e. one which 'modifies or controls electrical signals by amplification, switching action

52

or modulation of the signal in a circuit', as opposed to a <u>passive</u> component, which does not change the energy of a signal. More generally, active <u>solid state</u> components are based on material which has semiconducting properties, of which silicon is the best known. Semiconductors may be of several types, especially <u>discretes</u>, which are individual components like transistors, or <u>integrated circuits</u> ('IC's). Integrated circuits may be <u>microprocessors</u>, which perform computing functions, or <u>memories</u>. A <u>chip</u> is a small piece of semiconducting material on which an IC is fabricated, and the term 'chip' is often used synonymously with ICs (OECD, 1985, pp.8-11). ICs, and other electronic components, are normally placed on a <u>printed circuit board</u> ('PCB'), and this forms the core of an electronics product, such as a micro computer. The placing of components on to a PCB is known as PCB <u>assembly</u>, and has itself been subject to considerable technical change. Some applications, such as mini-computers, require multilayered PCBs.

37. Exports to the US were greatly aided too by the policies of American chain stores, who actively sought out cheap sources of supply from Asia, in the face of highly cartelized Western radio production (Gregory, 1982, pp.45-6).

38. The regulations about the exporting of capital from Japan were liberalized in 1968.

39. The McKinsey report included material based on interviews with 30 major companies: British Aerospace, Ferranti, GEC-Marconi, Plessey, Racal, STC-ICL, Thorn EMI, and Logica of the UK; eight American companies including IBM, Apple, and Digital; six Japanese, six continental European, and two South Korean.

40. The British companies maintained only an 8.9% share of electronic components sales, 22.6% of the computers and automation market, though over 80% of software sales (NEDC, 1988, pp.11,18).

41. Though the largest customer is computing/electronic data processing, which accounts for almost two-thirds of the sales of the member companies of the Association of Contract Electronics Manufacturers (interview, September 1991).

42. See note 40.

43. IBM's market share of the world market fell from 60% in 1967 to 40% in 1980. The company fought back against competition, especially with the introduction of its micro-computer, the PC, which rapidly became a market leader. By 1984, it had a 76% share of the world mainframe computer market, and 45% of the micro-computer market (Morgan and Sayer, 1988, pp. 82-3)

4 The engineering companies

This chapter considers the experience of subcontracting among four principals and five subcontractors in the UK engineering industry, and two principals and three subcontractors in Japan (1). Section 1 introduces the sample of companies. Section 2 considers the factors underlying the decision to subcontract, how this has changed in Britain in the last decade, and how it compares to the situation in Japan. Section 3 looks at issues of supply chain management, how British companies are changing their views on the subcontracting relation, and how such relations are conducted among the Japanese companies interviewed. This section mainly takes the principals' viewpoint, though some subcontractor material is introduced too. Section 4 asks how subcontracting appears from the perspective of the British and Japanese subcontractors.

4.1 The companies

Introductory profiles of the engineering principals are given in Table 4.1. Table 4.2 introduces the subcontractors. Although information was collected on companies' employment, date of foundation, share of exports in turnover, detailed product mix, and so on, this is normally suppressed so as to preserve the companies' anonymity. This is done especially where principals are concerned, who are likely to be more easily recognisable than subcontractors. All the British and Japanese principals are well-established companies. The British principals vary in size from a few hundred employees to over a thousand, while the Japanese principals are somewhat smaller. Of the British subcontractors, all but one have under a hundred employees, while the Japanese subcontractors, though still small companies, are a little larger on average than the British ones. All the principals, British and Japanese, are significantly involved in export markets, some very heavily so.

Table 4.1
The Engineering Principals

Company	Main Products	Items on Subcontract	Attitude to Subcontracting
British Principals ENG-GB-P1	Heavy and medium engineering products	Heat treatment, large machining jobs, plastic work, electronics	Normally try to do as much in-house as possible but now considering putting more work out
ENG-GB-P2	Machine tools	Complete assemblies, turned parts, cyanide hardening, and many others	Outsource as much as possible to concentrate on core business
ENG-GB-P3	Machine tools	In state of flux	Until now, do as much in-house as possible, but on verge of major reorganization towards outsourcing
ENG-GB-P4	Machine tools	Castings, electronic control equipment, sheet metal work, small machined items	Concentrate on major items, and outsource everything else
Japanese Principals ENG-J-P1	Machine tools	Key specialized parts such as machine heads, complete simpler versions of main product	Outsource to concentrate firm's resources for growth on core activities. Maintain in-house capability for key subcontracted items
ENG-J-P2	Machine tools	Subassembly and fabrication, design of optional special features	Outsource to access cheaper hourly rates, and to reduce effect of business fluctuations.

55

Table 4.2
The Engineering Subcontractors

Company	Main Products	Main Industries Supplied	Attitude to Subcontracting
British Subcontractors			
ENG-GB-S1	Specialist engineering (non-CNC), items for prototypes, one-off machine tools	Machine tools	Worried by severe price cutting by other subcontractors in 1990-1 during recession
ENG-GB-S2	General precision engineering, mainly with CNC equipment	Telecommunications, printing, and others	Subcontracting has improved as many of the worst customers failed during the early 1980s recession
ENG-GB-S3	High quality electronic pressings	Wide variety of industries (including motor industry)	Feels customers do not nurture suppliers enough
ENG-GB-S4	Machinery designing and manufacture	Engineering, oil and others (including motor industry)	Could expand by taking on more subcontracting, but reluctant to do so because of periodic recession
ENG-GB-S5	High precision engineering, both conventional and CNC	Food, medical, defence and others (including motor industry)	Regards subcontracting as a somewhat hostile environment, and is diversifying into own end products to some extent
Japanese Subcontractors			
ENG-J-S1	Machinery fabrication and assembly	Machine tools	Very appreciative of technical advice and help received from main customer
ENG-J-S2	Structural steelwork	Engineering subcontracting, food industry	Appreciates ability to grow rapidly with main customer
ENG-J-S3	Machinery manufacture	Industrial machinery	Accustomed to long and close relation with main customer

4.2 The subcontracting decision

4.2.1 The British principals

Among the British engineering principals there is clear evidence of a radical rethinking of what the efficient (vertical) boundary of the firm should be. As discussed in chapter 3, engineering has been seriously affected by foreign competition, in both export and home markets. It was also hit hard by the recession of the early 1980s, and the early 1990s recession has further intensified pressure on the companies. All of the British principals were operating with workforces at least 50% less than at the end of the 1970s. Thus reorganization has seemed a necessary condition for survival. For the three British machine tool companies, redefining the core of the business, shrinking to that core and putting other operations out to subcontract, has been the central feature. The reorganizations have been accompanied by other changes, but these have been closely linked to outsourcing policy. The more traditional engineering company, ENG-GB-P1 has reorganized too, but subcontracting has been less subject to change than in the others.

The machine tool company, ENG-GB-P2, exemplifies these changes in the boundary of the firm. Having built up a strong export position, and achieved a substantial share of the UK market, based on a fairly standard machine tool produced in large volumes, GB-P2 encountered competition from Taiwan, South Korea and India. While the East Asian competitors initially produced a cheaper but inferior product, though often superficially an exact copy, the Asian products eventually achieved comparable quality. The British company also admits it was slow in seeing the implications of technical change, especially the applications of electronics.

Faced with production at little more than a quarter of capacity in the early 1980s, GB-P2's reorganization involved:
-reassessing the organization of work on the company's site; 'we measured our chaos and tried to eliminate it'. An important aspect of reducing this chaos was drastically to cut stock-holdings on-site with a view to arranging just-in-time delivery from suppliers.
-reducing the site size, and concentrating production on one area of the old site.
-redesigning the main product to make a more sophisticated machine with better cutting characteristics and bigger throughput, at little more than the original cost. In particular, it replaced mechanical parts with electronics as far as possible.

A changing policy towards outsourcing went together with the other organizational changes. The new product was designed, and several updated older products too were redesigned. This was to reduce the number and the complexity of parts, and to standardize parts between machines, all with a view to using parts which could be put out to subcontractors.

At the same time, GB-P2 conducted an exercise, lasting six months, which graded parts into three categories, according to which a part would be definitely for in-house production, or would be one for which a subcontractor would be sought, and there was an intermediate category where subcontracting would depend on the competence of the suppliers available. The main criterion was to put to outside supply those parts which were expensive to make in-house but which a specialist supplier with larger volumes could do more cheaply. These included various turned parts, small shafts and gears, small levers. Items to be retained in-house were those which had required very heavy investment and specialist expertise, such as the machines beds and major prismatics (e.g. big gearboxes), and where it was expected that an outside supplier could not provide adequate service. The changes in supply chain management implied by this reorganization are taken up in the next section.

The basic experience of ENG-GB-P3 is very similar to that of GB-P2. A major player in the British and world market for its product, it has been heavily hit by the recessions of the past decade. Although it has faced East Asian competition, sometimes by superficially exact copies too, the East Asian competitors have not been able yet to match the quality and durability of its product range. Like the (reorganized) GB-P2 it also has been able to match Japanese competition both on quality and price, and has actually mainly faced competition from European producers. The early 1990s recession has been the final factor in pushing it in towards the major reorganization on which it is now on the verge. Under GB-P3's reorganization it plans to more than quadruple the amount it puts out to subcontract, having previously done as much in-house as possible. It wants to put out non-crucial, low profit items like small-turn parts. These occupy factory space and can be done easily and more cheaply by specialist subcontractors with lower overheads, on the basis of drawings supplied by the principal. Similarly, gear-cutting will be outsourced and the old, existing gear-cutting machines in-house will not be replaced. The company also stresses its wish to outsource complete assemblies of particular items rather than just parts, because it does not want to incur overheads on the organization of different components of an assembly. The core items which will be retained in-house are: the main machine build, big components such as machine beds, and crucial items like spindles. In part the desire to outsource is to avoid too drastic contraction in the downturns in business which have seemed to come every four years, but the company recognises it cannot just pull back from suppliers in bad times and expect easily to reestablish contact in the revival. Like GB-P2, the company also is aiming at an organization which will allow it to survive with a very small order book in bad times, while maintaining ability to expand when demand revives. Both companies feel they have never really come out of the early 1980s recession, and that a depressed UK market has meant an undue dependence on export sales. Some bitterness was expressed at lack of government financial help for restructuring, both compared to European competitors and with British agriculture. GB-P2 had found the Department of Trade and Industry's 'Managing into the 90s' initiative's activities on partnership purchasing a useful forum in which to exchange information with other companies, but the other companies were unaware of it.

ENG-GB-P4, the third British machine tool company interviewed, had reorganized at an earlier stage. In a similar position to GB-P2, it had built up by the late 1970s a leading position in world markets for its machines. More far-sighted perhaps than GB-P2, it had anticipated loss of market share if it did not develop a new product incorporating the new technology it saw being developed, especially in Japan. This company searched for a partner already more advanced in the application of electronics than itself. As a result, it initially added a Japanese machine under licence to its product range, and subsequently jointly designed a further, newer machine with the Japanese partner.The development of this advanced product range was accompanied by what was described as a 'culture change' in the company's organization. There were changes in factory layout, inventory holding and delivery of supplies, and changes in subcontracting, though it seemed that the company anyway had somewhat less of a tradition of doing everything in-house than the other British engineering principals interviewed. Subcontracting was facilitated by the fact that the number of parts in the new machines was reduced to about 400, compared to 2000 in the old products. By the early 1980s the company had achieved its present structure, and it enjoyed boom conditions in the mid 1980s. It was faced with competition from similar machines from Taiwan. Again, these were exactly copied (even down to typing mistakes in the operating manual!), but they only had a third of the operating life of the British machine and deteriorated in terms of accuracy. Reorganization has helped the company to survive so far the early 1990s slump in the UK, which it describes as exceptionally severe, and which has caused it to rely almost entirely on export markets for sales.

GB-P4's manufacturing philisophy has been to produce in-house only the 'majors', the principal components of its machine. These are mostly castings which are bought-in and then machined in-house to an exceptional standard of accuracy. This work uses equipment, several individual items of which represent over £1 million of investment, and are not available in prospective subcontractors. During its phases of expansion, the company decided to concentrate its investment expenditure in the latest equipment in these key areas. GB-P4's main areas of outsourcing, representing a spend equivalent to over 15% of the main factory's turnover, were for castings and electronic control equipment, obviously specialized items. Other items subcontracted were sheet metal work, and various items which small subcontractors could supply at low cost such as small shafts, handles, pulleys, and many gears.

Compared to these initiatives, changes in subcontracting within ENG-GB-P1, the more traditional engineering company, were limited, although a new parent company was pushing it in this direction to some extent. Pride had been taken in the ability to do as much as possible in-house, to maximize total value-added. In the difficult times of the early 1980s, fearing redundancies, there had been much workforce resistance to outsourcing, which was seen as a loss of employment for the existing workers and a lack of confidence in their ability. Of course, some items were subcontracted which were obviously outside the company's mainstream activities. Of the company's total outsourcing of non-standard items, three-quarters was overflow work, and only a quarter was work put out permanently. Indeed, the company understood the term 'subcontracting' only to mean putting out work which it itself had the ability but not the current capacity to do in-house. Nevertheless some changes have been made. Finding its machinery for small-turn parts constantly underutilized, for instance, the factory disposed of it, retrained the workers, and put the work out to local machine shops. Some general reorganization has taken place too, such as splitting various product operations into different profit centres.

4.2.2 The Japanese principals

The context in which the companies interviewed in Japan operate - principals and subcontractors - differs from that of the UK in at least two immediate respects:
-all but one company (in late 1990) claimed to have experienced rapid growth in sales for the last five years. The one exception had

experienced problems in depressed conditions in 1986, but its sales subsequently had revived. This growth was in spite of the fact that several companies spoke of difficulties caused by the business cycle in engineering, and especially in machine tools. Also, the domestic Japanese market was said by the companies to be intensively competitive, and export-orientated sales would have been impeded by the high Yen exchange rate of the late 1980s.

-virtually all Japanese companies spoke of a severe labour shortage, at least in major industrial regions like greater Tokyo and Nagoya. This has been an incentive to conserve their own labour force for production of items which rely most on the firm's specialist in-house expertise, and to seek subcontractors for other production.

Despite the general impression that Japanese industry has been involved heavily in subcontracting for much longer than in the UK, both Japanese engineering principals had made their main moves towards subcontracting within fairly recent years. One had moved to outsourcing in the face of depressed home market conditions in the mid-1980s, and the other had done so in the mid-1970s, when the Japanese economy was readjusting to the first oil shock.

In the case of ENG-J-P1, 80% of its requirements for what it described as key parts for its main product (equivalent to 10% of its total materials purchases) were gradually put to outside supply from 1975 to 1980. J-P1 gradually became more specialized in terms of its own machinery, in the face of technical change in the industry. It approached possible subcontractors, found ones who could perform up to its own standard. It now uses ten companies for these parts, of whom two are particularly important, within a overall supplier base of 200. It retains in-house expertise for these companents, lest there ever should be a position where outside supply should become unavailable, and perhaps because ability to make the part is conducive to more general design improvements. J-P1 felt that any diversification into other activities, including bringing in-house items which were supplied by subcontractors, would have been precluded by the labour shortage, and the unwillingness of younger workers to seek employment in the smaller kind of principal represented by J-P1. To conserve its equipment and workforce for production of its main product, this company also subcontracted the complete manufacture of a simpler machine; and it commented that its customers, out of loyalty, would not approach its subcontractor directly.

ENG-J-P2 attributed its move towards greater outsourcing in the mid 1980s to a straightforward desire to reduce costs on items which could be undertaken by specialist subcontractors, who had lower overheads and labour costs. It said it could buy-in work from such suppliers at about Y3-4000 an hour (£12-16), compared to Y10,000 (£40) in-house, and that its move towards outsourcing had greatly raised its profitablity. Three main subcontractors are used in fabrication and several in assembly. Machines often are designed with special features for customers, and this designing, which is relatively simple, is subcontracted too. The cessation of in-house production was accompanied by an upsurge of profits.

J-P2 thought that all other firms in its line of business also subcontracted to a similar extent. J-P1 thought really large engineering companies, at least two of which produced a similar product to its own, produced in-house the key parts which J-P1 subcontracted. These large companies, though, produced a standard machine, whereas P1's was highly adapted to the requirements of individual customers.

Subcontracting decisions are made too by the subcontractors themselves, there being several tiers of subcontractors. This is taken up in subsection 4.3.3.

4.3 Supply chain management

4.3.1 Subcontractor selection, development and monitoring

The recent decisions by two of the British machine tool companies greatly to increase their outsourcing have been accompanied by a more thorough and carefully thought-out approach to choosing suppliers. GB-P2 is looking for suppliers who can fit in well with its just-in-time delivery system, supplying goods in packaging which can be used immediately (e.g.trays rather than boxes). It also wants suppliers whose paper work matches the delivery (i.e. if the delivery note sent by the supplier says 100 units, there should be exactly 100 delivered). Experience has shown that meeting delivery schedules sometimes has been at the expense of quality. Some suppliers (such as many foundries) find j-i-t delivery very difficult, and some suppliers have claimed to be able to meet requirements in order to get the business, without actually being able to do so. This principal puts emphasis on suppliers being able to give a quick response to problems, realizing that problems inevitably arise and the important issue is the supplier's willingness to tackle them within 24 hours. For this reason, suppliers within a 20 mile radius are preferred, so quick visits can be made, and 150 miles is regarded as an absolute maximum. GB-P3, in the early stages of major reorganization towards outsourcing, did not have such an explicit set of requirements, but both companies stressed the need for the supplier to do the quality control, so as to avoid the need for inward inspection.
GB-P2 was developing a supplier rating system, for appraising both new and existing suppliers. It already had a large supplier base, of 150 companies, of which it dealt very regularly with about a 100. Ideally, it would prefer a base of about 50. GB-P3 stressed the desire to put out complete assemblies rather than just individual parts - in order to devolve some supplier management problems onto its own suppliers, a point to be taken up later in regard to the multi-layered Japanese subcontracting system in engineering. This would involve dealing directly with a smaller number of suppliers. GB-P4, with its outsourcing already well-established, also felt it would like further to reduce its supplier base. This not particularly because of unsatisfactory supplier performance, but was to reduce administrative costs by single-sourcing many components. It felt the early 1990s recession had pushed it in this direction, a decision it had not previously faced making. It was very critical, however, of the government for the high nominal interest rates associated with the recession (P4 had had to pay 17% for bank finance).
GB-P2's supplier selection procedure is:
-identify the item required,
-identify potential suppliers from sources such as catalogues and subcontractor exhibitions (now a regular feature of the UK scene),
-call for quotations from a selection of suppliers, and have a quality assurance team from the principal visit them,
-then decide on an overall basis, on a combination of quality, ablility to meet production schedules, and the quality of the supplier's paperwork (see first paragraph of this subsection).
This principal, which itself had achieved British Standard 5750, would

seek this if possible from suppliers. It commented, though, that some suppliers with BS5750 did not actually live up to the standard's procedures, and there was no way of reporting this back to the British Standards Institute. GB-P2 was considering an explicit supplier rating system, based on the above criteria. It was also thinking of publishing a list of the top ten, and the bottom ten suppliers, in Japanese fashion in its factory. GB-P3 commented that it also looked for BS5750, but did not insist.It noted that during the current recession many potential subcontractors were looking for business, and that supplier prices were lower now. It felt that it had not reckoned sufficiently in the past with prospective supplier price volatility, a feature rather different from the Japanese emphasis on price stability or progressive price reduction.

ENG-GB-P4, with the longest history of outsourcing, was sceptical about the ability to find new suppliers easily, just as a result of 'policy change'. It stressed how it had carried out its selection of likely subcontractors as part of its supplier development programme. It had 'grown with' several key suppliers. It did mention the importance of BS 5750 as an indication of a supplier's status, however. Although it did not have a full just-in-time delivery from its suppliers, it operated strict inventory control based on monthly scheduling of work. Its deliveries were geared to the very fast progression through the factory from basic components to finished machine. It left quality control generally to suppliers, while maintaining a high degree of traceablity of each component, both with regard to the supplier and to operations within the factory. It retained these records for warranty and customer service.

ENG-GB-P1 did not appear to have an explicit supplier selection policy, and proceded on more of an ad hoc basis.

Neither Japanese principal appeared to have a formal policy for supplier selection, but each gave very definite indications of its requirements. J-P1 had found suppliers of its key parts whose technical level was as high as its own in-house production. It did not do inward inspection. It would reject a part if it failed to meet specification, in which case it would return it and expect the subcontractor to make good the loss. It commented, however, that its subcontractors hardly ever made such mistakes. J-P2, in its selection of a subcontractor, stressed the importance of the supplier possessing the appropriate capital equipment. If an existing supplier does not have equipment needed for a particular order, it does not mean a break in relations and P2 would try to give a reliable supplier other orders. A significant part of J-P2's output consists of machine tools for the motor industry, where frequent changes in vehicle model require frequent changes of machine tools, and four years ago J-P2 itself undertook major reinvestment in CNC equipment. J-P2 regarded reliable delivery as a key requirement for successsful subcontracting.

The issue of dropping suppliers is taken up below when principals' and subcontractors' attitudes to dependence are discussed.

None of the British engineering principals appeared to have an explicit policy on subcontractor development, with the partial exception of ENG-GB-P4. All were willing to transfer technology and give other practical help in particular instances where the supplier seemed to offer good long term prospects. GB-P1 was working with a prospective new subcontractor, giving technical advice, and running trial batches at the subcontractor with materials issued by the principal, with a view to the subcontractor undertaking most of the necessary quality control.

Specialized test equipment which the supplier needed to install was allowed to be amortized over the life of the proposed contract. Also, and for the first time, the principal had worked together with a new subcontractor when tendering for an order.

With regard to technology transfer to established suppliers, in this principal's case the main instance was a two-way technical interchange with a supplier of a raw material, which had to be specially suited to the principal's needs. Here the principal retained in-house expertise specially to liase with the supplier, in a very long-established relation.

One of the British machine tool companies described its relation with an existing supplier as an example of its supplier development methods. This supplier, which the principal initially used with satisfaction for urgent overflow work on small parts, ran into difficulties when given longer term scheduled work.Eventually it was taken over by an accountant, who visited the principal and expressed strong interest in developing the relation and meeting the principal's needs. As a result the supplier bought one of the machines made by the principal to do the work. In another case, the principal had two pieces of sophisticated machinery which it could not fully utilize, and it lent these to a subcontractor

GB-P4 came closest to supplier development on the Japanese model. It spoke of the need to 'grow' suppliers, some of which had developed with it over twenty years of operations. With one of its main suppliers of electronic control equipment it had developed a relation in which the supplier progressed from 'dumb optics' on to control equipment which was especially user-friendly and preferred by small company buyers. Another key supplier, a foundry, had sent one of its engineers to P4 for six weeks, at the foundry's own expense, to learn the details of P4's manufacturing process, especially its machining, so as to produce castings exactly to P4's requirements. One of GB-P4's most important suppliers of gear cutting and small parts had been with P4 for twenty years and had grown from a two-man operation to a firm of over a hundred workers, with constant close cooperation.

Two of the British machine tool companies disliked free-issuing materials for subcontractors to work on, but were willing to do so in times of difficulty for a subcontractor. They were also willing to use their own purchasing power to get lower materials prices for subcontractors. Even when under pressure from recession, the engineering principals said they tried to ensure payment to small, heavily dependent subcontractors to keep them in business, even if it meant the principal's manufacturing staff disputing with their accounts department! The third machine tool company was willing to free-issue, and found it satisfactory if it kept a close check on wastage, and if it required scrapped material to be returned to it. This company would help a subcontractor get cheaper materials, but only for its own work. Like the other British engineering principles, it never offered financial help.

Neither of the Japanese principals appeared to have an explicit policy on the development of their subcontractors' capabilities of the sort which have become familiar through the operations of large Japanese companies in the UK (see NEDC, 1991a, p.14). They were prepared to give considerable ad hoc help, however, and subsection 4.4.4 reports on help subcontractors received from principals.

4.3.2 Contractual arrangements and the subcontracting relationship

The two British machine tool companies who had recently reorganized, or were in process of it, saw the use of contracts as a new departure and as an integral part of their increased outsourcing. Contracts also were seen as an indication to suppliers of principals' seriousness and commitment. One already gave, and the other was planning to give, contracts of 1-2 years, and to single-source in exchange for a specified quantity at an agreed price and j-i-t delivery schedule. If the actual call-offs fell short of the agreed quantity, price could be renegotiated. Both saw contracts as something of a reward for meeting their requirements. The more traditional engineering company also was willing to give contracts at an agreed price, but, instead of a specified quantity, it gave an agreed percentage of the principal's usage. For a machining order it spoke of a contract for 1-2 years. The principal prefered not to single-source, in case of disruption of supply at any one subcontractor. GB-P4, however, with longer experience of subcontracting and stressing its good working relations with its suppliers, planned its work on a three-monthly basis. It gave its suppliers three-monthly orders, with a tentative order for a fourth month; all suppliers were treated equally in this regard, no matter how long or close the relation.

The Japanese principal, ENG-J-P1, until five years ago had only given its suppliers individual orders, even though it had had relations of 10-15 years with its main suppliers of key parts. However, after a subcontractor's former employee had divulged technological information to a rival, J-P1 had become afraid of similar behaviour from suppliers, and now requires the suppliers of key parts to sign a <u>nensho</u> document, which requires the supplier to keep secret any technological information supplied during the course of its relation with P1 (2). ENG-J-P2, which has had a 15 year relation with its main subcontractor for fabricating and sub-assembly, gives a one-year basic contract which specifies the annual expected orders, which agrees the general hourly rate at which the supplier's time will be charged,and circumstances under which that rate can be changed. Orders then specify exact prices according to that general formula. J-P2's arrangement is thus not very different from that being used or proposed by the British machine tool companies, GB-P2 and GB-P3. Details about the contracts received by Japanese subcontractors are given in subsection 4.4.3.

All the British machine tool companies were against a supplier being heavily dependent on sales to them, while recognising such dependence gave them more leverage. One stressed he wanted to be free to drop a supplier if necessary, and this was easier if the supplier was not too vulnerable. Taking 30-40% of a supplier's sales was mentioned by several as a good figure. Only GB-P4 had an explicit policy on supplier dependence. GB-P4's aim was that a supplier should supply 15-20% of its sales to GB-P4. If the figure rose above about 25%, P4 would visit the supplier and suggest that the supplier should expand with other business to get the precentage down, or P4 would reduce its purchases. Another machine tool company mentioned he had had to drop some suppliers who were heavily dependent, one for bad work, but the others because of falling orders. Several subcontractors had gone out of business as a result. It is hard to know, without extensive interviewing of the firms' subcontractors, whether this implies that the starting point for the new policy, as far as it concerns existing rather than new suppliers, is a history of confrontational relations. However, one of the company's suppliers who was interviewed independently (i.e. not at the principal's suggestion) spoke of a history of good relations and its own willingness to accommodate slow payment by the principal to help the principal out of present difficulties in the recession. This subcontractor, however, was dependent on the principal for only a small percentage of its sales

Principals' views in Japanese engineering on how dependent their suppliers should be were not so clear-cut as those in the UK. ENG-J-P1 was content to let J-S1 be dependent for half of its business on the principal, but here the principal had a small equity stake and had proved willing to give financial help in case of difficulty. ENG-J-P2, in contrast, said it did not like to have subcontractors dependent on it for more than 30% of their sales, and preferred them to sell to customers in several industries to try to spread risks of business fluctuations. Neither principal appeared to operate a policy of single-sourcing, and certainly had several suppliers for key items (and in J-P1's case, as mentioned above, maintained in-house capacity as a fall-back too).

Short-term changing of subcontractors seemed to be unusual among the Japanese companies. J-P1 and J-P2 would offer help to subcontractors in difficulty. J-P1 said that it would only definitely drop a subcontractor if that subcontractor failed to keep secret technology which was transferred to it by P1. All the relations of J-P1 and J-P2 with suppliers were long-term ones, in P2's case antedating its major expansion of subcontracting in the mid 1980s.

The British principals, in spite of the alleged short-term behaviour of British principals towards suppliers, had many relations of twenty years or more, including GB-P1's relation with its main technical materials supplier and several of the main suppliers of GB-P3 and GB-P4.

4.3.3 Sub-subcontracting

The use of multi-tiered subcontracting in Japanese engineering is in striking contrast to that of British industry, where further subcontracting by subcontractors is at best tolerated by principals and only for very specialized areas obviously outside subcontractors' competence. When asked directly about subcontractors themselves subcontracting further, British principals, especially the machine tool manufacturers, stressed they were wary of it, and would like to be assured about the sub-subcontractor's performance. If the subcontractor itself subcontracted the whole job, one principal simply regarded that as a failure on his part not to have found the ultimate subcontractor himself. However, implicit in the wish to subcontract whole assemblies, rather than components which are assembled in-house, is the likelihood that the more a subcontractor is expected to do, the more that subcontractor is likely to require outside expertise and perhaps capacity. This was made explicit by a principal in the motor industry (see chapter 5) who expressed envy at the Japanese ability to manage multi-layered subcontracting by devolving the management of lower levels to subcontractors. One of his major problems was putting different subcontractors in touch with each other, and then refereeing their disputes.

In Japan, ENG-J-S1 had ten subcontractors of its own, the largest of which is ENG-J-S2. Two of the other subcontractors make machinery frames and the rest make specialized parts.S1 would not consider bringing these items in-house because:

-they generally required special skills and equipment which J-S1 did not itself have.

-J-S1 was constrained in any expansion by its site size, and so growing while putting out more to subcontractors was attractive.

-because of the business cycle in engineering, J-S1 was reluctant anyway to grow greatly by in-house production.

In turn, J-S1's largest subcontractor, J-S2, itself had a supplier base of some 15 subcontractors, constituting a fourth layer of firms (including the principal). Two were doing large, structural steelwork in areas away from the main industrial centres, and were chosen to do overflow work and because they could access low-cost labour. The others were mostly very small firms, with perhaps 2-3 people, doing particular small parts, cutting, welding. For some contract maintenance work J-S2 employed skilled, labour-only subcontractors. Some 70% of S2's turnover was made up of payments to subcontractors. J-S3 also employed subcontractors of its own, though it did not specify numbers, and said they were mostly very small, with significantly lower wages than S3 itself paid.

4.4 The subcontractors' experience of subcontracting

4.4.1 Subcontractors' perceptions of their competitive advantage

The British subcontractors in the sample seemed to perceive their competitive advantage as consisting of a combination of specialized expertise and low overheads, but not low wages. Among the principals, the more traditional engineering company said that it could now buy-in machining at a rate of £12-£15 per hour, compared to its in-house production which it costed at £25 per hour. This was in spite of the fact that it had its own considerable in-house expertise in general engineering and a tradition of buying-in castings to machine itself. Very similar figures on relative costings between in-house and subcontractors were suggested by ENG-GB-P4. A small subcontractor, doing specialized work with non-CNC equipment, costed its general machining at £18 per hour. Another subcontractor, which had invested heavily in CNC equipment equipment, thought really large companies like British Aerospace might incur costs of £70 per hour. While this may well be an exaggeration, the subcontractor clearly felt he was clearly competitive on cost as well as expertise. He suggested that large companies only kept machining work in-house which required exceptionally heavy investment in individual pieces of machinery and exceptionally high precision. For instance, one of his large customers had just bought a £1.5 million grinding machine, an investment a small firm could not contemplate. ENG-GB-P4 mentioned that for-use of its largest and newest machines, £80 per hour would be a realistic costing, although its average in-house costing for machining was £25.

The founder of the small company, ENG-GB-S1, had anticipated the trends in larger firms, accelerated by the early 1980s recession, towards putting prototype work and special products out to subcontract. These were labour-intensive and not likely to require CNC equipment. This company, which worked with second-hand equipment which it had greatly modified and improved itself, had also invested in calibration equipment so as to achieve a higher level of accuracy than most of its customers. In spite of its low costing for machining, mentioned above, it paid wages comparable with those of the principals. Like the other subcontractors, it regarded high wages as essential to keeping the loyalty of its skilled workforce. Like one other subcontractor, it even gave its shopfloor workers subcriptions for BUPA (i.e. private) health care (a benefit not given in the UK to university lecturers, for example!).In general, the British subcontractors' wage levels are similar, or higher, than those of the principals.

ENG-GB-S2, a company which had developed initially by investment in CNC milling machinery, was the one subcontractor which seemed to occupy an exclusively specialist niche. Its customers were said to accept its need for a profit margin on turnover of about 40% to maintain its reinvestment programme. All the British subcontractors, however, appeared to have independent technological capacity. GB-S4 was marketing its own designed and built machines as well as doing subcontracting. GB-S5 too was developing its own final products. GB-S3 felt its niche sprang from its ability to make its own tooling for the pressings in which it specialized.

GB-S3 commented how improvements in equipment capacity and speed had been accompanied by great increases in the price of equipment. It said that worries about stop-go in the British economy made it hesitate to invest in best-practice. Among the other British subcontractors, however, S2, S4 and S5 were insistent at being near the technology frontier, while the founder of S1 took pride in his ability to modify cheap, second-hand equipment to a high level of precision.

Among the Japanese subcontractors, J-S1 was to a large extent doing overflow work, though of a permanent nature - the fabrication and assembly of one of J-P1's simpler machines, for which P1 did not want to use up limited in-house capacity. J-S2, working for J-S1, was doing specialized structural steelwork, making machinery frames for S1. J-S3 was making a small volume special-purpose product, for ultimate sales to manufacturers, via a principal making a mass-produced version. It seemed to be accepted that sucessively lower tiers of subcontractors would pay lower wages, though in part this was because they employed a more elderly workforce (3). Both J-S1 and J-S2 spoke of heavy recent investment in CNC equipment. J-S3's main equipment had been in place for over a decade, but it had a policy of adding new equipment about every five years. Both Japanese principals had taken considerable interest in the suitability of their subcontractors' capital equipment.

4.4.2 Subcontractor selection and monitoring

For the subcontractors, separating the process of selection and monitoring from the more general relationship and the contractual arrangements involved is arbitrary, since the selection procedure and the monitoring are perceived by subcontractors as essential expressions of the way in which the principals regard their suppliers.

All the British subcontractors interviewed had at least four or five major customers, and sometimes rather different experiences with each. Most of the British subcontractors mentioned cases of working together with new customers to set up a new product. One mentioned working on a prototype of a part for a new customer, knowing that when the order went out to quotation, it would have an advantage in getting the order having been in at the early stages. Nevertheless, the initial work was undertaken with no promise of orders for volume production.

Another British subcontractor mentioned how one customer, a large motor parts supplier, put drawings out to, say, six suppliers. It gave each a small order, with a repeat order for a few months if the work was satisfactory. The subcontractor, who referred to this sort of work as

67

'knife and forking', felt it was quite unsatisfactory, giving the subcontractor no opportunity or incentive to plan ahead to set up a production line. This buyer, however, after a year, had started to give six-month rolling orders; so in fact a selection procedure was being operated, but one which lost subcontractors' goodwill. The same subcontractor had set up a special production facility for one customer, with equipment with little alternative use, where the customer would prefer its final customers not to know it did not do the operation in-house (!). Here the subcontractor had felt confident to make the investment, since the customer was willing to single-source and since a new subcontractor could not be set up in a short space of time.

Willingness to give contracts, or orders for several months ahead, rather than one-off orders was generally seen as an expression of a principal's goodwill and commitment in British engineering, though examples of good relations were found where principals had given continued one-off orders over the years.

ENG-J-S1 and ENG-J-S2 had formed their business links with their main customers many years ago and did not provide much detail about how they were selected as suppliers.With regard to monitoring, J-S1 said that, although its principal is generous with technological help, it does not interfere in management. S-2 was closely involved in joint designing with its main customer, and did not discuss monitoring methods for its own share of the work. ENG-J-S3 was a bigger company than the other subcontractors and made a complete product for sale by a large company under the large company's own brand name, as also did several other subcontractors for that principal.Its product was a more specialized version of the principal's mass-produced product. J-S3 has its own, independent designing capacity, and submits its design to the principal for approval. Representatives of the principal visit J-S3's factory several times a month, but actually they now leave the supervision of production almost entirely to S3. J-S3's principal, in fact, had long ago been involved with the setting up of S-3 as a company

One of the Japanese subcontractors, who also did work for the motor industry, said the company was approached by a large motor manufacturer in the 1950s, who thought (correctly) that the subcontractor's existing product would give it expertise to diversify into making motor parts.

4.4.3 Contractual relations

There was considerable variation among the five British subcontractors in the contracts they received. There were variations among the different customers of individual contractors, and also among the arrangements the same customer gave to different suppliers. One-off orders were very common, and GB-S3 received nothing else. The longest formal contract was one year (for GB-S5), and orders of one or two months, perhaps with projections for a similar period in the future, were the most common arrangement after one-offs. This lack of formal contracting was sometimes in the context of a longer term arrangement. In the case of GB-S2, this was formalized in an agreement which promised that the principal would sole-source so long as the supplier maintained adequate quality and delivery. There was also provision for price renegotiation in the light of general inflation, though the subcontractor mentioned that in fact his margins had been eroded slightly over recent years. The agreement had remained in force during a four year association, which was continuing, and the supplier had been heavily involved in the original design. This subcontractor was the only one who thought his customers (and the agreement was with the largest customer) largely had avoided the effects of the early 1990s recession. GB-S4 had a two-month order, plus a two-month projection from a car manufacturer (not its largest customer), but felt there was an unwritten understanding that orders would continue for the life of the present model of car.The subcontractor mentioned, however,that he rarely saw anyone from the motor manufacturer, no attempt being made at a Japanese-style relation. The only subcontractor, GB-S1, who supplied one-off orders under a principal's 'supplier partnership programme' encountered one of the only two serious cases of ruthless opportunism found in the whole British interviewing programme of three industries! This case is discussed below in subsection 4.4.5.

Among the Japanese subcontractors, J-S1 received only individual orders from its largest customer, whom it had served for 25 years. From some others it got a basic document in addition, which specified orders for 3-4 months ahead. It gave no indication that this lack of contractual obligation caused it any anxiety or that it expected orders to be switched - indeed, it had never been dropped as a supplier by any principal. J-S2, in dealing with its own largest customer, had to sign a document pledging never to reveal technical information gained in the relation with the customer [see also chapter 7], but otherwise it simply got one-off orders in the context of a relation which had lasted over 15 years. This secrecy provision was like that imposed on J-P1's suppliers. J-S3 did not go into details about its contractual relation, but it had been dealing with its main customer for more than 25 years.

All three Japanese subcontractors discussed the process of price formation. S1 said that, in dealing with its largest customer, S-1 itself set the price for small items, but for large items the customer set the price. However, S-1 felt the customer was very familiar with S-1's situation and behaved reasonably. S-2, with its main customer, went through a longer procedure; the customer would ask for a quotation, giving an idea of what it expected to pay, and S-2 would do an estimate, with negotiations if the two figures differed.When the price, payment conditions and delivery had been agreed, on order would be issued. J-S3, for a new product, would receive information from its customer specifying the final selling price which the customer expected for the product, and if S-3's costings differed, there would be negotiations. In each case, it appears the Japanese principals took a more active role in price setting than the British ones, but there was no mention of the progressive price reduction asked of suppliers which is a well-known feature of the Japanese motor industry.

4.4.4 Technology transfer and other help

As mentioned already in subsection 4.4.1, all the British engineering subcontractors spoke of having considerable technical expertise of their own, often more so than their customers. All had worked with various customers on complex orders. GB-S4 sold almost a third of its output as final product, and had customers come to it simply to tell it the kind of machine they wanted. GB-S5 was developing its own product too. They had not received explicit technical help, but had all been involved in joint development of items with customers. None had ever received financial help from principals.

Links through former employment or other association with principals were important, however.The founder of GB-S4, who had once worked for a large local engineering firm, said his former employer had been hostile to his leaving and told him not to expect orders, but this principal had relented once the subcontractor had got established.He mentioned that many subcontractors in the region had once worked for the same large company. GB-S1 got substantial orders from a large firm for whom he had worked, and GB-S2 initially grew as a subcontractor to an electronics company with which he had been associated.

Of the three Japanese subcontractors, J-S1 was a subcontractor to one of the two principals, and J-S2, in turn, was a subcontractor to J-S1. These, and J-S3, gave indications of help they had received. J-S1 had got into some difficulties in the mid-1980s, when it had failed to get payment from a foreign customer. This was also a time when there was some surplus capacity in Japanese engineering. J-S1 referred with gratitude to help it had received from its main customer, including a relaxation of payment requirements. This customer subsequently took a small equity stake in S1,but, while it was said to be generous with technical help, it did not interfere with management. ENG-J-P2, doing structural steelwork, spoke of its own need to invest. During the 1980s there had been an acceleration of technical progress, and new equipment had allowed it to cope with the labour shortage by expanding output with a contracting workforce. CNC equipment had allowed inexperienced workers to operate with less supervision. Much of its new equipment had been leased, for tax purposes, from specialized leasing firms set up by insurance companies. J-S2 cooperated very closely with its largest customer (not J-S1, and not interviewed), which would provide the basic design of a factory, and leave the design of individual areas to S2, with other firms supplying the actual machinery. S2 has greatly shared in this customers rapid expansion, which has generated profits for S2's own growth.S2 mentioned it gave advice to its own subcontractors (i.e. the fourth tier), for example giving them information on the overall design in which their components had to fit.

In the case of ENG-J-S3, the principal has a very small capital stake in the subcontractor, although S3 itself has no ownership in any of its own subcontractors. J-S3 has received considerable help in the past on production management from its principal, as well as benefitting from the principal's extensive sales organization.

4.4.5 Dependence, dualism and opportunism?

All the British subcontractors interviewed tried to avoid overdependence on individual customers. All had at least four or five major customers. None sold more than 30% of their turnover to any one principal. GB-S2 set a 30% maximum, and would try hard to expand with other customers if one customer rose above this. GB-S4 expressed a similar view, and professed fear of some large companies who would come in with a big order and then drop the supplier.

GB-S4 felt many large companies were quite ruthless. This was a view widely shared, although GB-S5 felt it was not too difficult to spot potential cheats (principally non-payers) and to deal with them firmly through the law when necessary. One of GB-S5's managers, however, described subcontracting as being in a 'hostile environment', even though the company appeared satisfied with many of its relations with particular customers. Every British subcontractor spoke of payment delays by customers. This was being made worse by the early 1990s recession, but some large companies had been doing it as a matter of deliberate policy for long time. Legislation (like that of Japan) was needed to ensure faster payment,several subcontractors thought, although there was willingness to accept slow payment by trusted principals in genuine difficulty.

Single-sourcing by principals was thought to be a growing trend, because of economies of scale, but still a little unusual. GB-S5's customer, for whom S5 had installed special equipment and who single-sourced, was investigating the possibility of an ownership link with S5, presumably to lessen the danger of opportunism by the subcontractor. In any case, S5 did not do a large proportion of its business with that principal.

The spread of customers usually also meant a spread between industries. In one case, that of GB-S4, work for the oil industry had helped cushion falls in customer business in engineering and other industries during the early 1990s recession. S4 had felt the recession mainly in the form of orders coming in with less notice than usual and needing fast handling. GB-S2's customers had been little affected by the recession, the subcontractor felt, but GB-S1's customers had mostly been hard hit. Subcontractors in British engineering,especially those like S1 supplying mainly the machine tool industry, were well aware of the cyclical nature of the industry, with a cycle of 4-5 years. Frequent upswings and downswings had inhibited GB-S4 from expanding, even though it had experienced little problem in getting orders.

GB-S5, which normally delivered direct to stock for customers, felt just-in-time delivery was largely a device to push the stock-holding function onto the subcontractor, and tried to charge a higher price when this was required to cover the extra costs! This subcontractor had experienced rapid growth, and had a solid base of long term customers, but it felt subcontracting was a relatively low-profit activity, and was diversifying into its own final products, as was GB-S4. S5 also mentioned what it considered to be a very negative and badly informed attitude on the part of its bank towards the financing of even a successful subcontractor,a view widely endorsed by other British small companies.

Payment delays aside, the only serious case of opportunism in the British sample of engineering companies was encountered by ENG-GB-S1. S1's main customer at the time, taking some 25-30% of its sales, gave one-off orders but in the context of a formal Supplier Partnership Programme. The principal gave documentation on 'partnership' to suppliers, and held suppliers conferences. S1's product was a key part of a machine tool for making aero engines and for aero engine maintenance. The part was about 1% of the machine tool's value, but its precision was vital, and S1 had spent several months, in consultation with the principal, developing and adapting his equipment to make it. The principal, as part of the partnership,had even, Japanese-style, asked for access to S1's accounts. S1 had refused but, interestingly, he commented in the interview that he might have been willing to do so if a long contract (he mentioned five years) had been in the offing.S1 knew the director in charge of the supplier programme well and trusted him, and on this basis was willing to proceed without a long term contract. This 'obligational contractual relationship' did not, however, survive that director's transfer to another part of the organization, and his replacement by a new purchasing officer. The new man, a new broom sweeping clean, was determined to cut costs and sought other subcontractors. GB-S1 says the principal's manufacturing department was amazed he was dropped, but could not override the purchasing department. S1 said the principal's experience with the first new, and much cheaper, subcontractor had been unsatisfactory, but that a subsequent

71

subcontractor could be used and the lessons learned by the principal during the development work undertaken by S1 would lessen the time taken to instruct a new subcontractor. GB-S1 was extremely aggrieved, and clearly felt his trust had been abused.

No cases similar to the experience of ENG-GB-S1 were found in the Japanese sample. J-S1 said it had never been dropped as a supplier and never had dropped any of its own subcontractors. The only case of opportunism of any kind, as already mentioned, was where a former employee of a subcontractor of ENG-J-P1 had sold the design of a major part on one of J-P1's machines to a rival manufacturer. This had made J-P1 very wary about any similar behaviour by a subcontractor, and it included special and explicit provisions in its written agreements with subcontractors about keeping secrecy [see also chapter 7].

Several Japanese subcontractors tried to avoid overdependence, and even J-S1, which sold 50% of its output to its main customer, had several other customers in long-term relations. J-S2, though doing over a third of its business with one customer, had made a conscious attempt to diversify to lessen the cyclical nature of the engineering industry, and worked for food and brewery companies too. J-S3 was highly dependent on its principal, but was part of a group of small companies with a diversified range of customers.

NOTES

1. One Japanese company is not discussed here, or in the next two chapters. This was a company making switches, which seemed to lie between engineering and electronics without generating lessons of direct relevance to either industry. It does make an appearance, however, in chapter 7.

2. For further discussion of Japanese provisions for keeping secrecy, and of Japanese contractual arrangements more generally, see chapter 7, written by Makoto Takashima.

3. Although wages in smaller companies do rise with age, the progression is much less marked for blue-collar workers in small companies compared to blue-collar workers in large companies. Since differentials between small and large companies therefore are greater with respect to older workers than with respect to younger workers, differentials between small and large firms will be increased if the former have a higher proportion of elderly employees than the latter [see also chapter 2, section 2].

5 The motor industry companies

This chapter considers the experience of subcontracting among two principals and three subcontractors in the UK motor industry, and two principals and five subcontractors in Japan. Following the same format as the previous chapter, section 1 introduces the sample of companies. Section 2 considers the factors underlying the decision to subcontract, how this has changed in Britain in the last decade, and how it compares to the situation in Japan. Section 3 looks at issues of supply chain management, how British companies view the subcontracting relation, and how such relations are conducted among the Japanese companies interviewed. This section mainly takes the principals' viewpoint, though some subcontractor material is introduced too. Section 4 asks how subcontracting appears from the perspective of the British and Japanese subcontractors.

5.1 The companies

Introductory profiles of the motor industry principals are given in Table 5-1, and Table 5-2 introduces the subcontractors. As in chapter 4, although information was collected on companies' employment, date of foundation, share of exports in turnover, detailed product mix, and so on, this is normally suppressed so as to preserve the companies' anonymity. This is done especially where principals are concerned, who are likely to be more easily recognisable than subcontractors, though some suppliers in the motor industry in both countries also are large. All the British and Japanese principals are well-established companies, and all are larger than the principals in the engineering sample of chapter 4. The Japanese subcontractors also include companies at least as large as the engineering principals of chapter 4. All the principals, British and Japanese, are significantly involved in export markets, some very heavily so. Several of the Japanese companies, subcontractors as well as principals, have production overseas. The British subcontractors have appeared before, in chapter 4, and are included in both chapters since they depend both on the motor industry and on other industries too for significant amounts of business. In both countries, one principal is a motor manufacturer - a major one in the case of Japan, and in the UK a company belonging to a larger automotive group. The second principal in each country is a motor industry supplier, too independent in terms of design capability, size, and economic status to be considered a subcontractor, and who, in both countries, mainly supplied information about relations with its own subcontractors.

5.2 The subcontracting decision

5.2.1 The British principals

The British car manufacturer, MOT-GB-P1, has greatly changed its policy towards outsourcing during the past decade. This has been in the context of a major expansion, currently (1991-2) hit somewhat by the recession. A new model was planned with the intention that much more would be bought out, since the company would be producing at a higher volume than in the past. Castings, which were previously machined in-house, were put out to subcontract. Pressing was put out too. This was because the principal did not want to make heavy investment in presses for its expanded car output, when it could not have kept the presses fully utilized with its own demand. The principal put substantial investment into the tooling for the main subcontractor, but this tooling was specific to the needs of the principal and, of course, the cost was much less than for the presses themselves. These moves towards greater outsourcing were accompanied by more general reorganization in terms of factory layout, throughput, and stock control, along somewhat Japanese lines (though not acknowledgely so). Whereas in the British machine tool companies of chapter 4 such changes were intimately linked with expanded outsourcing, in the case of MOT-GB-P1, increased outsourcing had preceded them. Indeed, the improved use of space resulting from the reorganization allowed the company to bring back some items in-house, so as to avoid workers being made redundant. This principal commented that, because of regional wage differentials, it paid <u>lower</u> wages than some of its subcontractors, and that this also gave it some possibility of bringing items back in-house.

MOT-GB-P2, the major component manufacturer, does not exclusively serve the motor industry, but the motor industry is a major customer. Over the past five years it has put increasing amounts out to subcontract, particularly the machining of castings. Castings have been put out for many years, for classic reasons in terms of the economics of transactions costs, i.e. they are subject to economies of scale which the principal could not exhaust and they do not require highly specific capital assets. Thus, foundries can supply a range of customers more cheaply than customers could supply in-house. The decision to put more and more machining out to subcontract reflects a feeling that 'we want to design, assemble, and test'. With limited capital funds available, GB-P2 does not want to buy machine tools for jobs best left to suppliers, who are more specialized and have lower overheads. GB-P2 also mentioned that more specialist suppliers could pay bonuses to good workers more easily than it could itself, since it had production lines running at fixed rates. However, GB-P2's main interest was how its already extensive subcontracting should be managed. This in part is associated with preference to outsource a larger number of complete subassemblies, and is discussed further in section 5.3.

Table 5.1
The Motor Industry Principals

Company	Main Products	Items on Subcontract	Attitude to Subcontracting
British Principals MOT-GB-P1	Motor vehicles	Castings, heavy machining, fabrication and press work, prototype work	Moved from doing most stages in-house to being more of an assembler than a manufacturer
MOT-GB-P2	A major component	Castings, machining	Feels subcontracting system could be improved
Japanese Principals MOT-J-P1	Motor vehicles	Castings,machining,	Regards its extensive and complex subcontracting system as essential to its strong competitive position
MOT-J-P2	Major components	Any parts for which technology has become standardized	Keeps key items in-house so it can continue to develop their technology. Also makes some of own capital equipment in-house

Table 5.2
The Motor Industry Subcontractors

Company	Main Products	Main Industries Supplied	Attitude to Subcontracting
British Subcontractors [see also Table 4.2]			
ENG-GB-S3	High quality electronic pressing	Motor industry and wide variety of other industries	Feels customers do not nurture suppliers enough
ENG-GB-S4	Machinery manufacturing and design	Motor industry, engineering, oil and others	Could expand by taking on more subcontracting, but reluctant to do so because of periodic recession
ENG-GB-S5	High precision engineering, both conventional and CNC	Motor industry, food, medical, defence and others	Regards subcontracting as a somewhat "hostile environment", and is diversifying into own end products to some extent
Japanese Subcontractors MOT-J-S1	Body work	Motor industry alone	Notices competition from other subcontractors in its line of business
MOT-J-S2	Forgings	Motor industry, agricultural machinery	Appreciates opportunity to grow in the wake of its main principal, but mindful of competition from other subcontractors
MOT-J-S3	Machining	Motor industry, general engineering	Feels motor industry principals more willing to have longer-term relation than are some other industries
MOT-J-S4	Hydraulics and related products	Motor industry, and many others	Tries to reap advantages of mass production of particular parts

5.2.2 The Japanese principals

MOT-J-P1, the Japanese motor manufacturer, has a long history of outsourcing. Purchases from other companies account for some 70% of J-P1's sales value, and three quarters of its production costs. Well over 80% of its purchases from other companies are from 'cooperating companies' (a general term for subcontractors and suppliers), the rest of the purchases being of standard inputs like steel and some items of equipment. The company feels it achieves great cost reduction by outsourcing, since its suppliers are very effective in their own specific fields. However, when the Japanese motor industry was developed after the second world war, suppliers were used as buffers during the business cycle [see also chapter 7].

J-P1 identified four main factors in its subcontracting decisions:
-investment cost: if this is high, then J-P1 would search for a supplier who already had the equipment (1).
-duration of development required: if this is long, the principal would try to buy-in so as not to burden internal resources.
-relative production cost.
-number of workers needed: the principal would try to buy-in if this large numbers of workers would be required, and this buying-in may involve a wide range of subcontractors each doing a specialized item.

J-P1 has about 800 suppliers in a complicated hierarchy, discussed in section 5.3 [and also in chapter 7].

MOT-J-P2 is a substantial company, with sales to a range of motor manufacturers. It has a clearly thought out policy towards its make/buy decisions, which essentially centres on product maturity. J-P2 would produce in-house:
-if the product is new. When a item becomes standardized, J-P2 puts it out to subcontract, and only does the assembly in-house.
-if necessary to maintain secrecy. J-P2 is a company which spends an amount equivalent to nearly a fifth of its turnover on investment and R&D, and new product development is a key part of its strategy.
-if heavy capital investment is needed and no existing supplier can be found.

There are about 60 members in J-P2's association of supplying companies. This includes affiliates who supply parts, the smallest having some 20-30 workers. There are also 20 companies supplying machinery for specific uses, with drawings supplied by J-P2.

5.3 Supply chain management

5.3.1 Subcontractor selection, development and monitoring

The British motor manufacturer, MOT-GB-P1, did not provide much information on its subcontractor selection procedure, except to say that it responded to enquiries by prospective subcontractors. However, at least one subcontractor interviewed was approached by the motor manufacturer. GB-P1 speads its press work and fabrication around a variety of small subcontractors, who are not particularly specialized. It also spreads its prototype development work, an important part of its operation, around a large number of very specialist subcontractors (one of whom was interviewed, though not via the principal).

The British major component manufacturer, MOT-GB-P2, was very interested in issues relating to selection of suppliers. This was not because it wished to greatly to extend its subcontracting, which was already extensive and had recently been increased, but because it felt its subcontracting system could be improved. In the context of planning a small reduction in its supplier base, it was reviewing its own behaviour towards subcontractors, and its expectations of them. Customers, it said, were demanding quality as never before, and GB-P2 was trying to pass this message to subcontractors, although it felt that improved quality would involve almost inevitably some increases in price along the supply chain. However, there would be benefits not only in an improved competitive position, but in reduced costs of repairs to its products under warranty. GB-P2 monitored suppliers, rating them A, B, or C according to a points system, where quality was scored out of 40 percentage points, delivery out of 40, and 20 points were allocated to a more subjective appraisal of the subcontractor's management ability, and ability to make cost-saving suggestions. It looked for flexibility in subcontractors, and whether they had been investing. GB-P2 sometimes asked to look at subcontractors' books in an attempt, it said, to keep suppliers solvent, and felt it perhaps should do more of this. GB-P2 was interested in subcontractors's ability to produce complete sub-assemblies, to avoid the monitoring costs of dealing with several different levels of subcontractors for the same assembly.

The Japanese motor manufacture, MOT-J-P1, has a elaborate and well-established family of suppliers. It mentioned that the motor industry in Japan had become very 'modernized', in the sense that J-P1 would not maintain a relation with a subcontractor just because of a long past connection. Model changes in the motor industry were occuring on virtually a two-year cycle, and suppliers had to keep up with technical change. It compared this attitude to that in machinery and construction, which it regarded as more traditional sectors.

MOT-J-P1's network of suppliers comprises a small number of subsidiaries (i.e. more than 50% owned by J-1), about 60 'vendors' (who provide their own designs, and in whom J-P1 often has some ownership, but rarely more than 20%), and about 700 'subcontractors' proper, who work with designs supplied and where P-1 usually holds no share in the ownership. There were also some overseas suppliers. Of all the suppliers, some 50 provide 60% of P1's total materials purchases. Approximately the same total number or workers is employed in the subcontractors, narrowly defined, as in the principal, and the ratio of employment in vendors to that in the principal is between 1.3 and 1.5. It also buys supplies from other companies within the group with which it is associated. The selection procedure for suppliers was not set out in detail by J-P1, but for 'vendors' it was described in terms of stages of contractual arrangement (see subsection 5.3.2), which involves a vendor's engineers being attached to the principal, and trials of the vendor's product. For 'subcontractors', the principal supplies a design and proposes a cost.

Although the principal, J-P1, would like a long-term relation, it reviews the suppliers at each stage of a new model, which is brought in about every two years. Suppliers are expected to fit in with an elaborate just-in-time system, which involves parts being delivered to the production line at just the point where required. J-P1 claims not to hold stocks of parts itself. Most parts were not checked until the motor vehicle was finally assembled, but exceptions were made for brakes, steering and engines, which by government regulations had to be checked prior to assembly. MOT-J-P2 did not provide details of its subcontractor selection procedure, but in an industry where the product cycle in the applications of electronics to automobile components is shortening, technological capabilities will be important.

MOT-GB-P1 did not specify any explicit policy for subcontractor development, and the impression from talking to several of its subcontractors is that it tended to expect a subcontractor to be fully developed by itself prior to starting business.

As part of its conscious efforts to improve its supply chain management, MOT-GB-P2 was willing to help suppliers achieve its desired standards. It had a team of quality assurance engineers who spent a lot of time 'on the road' looking at suppliers and helping them become rated in GB-P2's quality manual (2) GB-P2 said it tried to get its suppliers involved at an early stage of a new project, and that it was getting a message from many of its suppliers that they would like to be involved at the design stage. It did supply some subcontractors with tooling, specific to its own needs.

MOT-J-P1's policy of having its vendors engineers come to the principal on secondment has already been mentioned. With regard to financial help, J-P1 had taken limited ownership in a variety of vendors (i.e. firms working to their own designs), as also mentioned above. For subcontractors, where there only rarely was ownership, the principal supplied designs.

J-P1 does not normally help by supplying its suppliers with equipment, although it has done so on a few occasions, but it may give financial support for equipment purchase. It feels actually supplying equipment may retard the supplier technologically. It would be reluctant to help a supplier in difficulty, especially if the firm had made no effort of its own to keep abreast of new technology. It might help, however, for social reasons (e.g. if substantial unemployment would result from the supplier closing), or if the principal felt itself to be partly to blame for the supplier's problems.

MOT-J-P2 has had an explicit policy for several decades of helping subcontractors to upgrade their production capabilities. Its own relation with the motor manufacturer which is its largest customer has been founded on the closest exchange of technical information, and J-P2 prides itself on bring to make significant technical suggestions of its own, especially of new electronics-based components.

5.3.2 Contractual arrangements and the subcontracting relationship (3)

MOT-GB-P1 tended to give formal contracts, usually of several years duration, to its largest suppliers, but not to others. It did not feel able to impose progressive price reductions on suppliers in the way reportedly done in the Japanese motor industry (Asanuma, 1989a, p.20), but it was working towards contracts where suppliers could not raise price because of inflation. GB-P1 mentioned, however, that at least one other firm in the British motor industry, to its knowledge, was imposing progressive price reduction on suppliers in exchange for long contracts. Quality requirements for subcontractors were specified according to GB-P1's quality manual.

Having almost halved its supplier base already, MOT-GB-P2, was in process of changing its contractual arrangements. It saw the giving of contracts as important indications to subcontractors of its goodwill. In particular, it wanted to show its willingness to change its past policy of shopping around for cheapness, changing its subcontractors frequently, and using this as a threat with the remaining suppliers to get better prices. However, some of its relationships with large

79

subcontractors were very long term, stretching back over decades. It was introducing with good, selected suppliers a longer term arrangement in the form of a supply agreement/letter of understanding. This would guarantee orders if supply, quality and price requirements were met.This was not unlike a Japanese arrangement found in mechanical engineering, except that it was time-limited. It was also willing to single-source with good suppliers. There was much discussion with subcontractors about costs. GB-P2 had tried to get rises in subcontractors's labour costs self-financed by the subcontractors, but this only worked to a limited extent.

MOT-J-P1 gave details about contractual arrangements with its vendors, which are in three stages:
-a basic document is exchanged. This is to open the relationship, may lead to future orders, and specifies general conditions only. It is initially for two years, and then is renewable annually unless either side objects.
-following agreement to sign the basic document, a contract is issued to arrange the dispatching engineers from the vendor to the principal as guest engineers.
-a contract is issued after the guest engineers have understood the principal's requirements and trial production has been done by the supplier.At this stage,no specific amount of goods, or unit prices, are specified. Subsequently, J-P1 will specify volumes and there will be discussion about price.

Every six months, vendors and subcontractors are sent information about volumes to be ordered in the next six months and about prices of prices of raw materials, about wages and productivity advances in product design. There in an association of J-P1's suppliers, and J-P1's top management informs suppliers about its production forecasts and investment plans through this organization.

MOT-J-P2 has a policy of keeping long-term relations with its suppliers, not just to look for the lowest current cost. A basic contract is exchanged with subcontractors, which contains general conditions about quality, handling claims, and giving forecasts. This is renewed annually unless either side objects, and within this framework the principal gives its subcontractors specific orders. Unit costs are reviewed twice a year.

MOT-GB-P1 did not express explicit views on subcontractor dependence, but in practice it tended to spread its orders around, and most subcontractors about whom information was obtained (either directly or via GB-P1) appeared to have a range of customers. In MOT-GB-P2's case, although it said it preferred subcontractors not to be heavily dependent, it was aware that some of its subcontractors were so. In part this relected the subcontractors' specialization on particular components which were highly specific to the manufacture of products like GB-P2's, but GB-P2 also thought some subcontractors found reliance on one major customer made for an easy life. MOT-J-P1 had clear views on subcontractor dependence; it advised subcontractors to have at least three customers, at least one of which should be outside the motor industry. It had a policy of not single-sourcing, except for a few very specialized parts for specific models. Information on dependence was not obtained from J-P2.

5.3.3 Sub-subcontracting

Further subcontracting by the British subcontractors has already been discussed in chapter 4, and there was no indication that its pattern differed significantly between work for the motor industry and for other customers. Though common, it was confined to a few specialist activities, and was equivalent to only a small proportion of turnover.

Sub-subcontracting is an essential feature of the Japanese motor industry. In the case of MOT-J-P1's production, there were three tiers of suppliers, generally of descending size of firm. J-P1 said that firms in the first tier were of an average size of 400 workers, 200 workers in second tier firms, and under 50 workers in the third tier firms. Unlike the Japanese mechanical engineering industry of chapter 4, J-P1 as principal kept a check on firms in the second as well as the first tier of suppliers (where components subject to safely regulations were concerned). It did not enquire about the activities of the small firms in the third tier, leaving that to its own suppliers.

MOT-J-P1's subcontractor, J-S2 (the forgings company), had 5 or 6 main subcontractors of its own, ranging in size from 30 to 80 workers, with all of whom it had maintained relations for at least ten years, and in the longest case thirty years. Payments to these subcontractors (and to two affiliates) accounted for an amount equivalent to about 30% of its sales. These second-tier subcontractors did not, however, have a layer below them. J-S2 said it subcontracted on because:
-its sub-subcontractors could pay lower wages than J-S2 itself,
-the sub-subcontractors had specialized equipment not possessed by J-S2
-for some specific parts the sub-subcontractors could do a better job than J-S2.

Similarly, MOT-J-S3 (a machinist), had five subcontractors of its own, each with 10-20 workers, and purchases from subcontractors were about 10% of total costs. It had to report to its main principal (which also was MOT-J-P1) when it put out work to these subcontractors, and the sub-subcontractors did not themselve subcontract further.

The subcontractor MOT-J-S4 (making hydraulics) is rather larger than the other Japanese subcontractors, and sub-subcontracts to an extent equal to nearly half of its total costs. However, it still is better regarded as a supplier than a principal, because it makes only parts rather than assembling products, and because it tries to keep in-house anything where there are economies of scale. J-S4 sub-subcontracts where:
-it lacks some specialist capacity, e.g. for the manufacture of castings
-for overflow work,
-for small batch production, where a subcontractor may be cheaper.
It will produce in-house where a part has new technology it wants to keep to itself. J-S4 has a subcontracting network of its own, with some 130 suppliers, whom it divides into two groups according to whether or not the subcontractors have the designs supplied by S-4. S-4 does not require its own subcontractors to report if they subcontract further, and expects quality and delivery to be ensured by its own first layer.

The subcontractor MOT-J-S1 (making specialist autobodies) also sub-subcontracted, with twenty small companies, for particular items, and mentioned the lower wages of its sub-contractors as a factor.

In the case of MOT-J-P2 (making electric and electronic equipment), which had a smaller range of subcontractors than J-P1, the principal was aware that some subcontractors would sub-subcontract, but it simply expected the first level of subcontractors to meet requirements. For products used for safety purposes, however, subcontractors had to consult with the principal before subcontracting on.

The British major component manufacturer, MOT-GB-P2, was especially

81

envious of the Japanese layered system of subcontracting. He often had
to adjudicate on disputes between subcontractors at different functional
levels, e.g. foundries wishing to supply more castings to machinists at
any one time than the machinists wished to take. He hankered after
dealing with only one level. However, in the British system, vertical
integration between machinists and foundaries has also been seen as a
possible solution (DTI, 1990b). MOT-GB-P1 did not mention any similar
problems, and its subcontractors who were interviewed only subcontracted
minor, rather specialized jobs.

5.4 The subcontractors' experience of subcontracting (4)

5.4.1 Subcontractors' perceptions of their competitive advantage

ENG-GB-S3 regarded itself as a high quality producer of basic
engineering products. It especially prided itself on its ability to make
press tools, though it preferred to use these itself for pressings
rather than sell them. GB-S4 felt it had very specialist expertise,
especially in machine design, and very up-to-date equipment. GB-S5
worked for a wider range of motor industry customers, and was doing
prototype work based on high precision engineering skills,with both CNC
and conventional equipment.

MOT-J-S1 (doing body work) regarded its specialist activity as being
highly labour-intensive. Its wage payments per worker were about 30%
lower than its main principal's, and its own sub-subcontractors paid
wages at least 25% lower than its own. It commented that it found it
hard to get workers, especially younger ones, to do its kind of fairly
arduous work. It said its sub-subcontrators relied heavily on elderly
workers. J-S1 had its own design capacity.

MOT-J-S2, a manufacturer of forgings, had been formed as a largely
independent company when its main principal decided to give up its in-
house production of forgings, and had transferred its existing
equipment to J-S2. Since then, J-S2 had made equipment purchases of its
own, and regarded itself as being in heavy competition with another 4-5
forging manufacturers supplying the principal. It mentioned it was asked
for periodic price reductions, and seemed to see this as an inevitable
result of this competition.

MOT-J-S3 (doing machining) felt it had a very specialized niche,
machining castings for its main principal's engine plant. MOT-J-S4
(making hydraulics) has even more of a speciality niche, having its own
very high technology specialist production, and serving a range of
industries.

5.4.2 Subcontractor selection and monitoring

ENG-GB-S3 provided no information on how it had been selected by its one
customer from the motor industry. It mentioned it regularly advertised
at exhibitions.GB-S4 said that in general growth had been easy and it
had never had to go and look for orders. The motor manufacture had come
looking, although GB-S4 nowadays rarely saw anyone from the motor
manufacturer, who was still an important customer. GB-S5 mentioned that
it signed secrecy agreements with a number of its motor industry
customers for whom it did development work. Some motor industry
customers 'selected' simply by putting out offers to tender to several
suppliers and giving them a series of short-term orders to see how they

coped.

MOT-J-S1 (making autobodies) had been selected by its main principal several decades ago when the Japanese motor industry was in a far less developed state than today. It commented that its main principal was rather strict on price, and tended to inspect its books to ensure that its prices were reasonable.

J-S2 (making forgings) had been in existence for some years, serving (among others) the agricultural machinery industry, before it received the forging equipment from its main motor industry principal. Its considerable experience presumably was a major factor in its selection. For current production, a general design is supplied by the principal, and the detailed designing is done by the subcontractor, and the principal specifies materials, and (for example) heat treatment. For new parts, trial production is performed at the subcontractor by the principal's engineers, who also do quality tests. There are also periodic inspections of the subcontractor's factory by the principal.

J-S3 (the machinist) also had been in existence for many years, and had had a long relation with its main principal. It did not provide details of how it had been selected as a supplier, but it had done high-precision work for an affiliate of its main principal during the Second World War, and its technical expertise hardly could have been in question. It received regular visits from its principal's engineers. S-3 did its own testing, but its dies were inspected monthly by the principal. On about half its work with its main principal, J-S3 did its own designing in the context of a general specification supplied by the principal.

MOT-J-S4 (hydraulics) is a larger firm than the other subcontractors, and has been well-established in its own right for many years, with advanced independent design capacity.

5.4.3 Contractual relations

ENG-GB-S3 said it received only one-off orders from the motor manufacturing principal, although this was typical of its other customers too. GB-S4 received a two-monthly schedule from the same motor manufacturer, which was the longest any customer gave, and felt there was an unwritten understanding that orders would continue for the life of the present model. GB-S5's contractual arrangements differed considerably between customers, even within the motor industry. It spoke of one motor industry customer (see also chapter 4) which eventually gave a six-month rolling order, but only after a series of short orders, which made production planning difficult.

MOT-J-S2's outline of its contractual relations with its main principal filled in a few additional details over what the principal had said. S2 receives a basic document, as the framework for the relationship. It receives a three-monthly forecast of orders at the start of every month. It must deliver every three days, and this requirement has gradually shortened over the years. Prices are reviewed every six months, and material price rises can be discussed as a counterbalance to requests for price reduction.

MOT-J-S3's contractual relations were very similar to those of J-S2, and with the same main principal. It had an annual, renewable basic contract, and a monthly set of order forecasts. It mentioned that the main principal every six months gave it a target for cost reduction, and then there were discussions about cost for each item.

MOT-J-S4 described its contractual arrangements with its motor industry customers in very similar terms to the other Japanese subcontractors. There was an annually renewable basic contract, together with a 3-4 month forecast of orders, which was issued monthly. Specific orders would come through every three or four days, with on-line communication. The principal would set a purchasing price target every six months, and a price would be agreed which could be reviewed in less than six months if special circumstances arose.

5.4.4 Technology transfer and other help

ENG-GB-S3 did not mention any transfer of technology from its motor manufacturing principal, and appears to have been used because of its already well-developed and well-proven ability in press tool manufacture. GB-S4's situation seemed similar. GB-S5 said it tended to work together with its better customers on a new job, more so than a decade ago, and that it tried for close contact with customers

MOT-J-S1 had received considerable advice from its main principal on management methods, such as inventory control, but it was independent and did not receive financial help.

J-S2 (the forging company) did not discuss technical help in the abstract, but it mentioned (see 5.4.2) visits by the principals engineers when new parts production was being started. J-S3 said it discussed its purchases of capital equipment with its main principal, but it had not received financial help for such purchases. However, it did have some equipment on loan from the principal, for which it paid a rental. It had never asked its main principal for advice on financial management, but felt it would have been forthcoming if required. J-S4 gave the impression that there was virtually complete freedom of technical information with its main motor industry customer, and this included a substantial flow from subcontractor to principal.

5.4.5 Dependence, dualism and opportunism?

ENG-GB-S3 stressed that it did not wish to be heavily dependent on any one customer, and had a wide range. It felt, in general, that principals did not nurture subcontractors enough, but it saw signs of some customers now taking a longer-term view. It specifically commented that there had been much technical change in the equipment it used (particularly higher running speeds), and that it would have invested more if it had been surer of its market prospects. GB-S4 had similar views on dependence, and felt its position to have been considerably strengthened in relation to customers by its ability to market its own machinery as an end-product. GB-S5 did not depend for more than 10% of sales on any one customer. It commented on the low profit rate on much subcontracting, especially in view of its heavy investment in CNC equipment, and said it was gradually developing end-products of its own. All the British subcontractors were noticing the effects of the early 1990s recession, though growth in the late 1980s had generally been rapid. All, however, had a range of customers outside the motor industry, and this had sheltered them to some extent from the severity of the British motor industry recession. MOT-S-S2 (the forging manufacturer) sold about 70% of its output to its single most important customer, though it has other customers within the motor industry, and some outside it with whom it had been dealing for decades. It was 8% owned by its main customer, and had had some of its equipment transferred from the main principal when the principal decided to give up in-house production more than twenty years ago. However, it had bought its newer equipment by itself. It felt its own main principal was less harsh than some other large motor manufacturers, who changed subcontractors more frequently, but it did feel under pressure on costs from the other forgings makers in the principal's group of subcontractors. In general, though, it thought it had been able to grow in its main principal's wake.

MOT-J-S3 (the machinist) sold nearly two-thirds of its output to its main principal, but it also had an electrical division with other customers. It felt there was little competition with regard to its sales to the main principal, and that the principal was willing to continue a very long term relation. However, it commented that on the electrical side of its business, it felt principals were harsher and more willing to change subcontractors in the short term.

MOT-J-S4 need hardly worry about dependence, having highly advanced design capacity in its speciality, and serving several industries. Its largest single company is a motor manufacturer, but only takes 20% of S4's sales. Clearly J-S4 is not a subcontractor in the sense that some of the much smaller firms interviewed are. It is included as such because of its insistence that it is not a 'large company', and that (consequently) it wants to keep for itself, through in-house production, any economies of scale in the production of parts.

NOTES

1. If no such supplier could be found, however, it was not clear (in part because of language problems in the interview) whether J-P1 would be more likely still to try to subcontract by inducing a supplier to invest, or do it in-house because of its own preferential access, as a large company, to sources of capital.

2. This point, and a few others, are from an interview with MOT-GB-P2 by Janet Anderson of the University of East Anglia's Economics Research Centre (see note 1, chapter 4). GB-P2 was interviewed subsequently, at greater length, by the present project after the company had evinced a strong interest in the results of the UK/Japan comparison.

3. See also chapter 7, which gives a Japanese perspective on the issues by Makoto Takashima

4. Since the British subcontractors have appeared before, in chapter 4, only their activities relating to the motor industry will be covered in the present chapter.

6 The electronics companies

This chapter considers the experience of subcontracting in the electronics industry in the UK and Japan. Following the format of the previous two chapters, section 1 introduces the sample of companies. Section 2 considers the factors underlying the decision to subcontract, how this has changed in Britain in the last decade, and how it compares to the situation in Japan. Section 3 looks at issues of supply chain management, how British companies view the subcontracting relation, and how such relations are conducted among the Japanese companies interviewed. This section mainly takes the principals' viewpoint, though some subcontractor material is introduced too. Section 4 asks how subcontracting appears from the perspective of the British and Japanese subcontractors.

6.1 The companies

Introductory profiles of the electronics principals are given in Table 6.1, while Table 6.2 sets out information about the subcontractors. As in chapters 4 and 5, although data was collected on companies' employment, date of foundation, share of exports in turnover, detailed product mix, and so on, this is normally suppressed so as to preserve the companies' anonymity (1). Of principals in Britain, four are computer companies, ranging from the largest computing multinational (see note 1) to two medium size company and one small one. There is also one principal making components. The British subcontractors include a manufacturer of printed circuit boards ('PCBs'), a maker of audio equipment, and a designer/manufacturer of automation system. Additionally, the association of contract electronics manufacturers [ACeM] was interviewed, which provided information about its members activities. In Japan, one large electronics company was interviewed, one of whose major product was computers; and one medium/large-sized Japanese computer company. The subcontractors were one firm working for the large principal, and one working for a consumer electronics manufacturer (2). There is some arbitrariness about which of the British companies is taken to be a principal and which a subcontractor. Several

Table 6.1
The Electronics Principals

Company	Main Products	Items on Subcontract	Attitude to Subcontracting
British Principals			
ELEC-GB-P1	Computer hardware, computing 'solutions'	Components, assemblies	Subcontract out as much as possible, anything not vital to core business
ELEC-GB-P2	Minicomputers, information systems	Metal work, plastic molding, prototype work	Subcontracts out items outside its expertise. Also trying to develop business as a subcontractor
ELEC-GB-P3	Intelligent terminals and workstations	Metal work, plastic work for housings and keyboard, overflow for large assembly orders	Willing to use overflow subcontracting to avoid fluctuations in workforce
ELEC-GB-P4	Electronic components, for minicomputers and other uses	Only for overflow work, or to source cheap labour (overseas)	Fear of subcontractors setting up as rivals
ELEC-GB-P5	Computer networking systems, design of printed circuit boards, software	Wiring of computer networks	Subcontracting limited by fear of setting up potential rivals
Japanese Principals			
ELEC-J-P1	Computer equipment, and other electronic products	Some integrated circuits, much fabrication and assembly	Willing to make heavy use of outsourcing, with complex network of suppliers
ELEC-J-P2	Computer equipment and information systems	Large volume printed circuit board assembly, many peripheral activities	Has adopted a relatively harsh attitude to subcontractors, in a context of rapid technological change and shortening product life cycles

Table 6.2
The Electronics Subcontractors

Company	Main Products	Main Industries Supplied	Attitude to Subcontracting
British Subcontractors			
ELEC-GB-S1	Bare printed circuit boards, some printed circuit board assembly	Wide range (but not high-volume consumer electronics)	Fear of very low profit margins, insufficient to finance essential investment in new technology. Feels customers very willing to switch suppliers for small price differences.
ELEC-GB-S2	Specialist audio design services and small batch manufacture	Entertainments industry	Very apprehensive about payment by customers, after bad experience
ELEC-GB-S3	Design and manufacture of automation systems	Motor industry, electronics industry	Feels customers often take insufficient interest
Japanese Subcontractors			
ELEC-J-S1	Intelligent terminals, and other computer peripherals	Almost all output sold to computer industry principal	Very content with the (long) relationship, but also developing own products to limited extent
ELEC-J-S2	Specialized, but high volume, printed circuit board assembly, some own products	Almost all subcontracted output sold to one consumer electronics principal	Feels the relation with its principal has stabilized the orders for its business

'principals' are far 'upstream', but they do not regard themselves as subcontractors because of their independence in terms of technological capacity. In contrast, the Japanese companies' positions in the principal/subcontractor hierarchy were much clearer. Since the five principals in Britain, and the first British subcontractor, cover most aspects of the computing sector of electronics, the other two subcontractors widen the field somewhat (without going into an entirely new area like consumer electonics) and are small, high technology companies operating on the interface between engineering and electronics (3).

6.2 The subcontracting decision

6.2.1 The British principals

In the world computing industry, in view of the company's dominance, 'it is scarcely an exaggeration to say that IBM is not so much a competitor to other firms as the environment in which they must operate' (Morgan and Sayer, 1988, p.81). The policy of IBM (ELEC-GB-P1 - see note 1) on subcontracting is of particular interest, and there is the clearest evidence of a move towards outsourcing by IBM in the face of international competitive pressure and accelerated technical change. In the early 1980s some 80% of work was done in-house and 80% put out. By the early 1990s the proportions have been almost reversed, with 70% put out to subcontract (4).

IBM subcontracts out:
-in order to maintain flexibility, so as to handle volume movements. A subcontractor say 30% dependent on IBM can increase volume by diverting sales to IBM, or by working extra shifts more easily than IBM could in-house.
-because IBM perceives itself as limited in its technical talents and wants to conserve them. 'If you try to reinvent things other people have already done, rather than use them as suppliers, you are likely to be 18 months behind the market' - a risky position in an industry where product cycles have themselves shortened to about 18 months (e.g. for laptop/notebook computers).
-but not primarily because of cost. IBM could usually match cost by in-house innovation. Low labour cost from overseas is not much of an issue, because the principal could automate.

Where heavy investments are required, and there is an established supplier, IBM normally will buy-in unless the item is crucial. IBM sees its market position as depending on keeping leadership in certain crucial areas, and buying-in just about everything else. For example, its two European semiconductor plants provide an in-house supply of leading edge processors and high density memories (Joselyn, 1991, p.51) (5). With 'bread and butter' items, it tries to buy in at the highest stage of assembly possible, which has implications for its supply chain management (see section 6.3). Its market position, it says, also depends on being able to persuade customers to pay more for 'front-end' products, where massive investment has been needed. There is severe competition from Japanese consumer electronics companies, who have entered the market for laptop and notebook computers, and who have extensive consumer sales outlets.

Heavy investment requirements are a problem, even for a very large company, and suppliers likely to have made them are sometimes competitors or may become so. For some items, no one company easily can go it alone - for example IBM has a joint venture with Toshiba, one of its main competitors in the portable computer market, to produce a flat colour screen, and IBM is also working with Siemens on chip development. In fact, some suppliers **are** competitors, which raises strategic problems. Some items of emerging technology, like flat screens, are only available from the Far East.

ELEC-GB-P2, a medium sized company making minicomputers which are highly customized to its clients, has not undergone the same profound changes in its approach to manufacturing as IBM. It has experienced almost a halving of its workforce from its peak in the 1980s, partly through recession but partly through technical change which has reduced hardware requirements (e.g. fewer PCBs per minicomputer). Its own subcontracting decisions are easily understood; it buys-in metal working (e.g. the frames for its minicomputers) and plastic molding work (such as casings for its workstations) from two specialist subcontractors, who have expertise the principal does not want to develop. It also uses a small subcontractor for prototype manufacture. In general, little of what GB-P2 buys-in is customized, since the customizing of standard items is its own main expertise; it survives against competition from larger computer companies by operating in a niche that larger companies would not consider worth their while. It buys-in bare PCBs, and could not justify in-house manufacture because of the economies of scale involved in PCB manufacture. This also appears to be the attitude of the larger contract electronics manufacturers, who are generally larger companies than GB-P2, but few of whom make bare PCBs in-house. GB-P2 was trying to expand through the early 1990s recession by developing business itself as a subcontractor. Only 10% of whose workforce is in manufacture (mainly assembling customized PCBs, the rest of the workforce being in design, software and customer services). It offers customers a complete service, by designing and supplying, say, a minicomputer system around a final customer's requirements. It is also willing to offer services such as specialized PCB design and layout, and a full procurement service, in the expectation that other, larger, suppliers will wish to subcontract these out.

ELEC-GB-P3, making intelligent terminals and workstations, all to customer requirements, subcontracted in a manner similar to that GB-P2. It used two subcontractors for metal fabrication, which it regarded as being outside its expertise. It preferred to dual-source for reasons of security, and it had provided the subcontractors with tooling. It retained ownership of the tooling and could, in principle, remove it if it changed subcontractor, but the tooling was specific to the extent that another subcontractor with different methods might not be able to fit it. It single-sourced for plastic housings for terminals, because of the high costs of the tooling it was required to provide. It also subcontracted the plastic manufacture for its keyboards. This was a company where the labour element of value-added was low, and the profit element high in order to cover heavy overheads. Non-standard, bought-in components were equivalent to over a third of turnover.

GB-P3 also illustrates some issues of economies of scale in electronics. Itself a fairly small company, in the past it subcontracted, as overflow, a large order it received, so as to avoid building up a workforce it could not later keep in employment. The main part of the subcontracting was printed circuit board assembly, i.e. putting components such as integrated circuits and resistors onto bare

PCBs. The large contract electronics manufacturers (members of ACeM) normally would only handle large volume work (say 5000 per annum or more), and GB-P3 was able to engage one of them for its large overflow order, which it would not normally have been able to do for smaller overflows. It mentioned that large computer companies now rarely assemble PCBs in-house, and that during the past 5-10 years there had been considerable use of Far Eastern assembler for this, who only would deal with much larger orders (20-25000 per year) However, since at least one big Western manufacturer had greatly reduced its use of Far Eastern assemblers, after those assemblers had put in capacity to service it, it was possible to source PCB assembly in countries like Taiwan and Korea in smaller volumes because of their shortage of work. Volumes were also significant in the purchase of bare PCBs (although they are much more of a standard purchase than PCB assembly); again, very large volumes could be sourced cheaply in the Far East, but Far Eastern producers were not interested in small orders. However, recall that IBM had mentioned problems of sourcing long-distance, particularly supply rigities, and now preferred European sourcing.

ELEC-GB-P4 is a manufacturer of a specialized component that is used on printed circuit boards, for minicomputers for example, though it has a range of other applications. It customizes about 60% of its output, but would strongly resist the idea of being regarded as a 'subcontractor' because it sees itself as having world leadership in the technology of its product. Hence it is included here, arbitrarily, as a principal; and in fact its experience as an 'upstream' producer illustrates aspects of both principal's and subcontractor's behaviour.GB-P4's growth has benefitted from the development of solid state technology in electronics, which has meant that almost all the large companies who previously produced in-house have ceased production of the component. The component now has more specialized uses only, and the absence of large standardized volumes protects GB-P4, it feels, from Japanese competition. Nevertheless, the production of the component is subject to substantial economies of scale in terms of setup time. This, together with the need for substantial R&D inputs, protects against potential rivals' in-house production. Technical change in the electronics industry has meant a changing customer base. GB-P4 prides itself on keeping as much of its production in-house as possible, which it regards as a selling point with customers. It subcontracts only overflow work, particularly soldering and assembly. This is to avoid fluctuations in the size of its workforce, which it feels would lose it goodwill in its community. It does subcontract some assembly work overseas, through an affiliate, to source cheap labour. But it has had some bad experience in this regard, when a supplier in Thailand started to contact GB-P4's customers with a view to setting up in business as a rival supplier. This has made it cautious about transferring knowhow.

ELEC-GB-P5, a small company operating largely independently within a large, diversified group, shares GB-P4's fear of subcontractors becoming rivals. Like GB-P4, P5 feels that its independent technological capability makes it more of a principal than a subcontractor. It is certainly a principal in the sense that it tends to deal directly with final customers, such as universities wanting to set up computer networking. In its early stages of growth, GB-P5 did its own wiring, but as it has grown larger it has tended to subcontract it. It does so especially for large jobs, so the subcontracting is to an extent overflow, and a larger company would use in-house facilities, P5 thought.

6.2.2 The Japanese principals

ELEC-J-P1 provides a good comparison with IBM (UK). It produces computing products as the largest item in its turnover, but also a range of other electronic and electrical products, some of which in the past were more important than computers. The interview concentrated on J-P1's computer operations, but a study by Sako (7) allows the company's operations to be seen in wider perspective. Useful material also was provided by one of J-P1's major suppliers, ELEC-J-S1.

Originally relying heavily on in-house production in order to control quality, when J-P1 rapidly expanded in the 1960s it moved towards using outside suppliers because of difficulties in increasing its core workforce to a sufficient extent. ELEC-J-P1 now has a total of 1,500 regular material and component suppliers to its headquarters and six divisional sites, plus another 1500 provisional suppliers who get one-off orders once or twice a year; and the total of suppliers rises to about 8,000 if suppliers to the company's subsidiary factories all over Japan are included (Sako,1990, pp.127, 129).

J-P1 makes about half of its integrated circuits in-house (Sako, 1990, p.127), to preserve its core technological capacity. J-P1's policy, it says, is to manufacture mass-production items itself, and to put smaller, more variegated products out to subcontractors.

Special features required to customize products are also put out, and subcontractors assemble them. When a product's volume starts to fall - in an industry with shortening product cycles - it will be put out to subcontract. ELEC-J-S1 thought that the part of J-P-1 with which it dealt had nearly 140 subcontractors making hardware, and about half that number producing software; in this grouping J-S1 was one of the largest suppliers. On the hardware side, the peripheral equipment such as terminals, printers, and disk drives were outsourced by J-P1, and also PCB assembly.

Heavy use of outsourcing is also made by ELEC-J-P2, a somewhat smaller, but still substantial, computer company (8). For one of its main factories (making workstations, business computers and laptops) in Japan it uses 1,000 suppliers, of whom 900 supply standard items, and the remaining 100 are the subcontractors proper (9). About 60% of printed circuit board assembly is put out to subcontract. The 40% of PCB assembly done in-house is of a small batch or prototype sort. In-house PCB assembly uses surface-mount techniques, which JP-2 notes is of a very advanced type requiring heavy investment expenditure. Note that in Britain, surface-mount technology has been a powerful factor in stimulating the growth of large, specialized contract PCB assemblers. J-P2's factory also buys-in cathode ray tubes for monitors, made to its specification, and other items such as cables, small assemblies, small power units, motors, cabinets, all rather obviously outside the core capabilities of a computer company. It also buys in floppy disk drives, however. J-P2 stressed the type and degree of outsourcing from product to product, but that the factory regarded its core skills as sophisticated mechanical assembly and final testing, besides the small batch and prototype PCB assembly already mentioned.

Whether or not the two Japanese manufacturers are more 'outsourced' than IBM can only be determined indirectly, in the absence of exact data. The accounts published for each major company by the Japanese Ministry of Finance show that J-P2's share of wages and salaries in total turnover is a few percentage points smaller than IBM's (which is 15.1%), while J-P1's is smaller still, but the presentation of the

92

Japanese accounts makes it difficult to compare the use of suppliers. J-P2's product mix is more similar to IBM's than is that of J-P1, but J-P1 is a company of more comparable stature.

6.3 Supply chain management

6.3.1 Subcontractor selection, development and monitoring

Increased outsourcing by IBM ('ELEC-GB-P1') has been accompanied by a sophisticated programme of supply chain management. It has 300 'preferred suppliers', which cover some 80% of the needs of its two main UK manufacturing plants, and who are mostly makers of components, though there also contract manufacturers (about whom more later) among them (Joselyn,1991,p. 51). It also has a tail of 3000 suppliers, accounting for the other 20% of its needs. For administrative reasons IBM would prefer to deal with a smaller number of suppliers, and is reducing its supplier base. This may mean a subcontractor should produce a complete subassembly rather than a component. This implies, in turn, that some supply chain management is devolved onto the supplier, and indeed capabilities in this regard are assessed when a supplier is evaluated.

IBM's selection procedure for a new supplier initially takes a year, and there is a second year during which the supplier is worked in. Suppliers are graded A,B, or C; a C-grade supplier either is on the way out, or will be upgraded to B. The British Standard 5750 is used as a guide, but there is increasing use of the US Baldridge Award (administered by the US Department of Industry) standard as a criterion. During a supplier's second year she might be used as a secondary supplier, a lot of technical effort would be put into the supplier's factory, and she would be required to deliver just-in-time. At a later stage this supplier might become a primary supplier, backed by a secondary one, and be able to come to IBM with suggestions of her own for new developments in the items supplied. Input into the supplier selection process also is provided by IBM's technical procurement centre in Bordeaux (Joselyn,1991), which provides information on European sourcing options, though apparently dealing more with 'consumables' than with transaction-specific items. IBM gives the impression (confirmed indirectly by other interviewees in course of discussion of their own sourcing), that it has sought to move out of sourcing in Asia and to look for European options, particularly because of the lack of flexibility from long shipping times and the possibility of supply disruption.

ELEC-GB-P2's choice of subcontractors is quite staightforward. It has chosen subcontractors within a 50 mile radius, since frequent visits and close personal contact is important to sort out minor problems quickly. It does not normally change its subcontractors, although it monitors their prices and would consider changing if prices became out of line with what GB-P2 considered standard. ELEC-GB-P3 would do a vendor rating exercise with any prospective new subcontractor, visiting their premises and checking their quality control. Like GB-P2, it preferred suppliers to be within 50 miles.

Although ELEC-GB-P4 has had bad experience with overseas subcontractors trying to set up in business as rival suppliers, it does use two small local companies for overspill assembly. It took some time to teach these two smallish companies what was required, which is one reason for only using two. GB-P5 uses a local wiring contractor mainly for overflow work, although it might use someone else for work outside the area. GB-P5, though satisfied with its present relation (especially since the subcontractor sometimes brings business to its attention), would hesitate to provide a subcontractor with too much advice lest the subcontractor entered into competition with it.GB-P5 very much wishes to keep financial control over the jobs it does.

The two Japanese computer principals had contrasting approaches to subcontractor choice. The smaller of the two, J-P2, took a much harsher attitude, and was interested in a subcontractor's ability to perform over the life of a product, with no commitment to a long-term relation [see note 8]. J-P1, while exercising considerable power and control over its subcontractors, was interested in an essentially long-term relation.

J-P2 approaches its choice of subcontractor, it explained, in the light of the fact that electronics subcontractors are more independent in their technological capabilities than, say, those in the motor industry, and that the product life cycle in computer products has been shortening rapidly. J-P2 spoke of computing power being quadrupled within the same space every four years, and how, over a two year period, portable computers have been reduced from laptop to book to notebook size, with technical change being driven by competition between manufacturers. J-P2's selection procedure for a new subcontractor takes 3-6 months. It would first give drawings to potential subcontractors and get estimates, with a view to finalizing on one or two. During the trial period, there would be severe quality control by P2. Towards the end of the product's life, P2 would look for new subcontractors and pick the best. The existing supplier have the advantage of not needing such a long trial period, but still might not be chosen. A subcontractor's ability (and willingness) to invest would be an important factor, and P2 said that often substantial new investment might be required of the subcontractor to move to production of the new product (10). J-P2 did, however, sometimes allow a subcontractor to buy equipment on J-P2's account and to use it for the life of the product. [It also mentioned, in passing, that for an operation it was running in the UK, it had brought a substantial range of equipment with it from Japan for the use of local subcontractors].

ELEC-J-P1, is looking for subcontractors in the expectation of a long relation, which it feels will produce good learning effects in them. J-P1 is particularly looking for subcontractors capable of assuming a joint role in new product development, and those who cannot are likely to find themselves producing only older products with narrow profit margins. In spite of having an association of existing suppliers, many of whom are of long standing, J-P1 maintains a lookout for new ones. A new supplier may be taken on on trial, and gradually moved up J-P1's supplier-rankings if appropriate, possibly displacing eventually higher ranked suppliers. Similarly, an unsatisfactory supplier will not be dropped immediately, but will be moved down the ranking and given reduced orders if its performance does not improve. New suppliers are subject to an appraisal procedure, asked to provide samples and small batches, which are subjected to a decreasing degree of inward inspection by J-P1. However, when the subcontractor is allowed to take on the responsibility for inspection of its products, it also takes on the responsibility for reimbursing the principal for any wastage caused if what it supplies proves faulty. (Sako, 1990, pp.130, 137)

J-P1 attempts to smooth orders to subcontractors and not to reduce them to zero for satisfactory suppliers even in bad times, in return for which they were expected to secure periodic cost reductions (Sako, 1990, pp.135, 142). Thus, J-P1 is by no means weakly benevolent, but has mechanisms for ensuring high performance by its suppliers. It explained one case where it had dropped a subcontractor, who had been given managerial and technical advice, and also more favourable payment terms in an attempt to help it out of difficulties; but could not recover from its difficulties. J-P1 also explained that the help it is willing to give its subcontractors is limited by the fact that many subcontractors work for other customers; something, however, which they are encouraged to do by J-P1, which does not wish to take full responsibility for their survival (11).

6.3.2 Contractual arrangements and the subcontracting relationship

IBM would give a supplier an indication of an annual programme of orders, and a profile of the life cycle of the final product over several years. There would be continuous updating of requirements, to maintain maximum flexibility, and there would be just-in-time supply. IBM prefers suppliers to do a substantial but not an overwhelming proportion of their business with them; a proportion of 10-30% of a supplier's sales going to IBM is considered ideal. If the proportion rises substantially above 30% - and this percentage is continually monitored by IBM - the supplier will be asked to reduce it. IBM does not want over-dependent suppliers who might go under if IBM changes its product line. IBM also rarely invests in suppliers, except for very large, joint-venture type projects.

The problems of IBM's suppliers sometimes being rivals has already been mentioned - and the suppliers include firms in Japan and Japanese foreign investors in the UK. There is also a problem of ensuring secrecy where technology is shared with a supplier who also supplies a rival - suppliers must 'fence in' IBM's information. IBM would not drop a supplier readily, and if one is dropped 'he would have seen it coming for a long time'. However, as IBM's UK purchasing manager pointed out (to Joselyn,1991), even the list of preferred existing suppliers is under constant review. There is likely to be a turnover of 30% within the next five years; 'the relationship must stay on a tough commercial footing and not be allowed to become cosy'

ELEC-GB-P2, making a specialized product and requiring only small volumes from its subcontractors, prefers not to give them contracts, and is willing to pay a higher price than otherwise in order to be able to give one-off orders. P2 would not wish its subcontractors to make supplies of items which might quickly become obsolete in a situation of rapid technical change. The subcontractors are financially independent. Like GB-P2, GB-P3 does not give contracts, but said its own subcontractors would not want to be tied to orders for more than three months ahead anyway. Its manager contrasted its own behaviour with that of a larger firm for which he had worked, which used larger companies such as ACeM members as subcontractors. There, a one-year contract would be given, for a specified quantity at an average selling price covering different items. GB-P4, the components supplier, normally receives one-year contracts from its customers, some of whom (representing at least 20% of sales) require substantial product adaptation. It gives a formal contract to its own two overspill subcontractors, scheduling orders. GB-P5 gives its wiring subcontractor only one-off orders, and gets detailed quotations about labour-time and other costs before a price is agreed. GB-P3 mentioned that it did not like subcontractors to be more than 25% dependent on it for sales.

In keeping with their different approaches to subcontractors, the two Japanese computer principals offered different contractual arrangements. The smaller and more specialized company, J-P2, with its hard attitude, offered detailed short-term (2-3 years) contracts (rather similar, it thought, to what would be used by principals in Britain!).The contract would include details on settlements, on how to treat defects, on volumes and on how price would vary with the volume demanded. J-P2 did not run a traditional group of subcontractors, and was rather scornful of this kind of approach, which it regarded as old-fashioned.

The long term relations of ELEC-J-P1 with its subcontractors have been mentioned in the previous section, and its contractual relations with them are broadly similar to those maintained by large principals with extensive subcontracting networks in other industries (e.g.MOT-J-P1). There is a general background contract, renewable annually unless either side objects, which includes conditions of payment and obligations for keeping secrecy In addition to this, there are various specification documents for particular products, and individual orders. Sako (1990,pp. 138-9) stresses the non-contractual nature of the basic contract, where ambiguities are to be settled by discussion [see also our chapter 7].

6.3.3 Sub-subcontracting

IBM is keen on subcontractors themselves subcontracting on, as it devolves some of the supply chain management onto the subcontractor. Sometimes it works through distributors who buy from groups of subcontractors.

However, although one might first suppose that layers of subcontractors exist for reasons determined by technological factors, supply chain management of the sort being developed by IBM also involves the active **organization** of suppliers into layers. Consider the constituent parts of a microcomputer - the screen, casing, keyboard, and the printed circuit board containing integrated circuits and other components. Key integrated circuits will be produced in-house as core technology. Assembly of components onto bare PCBs can be subcontracted out. There is a substantial group of largish firms with workforces up to 5000 or more, which specializes in this and is organized under the newly formed (in 1990) Association of Contract Electronics Manufacturers (ACeM, 1990). These firms work for a variety of electronics customers, including consumer electronics manufacturers as well as makers of computers. Their development has certainly been stimulated by new (surface-mount) technology, which has greatly raised investment costs and scale economics in PCB assembly. Although some work on the basis of free issued components, IBM encourages them to do their own purchasing - which raises the PCB assembler's profitably, and relieves IBM of the task of component purchasing from a range of suppliers. This creates the contract assembler of PCBs as a layer, who buys in components and bare boards.

ELEC-GB-P2,the minicomputer manufacturer, whose own subcontractors' role is minor and who do appear to subcontract further, is in process of forming itself into another layer in the supply chain by offering specialized services to other suppliers, such as procurement, and specialized aspects of design. GB-P2 itself was formed by a management buyout as an offshoot from a larger company some years ago. GB-P3, making intelligent terminals, would do its own PCB assembly in house for smaller orders, but would go to a lower layer of the subcontracting chain for overflow, using a larger contract electronics manufacturer for large orders. GB-P4, making components, prefers to keep in-house as much a possible, and tries only to subcontract overflow work. GB-P5's subcontractor, doing electrical wiring for computer networks, does not sub-subcontract.

ELEC-J-P1 said it dealt with only one layer of subcontractors. Since one of its largest subcontractors (ELEC-J-S1) itself subcontracts extensively, this suggests that J-P1 is able to devolve the management of the further upstream parts of its supply chain on to its first level subcontractors. J-P2 also appeared to expect its subcontractors to be able to manage their own subcontractors.

The larger of the two Japanese subcontractors, J-S1, operated its own subcontractor association, with a membership of 16, whose employment ranged from 70 to just 3-4. Other subcontractors were also used, and the criteria of membership of the organization was that S1 should be the main customer, that the relation should have been for more than three years, and there was also a minimum sales criterion from the sub-subcontractor to S1. These sub-subcontractors have under them (at most) one more layer of firms, thus there are a total of three layers below the principal in the supply chain. Clearly J-S1's role in the management of the supply chain is crucial, even though J-S1's own suppliers are responsible for the firms working under them. Indeed, in a foreign investment which J-P1 was planning in an Asian country, ELEC-J-S1 had gone on ahead to organize a local network of suppliers.

The smaller of the two Japanese subcontractors, J-S2 assembling very high-technology PCBs in high volume, worked very directly (i.e. in a shorter supply chain) with its principal, and only subcontracted itself to three very small firms. Nevertheless, J-S2 was responsible for over half the total purchases by its principal of PCB assembly of this type. Unlike the larger J-S1, which handled its own purchasing of components, J-S2 worked with components free-issued by its principal, again meaning less supply chain management devolved onto the subcontractor.

6.4 The subcontractors' experience of subcontracting

6.4.1 Subcontractors' perceptions of their competitive advantage

Staying competitive in printed circuit board manufacture is difficult, and depends on high volume and considerable investment, and the PCB manufacturer GB-S1 was having trouble in doing so. It lacked the volume to engage in sufficient bulk purchase of raw materials. It felt it needed investment (which its current level of profits could not sustain) in photographic plotting for more accuracy and less waste. There was severe competition from Taiwan and Korea. This was in spite of the fact that S1 was aiming at something of a niche market, producing highly bespoke products and not aiming at the mass market represented, say, by PCBs for televisions. GB-S1 felt the UK market for PCBs had been damaged severely by customers destocking during the early 1990s recession. Indeed, the market had been bad since the early 1980s.GB-S1 had diversified into PCB assembly (with the components supplied by customers on a free-issue basis), and was aware that large companies, led it said by IBM and Rank Xerox, were subcontracting more. GB-S1 was able to keep some particular customers by being able to put the right finish on its PCBs, which some competitors could not do.

The Japanese subcontractor, ELEC-J-S2, is in printed circuit board assembly. Its work was not for a computer company but (mainly) for a large manufacturer of consumer electronic products. It is an SME by Japanese standards, and belongs to a group unconnected with its principal. Its competitive advantage lies in the dualistic structure of the Japanese labour market; it can source low-cost part-time labour, which its principal would not employ in its core labour force (and would have union problems if it tried). The very complex PCBs which S2 is assembling can only be assembled in part by automatic insertion; there are many large components which require manual assembly. J-S2 explained that male workers, and young women, were not willing to do this repetitive, boring work, but that housewives found it acceptable, given that the company provided nursery facilities (12). This was in the context of Japan's overall labour shortage, which many companies mentioned. Since J-S2's principal supplied bare PCBs and the components on a free-issue basis, labour costs were equivalent to about half the value of J-S2's sales. The principal retained a small in-house capability to assemble boards of this type, both to maintain its technological development and also as a check on costs.

The Japanese electronics subcontractor J-S1 is a substantially larger firm than J-S2 (though much smaller than either Japanese principal), and is quite similar in its product mix to the British firm ELEC-GB-P3. The difference is that J-S1's intelligent terminals and other computer equipment are sold mainly to its main principal rather than to final customers. J-S1 competitive advantage lies in its specialized technological knowledge and investment (for example, it has bought two successive generations of PCB insertion machines). J-S1 also has something of a niche in the repair field, doing work small companies would not be able to undertake, and which larger companies would not take on.

Both ELEC-GB-S2 and ELEC-GB-S3 are outside the computer sector of electronics, which has been the main focus of this chapter, and their experience of subcontracting bridges the areas of the mechanical engineering of chapter 4 and electronics. They both are very small, highly specialized companies, combining mechanical engineering and electronics skills. GB-S2 designs and builds prototypes of audio and other electronic equipment. Its strength is its technical expertise, and it grew rapidly in the mid-1980s after many large companies closed down their in-house facilities in the early 1980s recession. It used to subcontract the engineering side of its business, but acquired an engineering workshop from a company which failed, and feels this allows it to have faster production and reduces the need for outside consultation. It does buy in printed circuit boards, 'to keep our capabilities for what we do best', also sheet metal work ('worth £10 an hour, whereas our machines can earn £20'), and 'tedious and repetitive work' like screen printing. It feels this sub-subcontracting greatly improves its position. GB-S3 buys in only standard items and its expertise lies in doing designing and building manufacturing systems which would not be within their customers' in-house expertise.

6.4.2 Subcontractor selection and monitoring

No detailed information was provided by GB-S1 (making printed circuit boards) on how it was chosen by customers. However, the strong impression was that customers were willing to switch suppliers quickly and in response to very small price differentials. Many of its customer contacts were more than a decade old, but it had sought new customers to try to increase volume to cut costs. GB-S2, designing audio equipment found customers through its reputation for highly skilled work, and had had a number of regular ones. GB-S3, designing manufacturing systems for the motor industry and electronics industries, and others, had many long-standing customers too. It commented, though, that it was hard to get British companies to take an interest in the work it did for them.

ELEC-J-S1 had been doing business for over 30 years with its main principal. The present chairman's father, who founded the business, was a former emplooyee of the principal. J-S1 previously worked as a subcontractor on an earlier area of production of the principal's, and as the principal moved into an electronic version, so J-S1 also moved into electronics, which was its avenue into computer-related business when the principal developed the computer side of its business. J-S1 mentioned apast event as being particularly important in its relation with its principal's computer peripherals department: ten years ago, when the department, and the principal's computer production generally had not been very profitable (because of intense foreign competition), J-S1 lent some of its best engineers to this department of J-P1's, and at low wages. Several other subcontractors had been asked to do the same, but had refused. From then on, J-S1 felt it had an exceptionally close relation with its principal (13). The monitoring of the quality of J-S1's products was done in three ways. For completely new products, the principal would come to the subcontractor's factory to do the testing, before delivery was started. For established products, the testing was left to S1. For products in between these extremes, the tests would be done by the principal on receipt.

ELEC-J-S2 had been selected as a result of approaching its main principal, who twenty years ago had set up a factory nearby. J-S2 had been in a declining industry, and simply removed its old plant and replaced it with equipment for electronic assembly in the same factory building. Many of S2's workers and engineers at that time were sent to the principal's main plant some distance away for three months training. Communication between subcontractor and principal is very close, with fax messages virtually every day, often with minor design and specification changes

6.4.3 Contractual relations

GB-S1's contractual arrangements varied greatly between customers, from 18 month contracts to one-off orders where the customers only paid when they actually used the boards. All GB-S2's customers gave only one-off orders, except for the company it claims seriously cheated it (see subsection 6.4.5), which gave a series of six month contracts! GB-S3 virtually only ever received one-off orders.

ELEC-J-S1 receives the basic contract already described from its principal ELEC-J-P1. It also receives an informal document which explains that an order will be sent but only giving an approximate indication to the amount. Even before this is done, there will have been communication between the engineers of the two companies to let S1 know what kind of demand is likely. In this prior stage, there is informal estimation of cost, which is then calculated on the basis of standard labour time and cost of materials. Then S1 sends the estimate to the principal, and a formal unit price is contained in the order document, when sent. However, production is started by S1 before receiving the formal order! J-S1 regarded itself as having a close relation with its principal, not just from close personal contact with the principal's personnel, but as the outcome of the accumulated experience of the principal with the subcontractor's performance over more than 30 years.

The contractual arrangements of ELEC-J-S2, the PCB assembler, with its major consumer electronics principal, are very similar to those of the other Japanese subcontractor, J-S1. There is a basic contract, renewable annually, and a variety of individual documents. The principal sends a design to the subcontractor, who makes an estimate. If the estimate is not in accord with the principal's expectations, there is further discussion, though this happens only rarely. As with J-S1, J-S2 starts production before the formal procedure for an order is completed.

6.4.4 Technology transfer and other help

GB-S1 had never received technical advice from a customer, although it would not necessarily have spurned it if offered; nor financial help. Both GB-S2 and S3 regarded their technological level as beyond that of their customers. GB-S3 would like to have had more involvement by customers in what it was doing for them, instead of simply being left with a problem to solve with insufficient consultation about the customer's real requirements. This was sometimes a problem because fixing a price was difficult at an early stage, and GB-S3 tried not to accept fix-price orders for this reason.

ELEC-J-S1 has a close relation with its (only) principal with regard to the exchange of technical information. The principal sends engineers to S1, and vice-versa. S1 discusses with its principal when it would like to introduce new capital equipment. Some of the principal's equipment is used on loan by S1, and it also has some older equipment the principal no longer needs.

ELEC-J-S2, besides having received considerable training for its workforce from its main principal at the start of the relation, frequently sends its people to the principal's factory to learn about new products or manufacturing techniques. The principal has no financial involvement with S2, but it does free-issue materials.

6.4.5 Dependence, dualism and opportunism?

Though GB-S1 said it tried to keep to a maximum dependence of 10% of sales to any one customer, in fact it was very much on the lookout for new business to ensure survival. Customers, themselves squeezed by import competition and recession in the UK, were behaving towards suppliers with great ruthlessness, and margins for producers of PCBs were being cut below the minimum necessary to finance new investment.

Both GB-S2 and S3, although having a high level of independent technology, found subcontracting in Britain a harsh climate. Both tried to make sales to final consumers too to diversify. S3 thought that the ruthlessness which larger companies showed towards subcontractors had improved in the mid 1980s, and a more cooperative spirit had developed, but that the early 1990s recession had worsened things again. S3 felt customers in the motor industry were especially unsatisfactory, wanting one-off jobs done extremely quickly and making no attempt to build any long term relation - S3 worked for several British-based motor companies, though not for the Japanese inward investors. Electronics companies, GB-S3 felt, were better customers, and regard price as less important than what the subcontractor can provide in the way of technological solutions.

The experience of ELEC-GB-S2 with its largest customer illustrates the continuing problem of opportunism in British industry. Although there was a formal contract, the customer (by now taking 75% of S2's business) simply deducted nearly 20% from the agreed price, when development work on an audio system was completed. This took most of GB-S2's profit on the work, and the customer threatened to withhold the rest if S2 took any legal action. S2, which regarded its work as in no way faulty, could not afford its cash flow to be so interrupted, and had to accept; but naturally feels highly aggrieved. S2 says the equipment is now made by several manufacturing subcontractors in exactly the same form which S-2 designed and trial-built.

The larger Japanese electronics principal, J-P1, argued that it wanted its subcontractors not to be highly dependent, and to have several customers. Sako's study (see note 7) has shown that the main group of P1's subcontractors are 60% dependent on P1, although there is a high variance. ELEC-J-P2 did not express a view on dependence, but in any case it was not looking for a long term relation with its subcontractors. Nevertheless, J-P1 also said it would hesitate to give much technical help to subcontractors also serving its competitors. Both our Japanese subcontractors had an extreme degree of sales dependence. The larger subcontractor, J-S1, sold 96% of its output to J-P1; J-S1 said that although it would suppose J-P1 would not like excessive dependence, in fact P1 had never raised the matter. J-S2 sold over 80% of its output to its main (consumer electronics) principal, and about 2% to a motor manufacturer. The rest of S2's sales were of a final product it developed, using its own electronics technology. J-S1 also had a limited development of its own final products, though it also tended to sell such items under its principal's brandname.

Neither Japanese subcontractor worried greatly about its high degree of sales dependence on one principal.Both felt their business had been helped to grow, and stabilized with constant orders from the principals. Neither had experienced any opportunistic behaviour on the part of a principal. The larger subcontractor, J-S1, felt its principal really wanted a close long term relation, but commented that other electronics principals were harsher, more willing to drop subcontractors. Both subcontractors felt their good relations with their principal depended on maintaining the growth of their technological capability and their quality control.

NOTES

1. The one exception to the anonymity rule in this book is ELEC-GB-P1, which is IBM, UK. When interviewed, it seemed that IBM's identity would be impossible to disguise, so my interview with the company was conducted on the basis that information given could be attributed. However, IBM is, of course, not responsible for any view expressed here; and any misunderstandings are my own! See also the published interview with IBM by Louise Joselyn (1991), which is a useful supplementary source on the company's purchasing policy.

2. An overseas associated company of the first subcontractor also was interviewed (in Hong Kong, on my return journey from Japan), to discuss its overseas subcontracting.

3. As also mentioned in chapter 4 (note 1), one Japanese company

which was interviewed is not included. It fell between engineering and electronics in terms of its activities (making switches), but it was not really on the 'interface' of those two industries, and its activities are difficult to relate directly to either. It does raise some points of interest, however, which are discussed in chapter 7.

4. IBM (UK)'s Annual Report for 1990 lists total value-added as 27.8% of its turnover in 1990, and 72.2% (£3.2 billion) as spent on purchased goods and services. Of this £3.2 billion, only 15% is spent outside Europe, and £500 million (equivalent to nearly 12% of total turnover) is spent within the UK (interview, 10.9.91). In the Annual Report, however, 'total expenditure with suppliers' is given as £1,341 million, which is 31% of turnover. In 1981 'expenditure with suppliers' was only about £150 million (c15% of turnover).

5. Presumably, purchases by IBM (UK) from other branches of IBM count as out-purchases in the 72.2% spend in note 4 above. Nevertheless, outsourcing from unrelated suppliers has increased greatly.

6. This information is from the Association of Contract Electronics Manufacturers, not from IBM.

7. ELEC-J-P1 was also interviewed by Mari Sako, as one of the three principals in the central case study of electronics in her Ph.D thesis on contractual relations in subcontracting (Sako, 1990, Ch.6; to be published as Sako,1992). Where any information from Sako's study is introduced here, it is specifically acknowledged; and information otherwise comes from the present study's own interviews with J-P1 and one of its major suppliers (ELEC-J-S1).

8. Note with with regard to the discussion of subcontracting relations from a Japanese viewpoint in chapter 7, by Makoto Takashima, that ELEC-J-P2 was seen separately from the interviewing programme organized by Takashima, and therefore is not discussed in chapter 7.

9. Sako (1990,p.133) says that of the 1500 suppliers of ELEC-J-P1, some 600 are subcontractors proper.

10. One of J-P2's engineers mentioned during the factory visit, however, that P2's cycle for replacement of its own equipment was about 7 years.

11. Sako (1990, p.133) notes that J-P1's central set of 600 subcontractors (see note 9) make on average 60% of their sales to J-P1, which suggests that J-P1's policy of having its subcontractors limit their dependence has some way to go.

12. They earned on average Y120,000 (£500) per month, for six hours a day/21 days a month.

13. See chapter 7 for further discussion of J-S1's relation with its principal.

7 The Japanese subcontracting relationship

7.1 Introduction

In order to investigate subcontracting relationships as a structural characteristic of Japanese manufacturing industry, to understand the division of work associated with these relationships, and to analyse their economic significance, we have first to make clear how such relationships are generally understood in Japan. Although the Japanese term shita-uke is translated into English as 'subcontract', the word has been used in both past and present Japanese society to express a rather specific relation between firms, while 'subcontract' appears to have a more general meaning in the Western world.

The term 'subcontracting relationship'(shita-uke kankei in Japanese) is usually used for the case where an ordering firm has some degree of control over a supplying firm in the production relations between them. This gives 'subcontracting' a meaning beyond the simple commissioning by one firm of work from another, instead of producing in its own factory. It cannot be said that in Japan we do not find any production commissioning relationships based on an occasional contract. Indeed, such relationships are found increasingly as there have appeared more independent small or medium-sized enterprises equipped with their own technology. However, 'subcontracting' in Japanese industry is mainly a continuous business relationship implying some form of control and subordination. This still prevails, although its characteristics gradually have undergone subtle changes in many respects. In other words, the shita-uke relationship is still the essential characteristic of 'subcontracting' in Japanese industry. As was noted in chapter 2 (section 2) it has been generally recognised that in the development process of the Japanese economy, small and medium firms were 'controlled' and 'subordinated' by monopolistic big firms, and that the latter made use of the former as a buffer in business cycles and exerted a controlling power over the small and medium firms in terms of pricing and other payment conditions. This relationship between them has been understood as producing problems of so-called shiwayose (loss-shifting) and shuudatsu (exploitation). With this as a background, the specific concept of shita-uke has been formed in Japanese society. The

terms <u>shita-uke jigyousha</u> (subcontractors) or <u>shita-uke</u> (subcontract)
are defined in the Shita-uke Chuu-shou-kigyou Shinkou Hou (Law for
Promotion of Small and Medium Subcontracting Enterprises), which is the
basic legislation governing policies toward subcontractors in Japan.
The same definition is used by the <u>Kougyou Jittai Kihon Chousa</u> (Survey
of Manufacturing Industries of Japan). These definitions do not
explicitly refer to 'controlling and subordinating relations'. However,
they clearly express size differences between 'parent' (ordering)
companies on the one hand, and subcontractors on the other, thus
showing an implicit intention to include that aspect of the
relationship in their terminology (1). In fact, the Promotion Law
clarifies its objective in its Article 1 of enabling small and medium
subcontractors to 'run their business of their own free will by
modernising the subcontracting relationship'. This shows that the Law
and policy-making authorities of Japan consider that such 'controlling
and subordinating relations' are the most important aspect of the
subcontracting relationship in Japanese industry and involve 'problems'
to be solved by government action [see also chapter 2, section 2].

In order to make clear the characteristics of subcontracting practice
in Japanese industry, and to analyse its economic meanings in
industries operating in world markets, we have to define terminology so
as to distinguish the Japanese characteristics of the subcontracting
relationship from those in Western societies. Thus it would be
impossible to understand those relations between firms that are
specific to Japanese industry, their changes over time and their
economic implications by relying upon, for example, a simple
classification of firms into ordering and supplying of parts by
'suppliers' and 'core firms', as in Asanuma (1989b).

We here define the Japanese 'subcontracting relationship' as a
continuous relationship between firms based on personal relations,
under which larger firms (in terms of capital, employment, or sales)
commission smaller firms to fabricate or process products, semi-
finished products or parts, or to provide services. This definition
does not include 'control and subordination'. Subcontracting relations
in Japan have become increasingly diverse in recent years. As a
significant number of small and medium firms have developed more
advanced technology of their own, their relations with big firms who
order from them have considerably changed. Thus it has become difficult
to consider 'control and subordination' as one of the elements involved
in the present Japanese subcontracting relationship. However, relative
size differences between firms remain a factor characterising that
relationship, and this contributes to the formation of steep pyramid-
shaped structures in the firm size distribution of Japanese industry.
Next, note that orders for fabrication, processing, or providing
services are accompanied by some special technical specifications or
directions from ordering firms, which is, of course, different from
orders with general specifications for standard goods. And the
relations between the firms tend to be based on personal relationships,
as opposed to a business relationship based on contract. In
consequence, both companies concerned are ready to be flexible in their
attitudes toward their partners on the basis of mutual trust. In this
relationship, a contract would be considered only secondary, and would
simply be an expression of general intentions and obligations.
Continuity is the last aspect of the definition of Japanese
subcontracting, which stresses the long-term nature of Japanese
subcontracting relationships.

The White Paper on Small and Medium Enterprises, which reports annually on SMEs and the policies taken toward them, and is produced by the Small and Medium Enterprises Agency (SMEA) of the Japanese government under the Chuu-shou Kigyou Kihonn Hou (Fundamental Law on Small and Medium Enterprises), says 'in key industries of our country, taking machinery as a typical example, the division of work relations between big firms and small and medium firms called shita-uke bungyou taisei (subcontracting division-of-work system) has developed to a high degree and this has greatly contributed to the growth of the Japanese economy' (SMEA, 1991a, p.86). This system described in the White Paper has developed over time [see also chapter 2, section 2]. First, in the period of high economic growth, assembly industries producing household electric appliances and automobiles were central to the Japanese economy, and were supported by small and medium firms as subcontractors, supplying parts in large quantities for mass production by the assemblers. The second period was one of difficulties for the Japanese economy, from the international monetary crisis and the subsequent oil crisis of 1973-4, and the White Paper says that in this period 'our industry was able to keep its vital enterprising attitude as a result of the contribution of its subcontracting division-of-work structure which showed remarkable efficiency in its working while it carried out its rationalisation by pursuing reduction of costs in management' (p.86). A third period is described by the 1991 White Paper as that when the reconstruction of the production system after 1973-4 began to prove successful, while in and after a fourth period Japanese industries were obliged again to cope with the convulsions in the world economy, that is, the second oil crisis and the rapid and substantial rise in the yen exchange rate after the Plaza Agreement in 1985. During those later periods, 'small and medium companies advanced in technical competence and improved their capability of production control in order to meet the demands to rationalize from their parent companies'. In this way, the recent improvement in technical competence and production control capability of small and medium enterprises has meant a considerable change in the traditional subcontracting division-of-work structure, giving birth to a diversification in subcontracting relationships which cannot be understood simply under the concept of 'loss-shifting' and 'exploitation'.

The 1991 White Paper reports that 15.8% of subcontracting small and medium firms belong to the group of 'exclusive contract type', defined as those doing subcontracted work under only one 'parent' company [i.e principal - see note 1] and with a ratio of subcontracted amount to total sales of more than 90%, and that 9.4% of SMEs are of the group 'dispersed contract type' which have more than 5 parent companies on average and dependency on subcontracting for less than 70% of the sales. [See Figure 7.1 and Table 7.1]. Small and medium subcontractors within the range between those two extreme groups are divided into a 'semi-extreme contract type and a 'semi-dispersed contract type', which are shown to have 36.8% and 38.0% of these firms, respectively. Comparing 1990 with 1987 (using data derived by the SMEA from the Fundamental Survey on Actual State of Industries, and shown in Table 7.1), we see that in recent years Japanese small and medium firms have shown rapid change in their business attitude, even over a three year period, away from dependence upon specific parent companies and towards more independence based on dealing with a wider range of parent companies.

In this way, the traditional subcontracting system in Japanese

Number of Parent Firms	1 parent	2 - 5 parents	More than 5 parents
Percentage amount subcontracted			
Over 90%	Exclusive contract type	Semi-exclusive contract type	
70 - 90%	Semi-exclusive contract type	Semi-dispersed contract type	
Less than 70%			Dispersed contract type

Source: SMEA (1991a, p.89)

Figure 7.1   Classification of Small and Medium Subcontracting Firms

Table 7.1
Changes in Type of Contract of Small and Medium Subcontractors in Japan

Type of contract held	1987 (% of subcontractors)	1990 (% of subcontractors)
Exclusive contract	34.5	15.8
Semi-exclusive contract	38.6	36.8
Semi-dispersed contract	24.5	38.0
Dispersed contract	2.4	9.4

Source: SMEA (1991a, p.89)
Notes: See Figure 7.1 for definitions of the contract types

manufacturing industry, which has a vertical multi-stratum structure of a pyramidal shape with a big parent company at the apex, has been gradually transformed in recent years. The changing conditions have been discussed among Japanese economists specializing in the small and medium enterprise problem, some of whom have changed their past views [for example, Sato(1984, 1985), Tatsumi (1979, 1986, 1987), Matsui(1989), Minato(1988), Watanabe(1983-84,1989))]. Many of them have tried to reconcile the recent 'transformation' of the subcontracting system with the traditional vertical structure. Examples of these explanations are: as subcontractors have to come to have higher productivity and there has developed the so-called 'multiplication of parent companies', the traditional 'vertical' hierarchical structure of industry has been horizontally diversified, and the 'horizontal' structure has been newly introduced in Japanese industrial system (Matsui, 1989); as competent small and medium firms specializing in specific technical work are able to find their customers in several mechanical industries related to the same work, the business relationship between firms has come to form a 'mountain range' structure (i.e a structure having multiple apexes, as opposed to the traditional structure of pyramidal shape with a specific parent company at the apex) (Watanabe, 1983-4, 1989).

These views are not suggesting that in present-day business relationships subcontractors have got rid of control by, and subordination to, their parent companies, or that they have established an equal position in relation to the big firms. There has only been a partial change in the traditional subcontracting system. However, there is also some case for arguing that there has been a change in the traditional relationship between big firms and small and medium firms towards a co-operative relationship between them of more equal standing. Thus the advances made in the technical and managerial capability of small and medium firms in recent years under changing economic circumstances have caused significant changes in subcontracting relations. These changes have involved an industrial structure of network type, which consists of vertical and horizontal relationships of close mutual dependency among self-supporting and independent firms.

To examine how far these alternative views represent the reality of present-day Japanese subcontracting, and to highlight the system's distinctive features, the next section discusses the subcontracting situation using material from interviews.

7.2   Japanese subcontracting relationships in practice

Although, as the previous section has suggested, the subcontracting system in Japan includes a diverse range of relationships between firms, the structure most commonly found is basically the multi-tier subcontracting division-of-work system. This is where firms are vertically related with each other, with small and medium firms forming the base layers. The subcontracting structure differs somewhat from industry to industry owing to the differences in technology and market. Also, each individual 'hierarchic system' with a particular parent company at the top may differ considerably from others in its organization of the actual vertical structure. In many cases even a parent company does not know fully what firms there are, how they are related, in the secondary, tertiary or lower strata of its subcontracting structure (2). It is the assembly industries, especially the manufacturers of automobiles and electric household appliances, which have attracted attention, in the sense that their strong performance is thought to have resulted from the Japanese-type subcontracting system. While the electric appliances industry has some variation in its division-of-work structures according to what product is being produced, the automobile industry has almost the same subcontracting structure for each of the big automobile manufacturers: a large parent company lies in the top of the production structure as a final assembler with many subcontractors in lower strata. The SMEA White Paper takes an example of the vertical multi-tier subcontracting composition of firms from a representative automobile manufacturer in Japan and examines the number of subcontractors belonging to each of the strata, as shown in Figure 7.2. It says that in the hierarchy of production of the car assembler more than 88% of all the member establishments are in the group of tertiary subcontractors forming the bottom of the pyramidal structure (inclusion of subcontractors in a lower than tertiary tier makes the proportion larger). A further 11 to 12% are members of the group situated in the tier just above that. On the other hand, according to the SMEA, it is the primary subcontractors that have a direct contract with their parent company A in production process and assume all responsibility directly toward the firm A for the work of supplying parts, including whole tasks undertaken by subcontractors in the secondary and lower contracting tiers. These primary subcontractors comprise only 167 firms out of the 47,308 subcontractors as a whole who belong to this production system under the one car assembler, a mere 0.4%. This example is very similar to that of Japanese manufacturing industry as a whole in terms of size distribution of firms, and of the subcontracting structure (i.e. one characterised by a steeply pyramidal shape with a vast base). Considering that up to 99.6% of firms working in the secondary or tertiary tiers in this system are playing an important part in maintaining the quantity and quality of final products at their parent, though they are not under a direct control of this car assembler, we can say that this kind of subcontracting structure exhibits a remarkable organisational effectiveness.

In order to investigate the actual state of relationships between parent companies and the small and medium firms which are incorporated into such subcontracting division-of-work systems, to identify the distinct characteristics of the structure, and to examine its economic significances, field research was conducted in Japan in 1990 by direct interviews with 16 firms (2 big parent companies, 3 companies of medium standing, and 11 small and medium sized subcontractors). [See also the discussion of the selection of these interviewees in chapter 3, section 3.1] Also interviewed was the All Japan Subcontractors Promotion Association which is the central agency implementing government policies for small and medium subcontractors based on the Subcontractors Promotion Law, and also the Small and Medium Enterprise Agency which is the administrative organ of the Japanese government in charge of policy towards SMEs. The firms for interviews were chosen among those in the automobile, electrical machinery, and general machinery industries because they have a comparatively large proportion of subcontractors and recently have attracted general attention for a rise in international competitiveness. For the big parent companies, one was taken from the automobile and electrical machinery industries respectively, for samples of companies of medium standing, one was chosen from each of those three industries, and three from automobile, four from electrical machinery, and three from general machinery were interviewed for samples of small and medium subcontractors. While the firms interviewed were not numerous, they were selected in good balance in terms of industries and firm sizes, and attention was paid to the inclusion of parents and their related subcontractors. Moreover, the additional interviews - with the agency operating policies for small and medium enterprises and the government body in charge of those policies - were carried out also with the intention of correcting bias caused by the small sample size.

On the basis of the interview material, five key aspects of the subcontracting relationship can be identified:

7.2.1 The basis of subcontract trading - a code of faith

The most important characteristic of relationships between firms in Japanese industry consists in performance on the basis of good faith, not of legal rights and duties agreed in a contract as in Western societies. This traditional practice has been maintained in the Japanese industrial world, despite the country's modernization. That attitude to the relationship between firms has not changed in principle even where Japanese industry structure and organization has undergone considerable change due to the internationalization of business and the progress in technology of firms of medium standing.

In general, some kinds of written contracts are exchanged between ordering firms (parent companies/principals) and supplying firms (subcontractors) concerning their subcontract trading in Japanese industry. The document exchanged between them in the first place is a Torihiki Kihon Keiyakusho (Basic Contract for Trading). It is understood to be a contract of opening accounts between them, which means that parent companies might possibly give an order to the subcontractors under this contract depending on the parents' needs. In terms of content, it is a sort of moral code emphasizing good faith and the obligation to keep any necessary secrets. It usually says that the details of appointed date of delivery, prices, terms of payments and so forth are all 'decided on the conditions separately set by the ordering company'. Usually the Basic Contract is not prepared on the basis of mutual agreement following the discussion between both parties, but is prepared by a parent company as a general contract in the same format with the same content to any subcontractor. It is presented to each of the subcontractors to accept as a whole without alteration. Thus the subcontractors are not allowed to examine each article in it and to express their opinion individually. It is true that almost all of the contents in the Basic Contract are moral regulations of general meaning and few of them are set out specifically. There is a traditional understanding with regard to Basic Contracts for Trading on the part of firms in Japanese industry that they are codes of sincerity and good faith with which both parties should maintain mutual cooperation in the long term. While the firms concerned take them seriously in this respect, not only subcontractors but also parent firms generally consider that the agreements on concrete matters and the items on penal regulations written into them should be taken flexibly according to individual background and circumstances. Thus in actual practice the Basic Contracts for Trading presented one-sidedly from the parent companies are accepted by their subcontractors without objection. The duration of the contracts is set to be one or two years at their outset, but it is prescribed that they are automatically renewed after the expiration of the preceding period for another one year unless either of the parties objects.

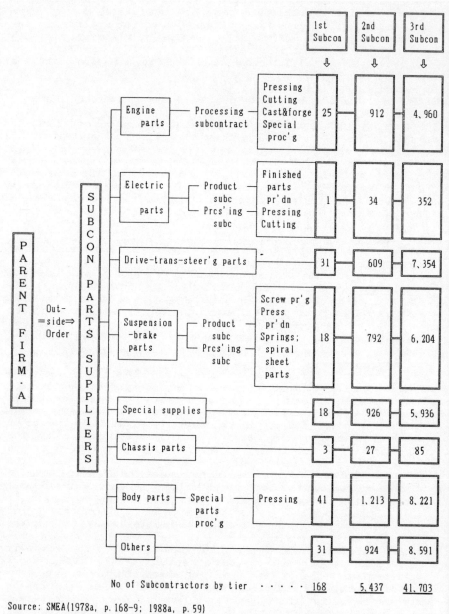

	1st Subcon	2nd Subcon	3rd Subcon
Engine parts — Processing subcontract — Pressing / Cutting / Cast&forge / Special proc'g	25	912	4,960
Electric parts — Product subc — Finished parts pr'dn / Prcs'ing subc — Pressing / Cutting	1	34	352
Drive-trans-steer'g parts	31	609	7,354
Suspension -brake parts — Product subc / Prcs'ing subc — Screw pr'g / Press pr'dn / Springs; spiral / sheet parts	18	792	6,204
Special supplies	18	926	5,936
Chassis parts	3	27	85
Body parts — Special parts proc'g — Pressing	41	1,213	8,221
Others	31	924	8,591

PARENT FIRM·A — Out=side⇒ Order — SUBCON PARTS SUPPLIERS

No of Subcontractors by tier · · · · · 168   5,437   41,703

Source: SMEA(1978a, p.168-9; 1988a, p.59)
Notes: The numbers of firms (enterprises) are those surveyed in 1977

Figure 7.2   The Subcontracting System in the Japanese Automobile
            Industry

The head of a small subcontracting firm working for a big machinery company told us that at the interview concerning this Basic Contract for Trading as follows:

Responsibility imposed on subcontractors is heavily stipulated in the Basic Contract. If we subcontractors examined carefully each article in the contract, it would be too dangerous for us to accept at all, because of the unreasonable responsibility placed on us - unless there is the traditionally common understanding that it will be applied flexibly.

In this way, the Basic Contracts for Trading place emphasis on the stipulation of moral responsibility, with an implicit understanding that these will be maintained on an ongoing trading relationship in the long term between parent companies and subcontractors. For matters of special importance (to the parent company) from past experience (for example, secrecy between both parties), the parent company sometimes asks its subcontractors to sign a document called a nen-sho (a sort of written oath) which is prepared separately from the Basic Contract.

For example, in the case of firm A, a machinery company of medium size (a parent company) which has many patents on its products registered at home and abroad, there was an incident where a former employee of one of its subcontractors B smuggled out plans and specifications of machines developed by the firm A and sold them to a Japan-UK venture company C which was one of its competitors. Firm A took firms B and C to court and won its suit in the long run, but it realized that the benefits for winning were not worth the considerable trouble it had had to go to. After this bitter experience, firm A asks its subcontractors to sign a nen-sho setting out a 'duty of secrecy' in addition to the Basic Contract for Trading, the managing director of Engineering Division of firm A told us in the interview.

From a Western viewpoint it might seem meaningless to exchange additionally such a written oath since a duty of secrecy is stipulated together with apparent penal regulations with regard to its violation in a Basic Contract for Trading. However, the preparation of a nen-sho for the matters deemed by parent companies to be of particular importance clearly shows the moral nature of Basic Contracts for Trading. That is to say, in the Japanese business world (though it is almost the same in other areas of Japanese society), it is not the penal regulations but the faithful relationship between both parties which ensures that contracts are observed, and it is the role of nen-sho to make certain of the code of faith concerning particularly important matters.

Subcontractors getting orders from their parent companies in accordance with the Basic Contracts for Trading sometimes pass a part or all of them to their own subcontractors (the second tier subcontractors). In this re-subcontracting, the first subcontractors place the orders at their own discretion without seeking approval from the ordering parent companies in many cases, though sometimes they are required to ask the ordering companies beforehand (for example, the case of re-subcontracting of manufacturing or processing certain safety-related parts in the automobile industry). It goes without saying that when re-subcontracting without permission in advance, the first subcontractors assume full responsibility to their ordering parent companies for the delivery time, quantity and quality of products for which the former originally received an order from the latter. The practice of tacit approval by parent companies of their subcontractors' re-subcontracting shows that the subcontracting relationship between them is maintained on the basis of a code of faith and mutual trust. Re-subcontracting by tacit consent is seen most often in the case of first-tier subcontractors with high technical competence. When a firm A places an order for manufacturing a certain product with one of its subcontractors B, and the firm B considers that the work is not worthy of being done by itself on account of the low level of technology needed to make the product, the firm B often passes on the whole of the order to a subcontractor of its own C (a second-tier subcontractor from viewpoint of firm A). If this were often the case with subcontractor B, then directly ordering from the second subcontractor C should be more profitable for firm A than continuing to order for this kind of work with subcontractor B. However, this is not done in business relationships among Japanese firms. This is because firm A understands that its relations with firm B are of an on-going nature based on a code of faith. If the firm A gave the order for manufacturing the product requiring only a low level of technology directly to firm C, passing over its first subcontractor B, it would injure the relationship based on personal contact and good faith between firms A and B. As a result, firm A would find it almost impossible after that to place an order with the firm B, even if A should actually need the help of B in order to make products requiring B's higher-level technology. Even if firm B did not refuse to accept further orders from firm A, the damage to mutual trust would make it impossible for engineers of both firms to continue communicating as smoothly as before. This would make it difficult for them to operate flexibly concerning prices, delivery dates, and so forth, and might give rise to problems about the quality of the final products of firm A. On the other hand, firm A does not regard it as contrary to the code of faith that firm B passes on the order from A to a subcontractor of its own without seeking A's permission in advance. During a continuing, long-term relationship between firms A and B, A as the parent company would feel able to make an apparently unreasonable demand on B with regard to say quantity, price, delivery date, but at some other time when A is not in a difficult situation A would give B an order for work which is very profitable to B or work requiring only a low level of technology (in which case B can make profit on it by re-subcontracting). In this way, A gives B compensation for B's losses from the work pressed on it by A when A was hard-pressed. Therefore, we can say that the ordering parent company A implicitly consents to subcontractor B passing on the order to one of B's subcontractors C without having A's permission beforehand. In other words, the subcontracting relationship in Japanese industry is such that on some occasions a parent company gives its subcontractors opportunities from which apparently benefit substantially, while on other occasions it asks them for sincere cooperation to meet its needs. Such relationships can only come into existence when both of them maintain relations in the long-term based on mutual trust, and not simply with the aim of making short-term profit. Such on-going relationships gives rise to the interchange and accumulation of information to all the firms concerned (A and B, or B and C), making for greater long-term efficiency for them all.

An <u>Individual Contract</u> is also exchanged, setting out agreements on a specific product and process contracted under the Basic Contract for Trading. Generally, this is also a one-sided document written by the parent companies, specifying the details of quantities, delivery dates, unit prices and so on and it is accompanied by various plans and technical specifications. Discussion then take place between a parent company and its subcontractor, with a view to moving to final agreement on the details proposed by a parent company in the document. When final agreement is reached on those details, the Demanded Delivery Date in the Individual Contract proposed by a parent company becomes the Promised Delivery Date, and that is written into an Order For Goods together with the quantities, unit prices and other matters settled at the same time in relation with the agreed date of delivery. Considering that actual agreements on the details of the contract are reached through this process of discussion, we find again that the understanding in the Japanese business world of what constitutes a contract in subcontracting is different from that in Western societies. In this process of preparing an Order for Goods on the basis of an Individual Contract, it is with regard to setting the contracted unit price that the difference in power between a parent company and its subcontractor is most apparent. The unit prices of contracted goods are usually reviewed every six months; and at that time parent companies naturally wish to set them in relation to the competitive situation in the market for their final products. On the other hand, subcontractors receiving orders from their parent companies estimate acceptable unit prices on the basis of their various costs of production. Thus, the unit prices proposed by both parties are rarely in accord, and in reconciling the differences in prices they sometimes have heated arguments. In order to have effective cost data to persuade their subcontractors, some parent companies do some small amount (say, 5% of the whole) of the same job in their own factories as what they order from their subcontractors. For example, Hitachi, the big electrical company was said by a subcontractor to do this.

However, the problem most worrying to subcontractors is a rise in cost coming from a change in the plan of their parent companies. Even after the final Order For Goods is issued on the basis of the Individual Contract, and the contracted work is in process, it is nothing out of the ordinary for plans or technical specifications originally proposed by parent companies in their orders to be changed. This naturally results in a change (usually, a rise) in the production cost of the subcontractors. Although contracted unit prices are determined by talks between a parent company and its subcontractor at the stage of making out an Order for Goods, in many case subcontractors, when they receive the order, must eventually bear the additional cost produced by any such changes in plans or specifications. Some economists regard this as a vestige of shuudatsu (exploitation) of small and medium subcontracting firms by monopolistic big companies, as Marxian economists have argued. However, one should remember that in the process of carrying out the subcontracted work, it appears that the mutual cooperation stimulates small and medium subcontractors to accumulate technical knowledge. We will take this point again in some detail in 7.2.3 below.

7.2.2 Ahum-no-kokyuu - 'breathing in harmony', or maintaining a
       cooperative attitude

It has already been shown that when business relations are established in Japanese industry some legal documents are generally exchanged for formality's sake but, especially in subcontracting relations, they normally are applied very flexibly in practice. The relationship between firms is maintained on the basis of mutual trust and personal contact between them, rather than on any rigid legal obligations stipulated in the written contracts. Therefore, a firm under such circumstances makes decisions as far as possible so as to harmonize its conduct with what the other party wishes. This is so even when it has to make an important management decision with regard to its own operations, not only when it carries out subcontracted work. For example, when a firm in a subcontracting relationship hesitates to make a request to another firm over a certain matter for fear of placing a burden on the latter, the latter perceives the need of the former and conducts itself in such a way as to meet the former's requirements as far as possible. This is to achieve a long-run profit for both, even if it may be unfavourable to the latter firm in the short run. This attitude is found not only in the business world but also in many groups maintaining special relationships in Japanese society. It is generally called ahum-no-kokyuu (breathing in harmony) (3).

In Western-type business society where formal contractual relations clearly stipulate rights and duties on each of those concerned, one firm states plainly its needs to the other, planning to make its profit as large as possible. The other party also decides its own attitude to the demands only with regard to maximising its profit. This admits of no cooperative attitude towards maximising the total profit of both parties - for example by considering a situation where the wish of the other party is not expressed explicitly. On the contrary, when one party happens to know a special circumstance or plan of the other party, the former will go forth into the action to increase its own profit by making use of that information. The cooperative attitude of self-restraint and 'breathing in harmony' seems in marked contrast to what Japanese perceive to be the Western behaviour of maximising one's own satisfaction. Thus we cannot truly discern the economic characteristics and the sources of performance of the Japanese business world, especially the behaviour of firms under subcontracting relationships, and the industrial structure associated with them, without taking account of this attitude towards cooperation.

It is the moral code of trust supporting contract relationship described in section 7.2.1 that provides the basis of this cooperative attitude. Therefore, even when the conduct of one firm concerned has an unfavourable effect on the other firm concerned, resulting in infringement of some specific clauses of the contract, the penal clauses are not immediately applied to that infringement. The latter firm affected says 'We'll let it pass for the sake of our long-term relationship with your company'. This is because the latter company understands that the conduct of the former company does not come from a non-cooperative attitude, but remains within the moral code of trust.

In connection with 'breathing in harmony', a young head of a subcontracting firm in the electronics industry, who succeeded to his father's company, described at interview an experience of crucial importance not only to that subcontracting company but also to its parent company, as follows:
his company S is a medium-sized enterprise with almost 200 employees, having, with both the head office and factory in the ward area of Tokyo (the residential area neighbouring upon central Tokyo). It had continuously done subcontracting work in assembling communications equipment and printed circuit boards for 36 years since 1955, receiving orders from its sole parent company N, which is one of the largest computer and communications equipment manufacturing companies in Japan. In 1980, S had a request to do the some sort of work for IBM in Japan. IBM is the toughest business rival against which S's parent company N had been competing in the domestic and foreign computer markets. To

receive an order from IBM, which had high technology and occupied as much as 70% of the world computer market, was thought to be favourable for future expansion of the subcontractor's business. It was also felt to be rather tempting for company S's technical advance. Thus there was a heated discussion within company S about whether they should accept the order from IBM or not, and they also sounded out the opinion of the parent company N. Company N did not show apparent disapproval to S about S's possible acceptance of the order from IBM. Instead, N expressed to S its intention of leaving that matter to S's own judgement, since company S was an independent business, although under contract with sole parent company N. Under these circumstances the company S eventually refused to accept the request from IBM. The young head of the company S said that the reason was as follows: being trusted by its sole parent company N, his company S had maintained an on-going cooperative relationship with N for a long time, even to the extent that S sent their engineers to the design group of N which was one of its most important departments, received technical guidance, and jointly developed new products. If his company S, with such long and deep personal relations with its parent company N, had accepted the request from IBM, which was N's greatest competitor, the long built-up relationship of human trust between the two companies would have been destroyed at a stroke. And above all, such conduct would have conflicted with the moral code of trust which formed the basis of their long-term subcontracting relationship. It would have not only destroyed the relationship with their parent company N, but would also have lost S its good reputation in Japanese industrial society, which would have caused S difficulties if it tried to seek new business relations with other companies.

After the company S refused IBM's request, the parent company N said to S, 'You might as well have accepted it ...', but the young head of S felt, 'I don't think it was in the heart of the company N, and I think still now that our judgement at that time was right, considering the relations with N after that.'

7.2.3 Joint development, technical assistance and other support: frequent personal communication

The relationship between parent companies and their subcontractors in the Japanese subcontracting system is characterized by their cooperative attitudes in the course of on-going relations based on a moral code of trust. Some of the system's important aspects can be seen in joint development of parts for new products, technical support of subcontractors by their parent companies, and the attitude of parent companies towards their subcontractors if the latter encounters difficulties in business.

As the Japanese economy has repeatedly encountered major unanticipated changes in international business conditions, there has been in recent years a perceptible change in the qualities which parent companies seek in their subcontractors. During the era up to the 1970s, when business's central aim was to extend its market using mass production, subcontractors were mainly used as suppliers of standardized parts in large quantities, or as producers of goods of special use and of low technology. Nowadays, in order to meet the need of reductions in costs caused by rapid technological innovation and required by annually intensifying competition, and to respond to changes in market demand for various kinds of goods in small quantities, parent companies have come to demand that their subcontractors equip themselves with technical skill to cope with such changes in economic conditions. Above all they want their subcontractors to be specialized and masters of a particular field of technology.

The recent rapid changes in the business environment have meant that larger companies can no longer remain in as comfortable a situation as previously, where they used to be able to run their business by relying on their own managerial resources, and utilized their subcontractors as supplementary producers or buffers in order to cope with the fluctuation of demand in the course of business cycle. Now they are required to take those subcontractors into their production system so as to create a functional combination with their own managerial resources. With repeated demands by parent companies to reduce costs, there has regularly occurred joint development of parts and products between parent companies and their subcontractors, and technical assistance by parent companies to any subcontractors of theirs in technical difficulties. This situation means parent companies require their subcontractors to have high technical skills. In particular, affected by the great changes since the 1970s produced by the two oil crises and the rapid rise in the Yen exchange rate after the Plaza agreement, large companies in the automobile and electrical industries already heavily dependent on international markets, have been pushed into a difficult situation. In these circumstances, these large companies have come to request their subcontractors to make progressive reductions in costs each time contracted unit prices are reviewed. Additionally they have started to send them frequent alterations in plans and specifications for the goods they order so as to adjust their business to the rapid changes in market conditions. The burden incurred by these requests usually falls on the subcontractors. Subcontractors sometimes resist, but usually they eventually take a cooperative attitude for the sake of keeping a long-lasting relationship. If subcontractors do refuse the requests from their parent companies, it results in the termination of the relationship, even long term ones, and generally the loss is greater to small and medium subcontractors than to their large parent companies.

Subcontractors try to respond to their parents requests in various ways. When they find it difficult to reduce costs with their existing level of technology, they usually request their ordering parent companies to give them technical assistance. Generally speaking, parent companies have all kinds of production technology regarding their products or parts which they subcontract to other firms (particularly in the automobile industry). As they know that there is a technical possibility of realising the cost reductions which they request of their subcontractors, they are ready to give the necessary technical support. With subcontractors achieving the cost reduction required of them in this way, the parent companies can maintain and strengthen their competitive position in the market for their own final products. At the same time, the subcontractors can acquire new technical knowledge in return for their strenous efforts at meeting the requests of their parent companies (see Figure 7.3).

The head of the technical section of the Small and Medium Enterprise Agency said at interview that he regards these relations as resulting in a distribution of the rewards such that 'all the profit realized by the cutting-down of costs goes to the ordering parent companies. The subcontracting small and medium firms which made efforts for it are satisfied to take <u>na</u> (fame) instead of <u>jitsu</u> (profit), citing an instance as follows:

116

in the middle of the 1980s, a Japanese representative car company T was asking its related subcontractors continuously to cut costs (semiannual reductions in ordering unit prices of 5%) whether they wished to or not. The company T demanded unilaterally this reduction in unit prices from one of those subcontract suppliers S, a manufacturer of hub-rings. In order to achieve the required reduction in costs, the subcontractor S tried to use steel for only the peripheral part of functional importance and to substitute less expensive cast metal for the material for the other part, in place of steel. In carrying this out, however, the problem of joining the steel part and the cast metal part was so difficult that it could not be solved by the subcontractor S. Thus, S asked its parent company T, which placed the order, for advice about this problem, and the technical division of T gave assistance to S. Thus the technical problem was solved in this way by the cooperation of the ordering parent company and its subcontract supplier.

With the cutting of costs being achieved by the joint efforts of the two companies, the parent company T not only was tided over difficulties caused by the rapid rise of the Yen exchange rate, but also further strengthened its international competitiveness. On the other hand, the subcontractors such as S obtained new technical skills by meeting the requests from their parent company. However, all the direct gains produced by the solution of such technical problems accrued to the parent company T, and the solution did not contribute directly to the growth of profit of the subcontractor S.

In connection with the procedures for the placing and receipt of orders for parts, where development activities are carried out with close and frequent personal cooperation between parent and subcontractors, the details of plans and technical specifications for new goods become known to the engineers of both companies. Thus a tacit understanding is reached between those engineers on the quantities, the dates of delivery, the unit prices and related matters concerning the newly developed goods, when the parent company places the order with its subcontractor. Accordingly, before the parent company issues a formal Order of Goods to the subcontractor, it informally notifies the detailed contents of the order to the production control section of the subcontractor. This is called naiji (an informal notification) of the order. Getting that naiji, the subcontractor instantly completes all the necessary preparations such as procuring the materials, and sets about production. That is to say, when cooperative activities are taken as far as joint development between a parent company and its subcontractor, the contents of the Individual Contract are virtually put into practice before that contract is formally issued on an Order for Goods, specifying the detailed conditions (such as goods or work to be ordered, quantities, dates of delivery, unit prices, and other related items). We can understand in this respect, too, the special meaning of a 'contract' in Japanese subcontracting relationships and the importance of the human trust supporting it, as already described in section 7.2.1 above.

In a subcontracting relationship, the extent to which parent companies are concerned with the management of subcontractors differs somewhat depending upon the business attitude of the parent company or the nature (the levels of technology, in particular) of subcontractors. However, it can generally be said that parent companies, as time goes by, gradually come to regard subcontractors as independent entities, leaving important matters specific to those subcontractors to their own judgement. Therefore, while they are always ready to give technical assistance, they do not concern themselves if subcontractors face financial

117

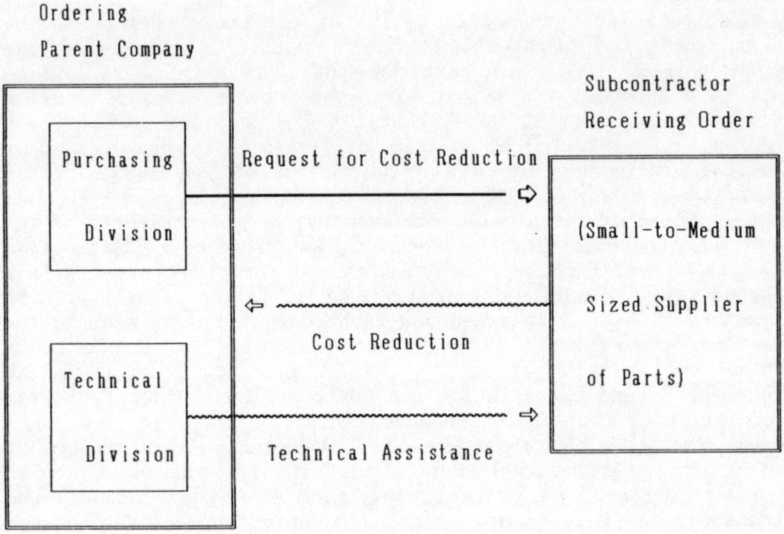

Ordering
Parent Company

Subcontractor
Receiving Order

Purchasing

Division

Request for Cost Reduction
⇨

(Small-to-Medium

Sized Supplier

⇦ ~~~~~~~~~~~~~~~~~~~~~~~

Cost Reduction

Technical

Division

of Parts)

~~~~~~~~~~~~~~~~~~~~~~~ ⇨

Technical Assistance

Figure 7.3   Distribution of the Rewards of Cost Reduction

problems. If giving help to such subcontractors, they generally limit themselves to relaxing payment terms. These days parent companies tend to judge whether they should give relief or assistance to subcontractors in difficulties by using the criteria of how much they themselves, as parent companies, are responsible for those difficulties, and how much they could profit in the future from giving the help. They decreasingly attach importance to the human relations specific to Japanese society such as 'goodwill from our old relationship'. A parent company in automobile industry gave an instance of one of its subcontractors, saying that despite its daily technical assistance, the subcontractor did not take a sincere attitude towards the technical improvement needed to deal with present rapid changes, but took on a risky job and fell into a managerial crisis. The parent company finally discontinued its help and dropped that subcontractor.

Generally, whether a parent company drops a subcontractor with managerial problems, the decision is not based on some particular facts, but on the judgement as to whether the situation as a whole has come to the loss of the relationship of mutual trust hitherto maintained over a long period between them. In this respect, we can newly understand the importance of the decision taken by the subcontractor S (in section 7.2.2) about the request from IBM, as the toughest rival in business to its parent company, to explain the attitudes of companies in Japanese subcontracting relationships.

7.2.4 Magokoro and shimbou (sincerity and patience) - the essence of the Japanese subcontracting system

It is said that the sources of the strong competitiveness of Japanese manufacturing industry at present lie in the extensive range of small-to-medium sized subcontractors acting as suppliers of good quality parts to a wide range of industries, and their sincere attitude towards mono-zukuri (making goods). It is also pointed out that the attitude sometimes goes as far as to leave profit out of consideration, and that the heads of those firms are more proud of gaining a high reputation in the business world, including their reputation in the eyes of their parent company, than anything else. This can be found in the attitude of subcontractors when they patiently endure frequent changes in plans and technical specifications, and harsh demands for as much reduction in costs as possible from their parent companies. They do finally meet the needs of those parent companies, and are themselves satisfied with only obtaining na (fame) and acquiring new technical skills, as we saw above.

In this connection, the head of the technical section of the SMEA, whose experience was cited previously, also argued that:
it can be safely said that one of the fundamental factors underlying the superior quality of Japanese products is the subcontracting system, where numerous small-to-medium sized subcontractors comprise a wide base and play the role of supplying parts and materials of good quality to a smaller number of larger companies manufacturing final products. The good quality of the products of those subcontractors comes from their magokoro (sincerity) towards 'making goods' - of wishing to make quality products - rather than from their superiority in technology. Small-to-medium subcontracting firms in Japan are acting more under the so-called 'rule of inertia' than running their business with the primary aim of making profits. That is to say, their primary concern is to continue today the work they have been doing up to yesterday, even though it does not make a large profit for them. They think it most important that they

maintain the security of the livelihood of employees, and of their own, by maintaining a good relationship with the parent company and making continuous efforts to meet the demands from it, persevering with them even though they sometimes seem hard.

Arguing that moral factors such as 'sincerity and patience' are the source of today's great differences in technology of production, and quality, of goods between Japan and Western industrial countries (and other Asian countries too), he continues:

for instance, when a subcontractor making bearings delivers the products to its parent company, the subcontractor normally makes observations of the operation of the machines (the final products of the parent company) which use those bearings. This is in order to see whether the quality of the bearings meets the subcontractors' own standards as producer. For example, if the subcontractor notices any unusual noise from their bearings in the machines, he immediately looks into the reasons. If some bearings are found to be cracked, for example, he replaces them with good ones on the spot, intending to prevent any breakdown due to failure of those bearings. Through this attention by subcontractors towards the parts they supply, their parent companies, and their parents' customers, can avoid producing defective goods (or can restrict to the greatest extent possible the volume of the defective goods produced). Subcontractors may even go to the factories of their parents' customers to observe the performance of the parts they supply.

As compared with this, in Western countries (and also Asian countries other than Japan) subcontractors or parts suppliers do not come to check the parts they supply until a breakdown occurs. In consequence, goods produced by the machines equipped with such parts may produce substantial numbers of defective or inferior quality goods (4).

7.2.5 Towards the coexistence of 'hierarchical organizations' and 'network organizations' - the result of technical advance in small and medium firms

The Japanese subcontracting system has generally been understood by economists specializing on small and medium enterprises to be characterized by a pyramidal-shaped structure; in other words a hierarchical structure formed on the basis of the relationship between companies controlling and those controlled, with a large parent company at the summit. These days, however, there appears to be a growing recognition among economists that the organizational structure has gradually changed, due to the technical improvement of small and medium firms. In this connection, suggestions have been made to reconcile the old view with the new reality by devising other types of structures such as 'horizontally-connected business' or 'mountain-range' structure. These views recognise the change in the present Japanese subcontracting system from one based on the old hierarchical-type organization (with relationship of 'control and obedience'), towards a new 'network-type' organization, where there is cooperation among a wide range of business enterprises including small-to-medium sized firms, with each company having its own professional skills and information.

An interesting example of such a business network working through information flows between companies mainly of medium standing, each having specialised technical skills, is a group of small-to-medium sized machine shops in the Keihin area. This area covers the region extending from residential districts in the southwest part of Tokyo to the southeast part of Kawasaki and Yokohama adjacent to them, where there

120

exists still as many as 18,000 small or medium businesses mainly making machine tools, or processing metals. These moved to the suburbs with the expansion of the city of Tokyo after the Meiji era, forming a large integrated industrial area (5). The main jobs those firms are doing today are making trial products related to research and development, or machines for research and development. They also do highly specialised machine processing for big businesses with headquarters in central Tokyo and mass production factories in many other areas of Japan and abroad. The industrially integrated group of firms in this area are characterised by this specialisation and by close cooperation with each other. Work such as making trial products or carrying out special machine processing is generally in small quantities and is always subject to change. On the other hand, each shop in the area has accumulated high technical skills in its highly specific field by specialising over a long period, although its scale of business is small. Thus one shop may devote itself exclusively to cutting, another to grinding. Neighbouring workshops keep close contact with each other through daily exchanges of business information, and through joint work. Thus this group of small-to-medium sized firms in this area can meet the specialised demands from customer companies in the manner and in their own time. As this area has high technical skills and can achieve tasks which are difficult for firms in other regions to undertake because of the diverse character and small size of the orders, there is great demand for work from this area from all over the country, irrespective of industry. Thus these firms have managed to stay in despite the managerial disadvantages of the small scale of business, high land prices in this area and so forth. They are closely connected with each other through the exchanges of information and are interdependent in making their respective jobs, while maintaining the independence of their own business. This style of division-of-work clearly represents an example of the 'information-network' type of structure.

This integrated industrial complex in the Keihin area was formed well before the high growth period of the Japanese economy in the 1960s, but in other areas of Japan, too, there have appeared recently small or medium sized firms which are not involved in the old relationship of control and obedience with parent companies. These independently seek to have customer companies in a variety of manufacturing fields by exclusively undertaking a specific task with highly specialized technical skills. Technical advance by small and medium enterprises was the most important factor in the development of such kinds of independent firms. What led them to that business stance at first was the need for saving energy during the oil crises of the 1970s, and for coping with the rapid rise in the Yen in the late 1980s. Japanese industries were compelled to find ways out of those difficulties by uniting all their efforts, including those of subcontractors. The detailed review of their whole production procedures resulted in the pursuit of deepening technical specialisation in the individual elements of production, and the reorganization of those elements into more effective systems (6). From around this period, there appeared a change in the stance of parent companies towards their subcontractors. According to the parent companies in our research (7) the most important qualification that they want their subcontractors to have is 'high technical skills so as to enable them to cope with rapid changes' or 'to make an effort to excel in a certain technical field'. They also wanted their subcontractors to maintain enough supply capacity to meet their demands as during the high growth period from the 1960s to 1970s.

Subcontractors themselves are fully aware of the need of having such technology, and gave the same response as to what was the main problem they had to tackle. Furthermore, in the course of the changes in subcontracting relations, parent companies have recently come to persuade their subcontractors, even those so far exclusively related to them, to develop relations with other parent companies too, and especially to find new customers in other industries.

This tendency for small and medium sized subcontractors to become independent by specialising in a certain field of work has resulted not only from the change in the business stance of parent companies towards their subcontractors, but also from the efforts of subcontractors at seeking new customers in the open market by developing products with their own technology. For instance, in case of a certain medium-sized company making switches, it receives orders for a variety of switches of special uses from its main customer company as before, and make those by drawing the plans according to specifications submitted by that company. At the same time it is making efforts to have relations with a wide range of other companies as a specialty supplier of switches. In addition, it always tries to adapt specialized products originally made for the parent company, towards mass production for general use. When design changes are expected, it tries to find a new mass market for them by advertising trial products in trade magazines and the like. That is to say, regarding firms of medium standing such as this, we can recognise that they are trying to set themselves into both the old pyramidal-type system and the new network-type system. This is with the aim of strengthening the basis of their business by utilising the merits of both. (8) It can also be said that a change in the attitude of parent companies towards their subcontractors since the oil crises has made subcontractors change their stance towards subcontracting.

The changes following the oil crises and the high Yen have not caused the Japanese subcontracting structure to change abruptly into the 'network' system from the old 'pyramidal' system based on control and obedience. However, parent companies and subcontractors are both at present trying to reconstruct their business relationships so as to achieve better results, by combining effectively the merits of both systems with their own managerial resources. Thus they are adapting themselves to the changing business environment in circumstances where both systems exist together. Although the 'network' system may seem like a type of business connection aimed at the pursuit of short-term profits, in reality it is usually introduced on the basis of the continuous business relationships hitherto maintained between a parent company and its subcontractor, still putting a special emphasis on the code of mutual trust. Thus, it must be emphasized that the 'network system does not represent a change in the basic way of thinking which permeates the Japanese subcontracting system as it has existed up to the present. (9)

NOTES

1. The definition of 'subcontractor' as used in the survey of subcontracting by the SMEA refers to a firm whose business is work done 'under commission from any corporate enterprise whose amount of capital is larger than that of the enterprise concerned or any individual enterprise whose regular payroll employees are more than those of it, (i) to manufacture products or related items for

the ordering enterprise or (ii) to manufacture production facilities or equipment for the ordering enterprise'. Although it does not specifically include any concrete characteristics of the business relationship, this definition coincides as a rule with ours, as set out in the text to follow.

[Note too that the terminology 'parent company', used in the present chapter, is that employed by Japanese economists to describe what would be called a 'principal' in Western writing on subcontracting. **'Parent' in this sense does not necessarily imply any ownership of the subcontractor by the principal, and certainly not that the subcontractor is a subsidiary of the principal. It simply implies that the 'parent' is an important customer of the subcontractor within a subcontracting relationship]**.

2. Generally speaking, as we shall see later, a parent company leaves to its direct subcontractor (i.e. a subcontractor in the first tier) the judgement as to whether the second subcontractor sends work commissioned by the parent on to a subcontractors in the second tier. The first subcontractor takes full responsibility towards the parent company for the work done by the second subcontractor. For important parts such as those concerned with automobile safety, however, a subcontractor in the first tier is sometimes requested to ask the ordering parent company in advance for its consent to re-subcontract the work to a second-tier subcontractor.

3. 'A' in Japanese is the first of all the characters and vowels, pronounced with the mouth open-wide, and '-hum' is the last, pronounced with the mouth closed. They show the situation where one person opens his mouth while the other closes it. When the words 'a-hum' made by the two people are coupled, we can envisage a state where the two persons are trying to harmonise with each other in their attitudes by listening to the other's breathing. In Sumo wrestling, for instance, this term is used when the two wrestlers, meeting face-to-face and on the point of fighting, try to keep in time with each other silently in order to stand up simultaneously to begin the contest.

4. In Britain, it was reported in The Times newspaper (24.3.92) that the Institute of Mechanical Engineers, claiming that more than £1.5 billion is lost every year to creaky machines, badly-oiled devices, simple design flaws and widgets that grind regardless rather than spin in low friction harmony, launched its War on Wear campaign. This was to encourage industry to pay attention to 'trigopology', meaning the science and technology of interacting surfaces in relative motion and of related practices, 'instead of worshipping Japanese-style management practices'. And it writes that perhaps the way to put the beef back into manufacturing industry is not through squeezing more productivity from the grumbling artisan, but through trigopology. However, it is questionable whether this kind of campaign will bring much improvement in productivity without reforming the attitude of workers in disregarding any unusual noise making machines if they are not on duty.

5. Since early days, the industrial integration of the Keihin area (the southern part of the Tokyo metropolitan area) has attracted

special attention not only from economists specialising in small and medium enterprises, but also those studying industrial organisation, because of its unique character as a group of suppliers. Analyses based on investigation into conditions in this area are Nihon-kaihatsu-ginkou, Setsubi-toushi-kenkyuusho (Institute of Investment of plant end equipment, Japan Development Bank) (1978), Shoukou-kumiai-chuuou-kinko, Chousa-bu (Research Department, Central Bank of Association of Commerce and Industry) (1977), Oota-ku (Ohta ward) (1986,1989), and others. Analyses from an economic-geography standpoint include Ide, Takeuchi, and Sawada (1977), Takeuchi (1978). Imai (1983, 1984), Imai and Kaneko (1988) and others look at this industrial integration from the view point of modern industrial organisation.

6. As the head of the technical section of the SMEA pointed out (see text) Japanese small and medium firms accumulated their technical skills especially after the oil crises. Imai and Kaneko (1988) further write that division-of-work links among firms proliferated during the period of these crises with the result that the division-of-work system was reorganised into that of a network-type. (pp. 42-43). Underlying the reorganisation was an accumulation of technical capabilities in small and medium firms which was accomplished through perseverance in meeting the severe demands from parent companies for cutting costs.

7. In addition to direct interviews, questionnaires were sent to about thirty other companies.

8. Generally speaking, the profitability of firms of medium standing specialising in a certain technical field of work is high compared with that of other firms. For instance, the switchmaking firm cited here has 74 employees and annual sales of about Y1.0 billion (£4.2 million), with a ratio of gross profit to sales of about 30%.

9. Therefore, it would seem that Imai and Kaneko (1988) go too far in saying 'the oil crises resulted in the reorganisation of the industrial system of Japan into a new 'network' type (p. 42).

8 Conclusions

As chapters 1 and 2 have suggested, an increased use of subcontracting is one among a variety of means with which firms can cope with a changing environment where there is greater market volatility, increased international competition, and accelerated technical change. This study has concentrated on engineering, broadly defined, and within engineering it has looked at mechanical engineering (with special reference to machine tools), the motor industry (especially passenger cars), and at electronics (especially computers). For the British principals in engineering, considerable reorganization has been taking place, and subcontracting has been a central part of it. This is especially the case for the machine tool companies. For the motor industry, supply chain management in an already highly outsourced situation has been a more important issue than the sheer volume of subcontracting; electronics has seen some major changes in subcontracting behaviour. The present study has been able to probe the details of this process through in-depth interviews, but it is reassuring to know that the general trends in engineering (broadly defined) have been confirmed by other work (1), including the large scale postal survey organized from the University of East Anglia (2)

While British companies have been moving to a more outsourced position, and improving the organization of their supply chains, Japan represents a standard of comparison with a system which has been in place for much longer. The Japanese system in its present form dates from the 1960s, but much subcontracting goes back further, to the Second World War and sometimes before. It has evolved sophisticated methods of selection, development and monitoring of subcontractors, and of encouraging innovation within the principal-subcontractor relationship. Of course, Japanese companies have experienced pressures too. It was macroeconomic restriction in the 1960s which pushed many large companies into drastic reorganizations of their subcontracting networks, towards the present system. The 1973-4 and 1979 oil crises also put pressure on profits. More recently there has been <u>endaka</u>, the high yen crisis, which started in late 1985. By squeezing export profits, this has been producing changes in the subcontracting system, including a harsher attitude to subcontractors.

Japanese companies in general have been far from mere passive responders to external pressures. Indeed, they have been the <u>source</u> of pressure on many Western industries, with a competitive strategy based on technical change. Chapter 3 has detailed for each of our three industries how, often starting from a weak position in the 1950s and 60s, the Japanese have become powerful competitors. They 'dematured' apparently mature industries in the case of electronics and the motor industry, and identified a crucial unfilled market niche in the case of machine tools by targeting the needs of small firms for technically advanced equipment. Japanese companies have been world leaders not only in many areas of electronics, but in the applications of electronics technology to production methods, and products, as in motor vehicles and machine tools. British companies, sadly, have been more reactive than proactive in these situations, and the pressure on them has been extreme, exacerbated by the current (1990-2) recession.

Section 1 summarises the pressures that British firms have faced and compares them to those experienced in Japan. Section 2 looks at the reasons why British and Japanese firms subcontract at present, while section 3 tries to show through what mechanisms the pressures outlined in section 1 actually lead to firms deciding to subcontract more. Section 4 considers what our research has to say about how subcontracting should best be organized, while section 5 looks at subcontractors' own experiences. Section 6 draws lessons from the Japanese subcontracting system and asks how those lessons can be applied to British industry, with some suggestions about government action.

8.1 Pressures for change

Chapter 3 has shown how British engineering employment has fallen drastically since the 1970s. Though this to some extent represents a labour shakeout, 'unmatched by declines in output, Britain's international competitive position has deteriorated in engineering overall. Even the growth in electronics has been unmatched by any employment increase, and has relied very heavily on inward investment, while domestic companies virtually have exited from many fields, notably in consumer electronics. Pressures from increased competition, accelerated technical advance and market volatility, though particularly intense in Britain, are broadly in line with those making for change in Western industry more generally, along the lines suggested by Piore and Sabel (1984). How have our British companies been affected by such pressures, and how does this compare with the experience of their Japanese counterparts? Although these pressures clearly overlap, for example where technical change has been promoted by overseas rivals as part of their competitive strategy, it is useful to make an attempt to consider their effects under separate headings.

8.1.1 Market volatility

In mechanical engineering, this has been in the form of the intensified business cycle normally experienced by capital goods sectors such as machine tools. The more recent volatility in consumer demand (Piore and Sabel, 1984, pp.190-191) has had only a limited direct effect on the companies interviewed. One Japanese company, making machine tools for the motor industry, spoke of its preference for producing a more standardized product, but accepted that it had to produce a highly

126

customized new machine each time there was a model change by a motor manufacturer.This company subcontracted the designing of optional features used in the customizing. More generally, the machine tools produced both by the British and the Japanese principals increasingly have included products designed to fit into small-scale and flexible manufacturing systems. While the Japanese had moved into this area somewhat sooner, the British principals were generally well-aware of its importance.

The business cycle, though an accepted problem in the industry, has been especially intense for British mechanical engineering companies over the last decade, and there was a feeling among most principals and many subcontractors that they had not fully come out of recession since the early 1980s. The 1990-2 recession was affecting even the most progressive companies, and their views about the role of the (Conservative) government and the banking sector were largely negative. Japanese companies too spoke of adverse effects of the cycle, and subcontracting was seen by most principals in both countries as a means of retaining flexibility in changing conditions of market demand. Subcontractors attempted in Britain to maintain a highly diversified customer base, and to cultivate niche markets as an insurance against demand fluctuations. This was true of the Japanese subcontracting too, but with more exceptions. The early 1980s recession was a proximate factor in pushing British engineering principals towards reorganization, and towards subcontracting in particular; but underlying it was a realization that their competitive position was being eroded in world markets, and increased subcontracting cannot simply be seen as a reaction to macroeconomic instability.

Japanese mechanical engineering companies experienced sharp cyclical fluctuations in demand. These sprang from export problems in the early 1980s associated with recession in the USA and Europe, trade frictions, and then the high Yen crisis. By the late 1980s, however, all the Japanese engineering companies interviewed were reporting rapid growth. Industrial machinery in Japan is highly export-orientated, with almost half of output sold abroad (KSK,1986). British mechanical engineering is slightly less export-orientated (see chapter 3, note 15), but the British machine tool companies had been pushed into much heavier dependence than usual on exports, as of mid-1991, because of the collapse of the home market in recession.

In the motor industry, the British motor manufacturer interviewed felt it had weathered recession better than many of its overseas rivals, and in the 1980s it had greatly increased output. The intensification of recession in 1992, since the interviews took place, undoubtedly has affected this company (and the British motor industry more generally) very severely, and the world recession is even affecting Japan in spite of its motor industry's strong competitive position.

In electronics, IBM announced its first-ever losses in 1991, and many European chip-makers and computer companies were in difficulties. Recession hit many Japanese computer companies too, with profits in 1991 substantially down (The Economist, 11.1.92).

Compared with many areas in electronics (especially consumer electronics and computing products, where the product cycle has been much shortened compared to the past) consumer market volatility in most branches of engineering is not so pronounced as, say, in textiles and clothing. There, seasonal fashion changes require extremely rapid producer responses (NEDC, 1987), and the idea of 'flexible specialization' to deal with continual change is most obviously relevant in this case (3).

8.1.2 Increased competition

Intensified international competition has been felt by all the export-orientated British mechanical engineering principals. According to them, competition in machine tools has been severe from Taiwan and other countries in East Asia. The extent to which East Asian producers have been able to match quality is debatable (4), but appears to be on an improving trend. Pressure on domestic customers' cash flow during the recession, including the effects of high interest rates, has helped the East Asians. A shorter-lived but cheaper machine becomes more attractive in these conditions than when customer firms can take a longer view. European competition was frequently mentioned, and there was a fear of the entry of Eastern European producers into the more 'downmarket' products. The British principals all claimed to be competitive against Japanese products, and most of them had taken a keen interest both in Japanese electronics technology and in Japanese manufacturing systems. The Japanese principals both spoke of intense competition in their domestic and overseas markets from other Japanese producers, and also in the machine tool industry from Western producers in particular product ranges.In the machine tool industry, one Japanese company suggested there was little wrong in terms of quality and performance with the particular British products against which it competed, but that Japanese producers were more cost-effective. The one British machine tool principal which had drastically reorganized its subcontracting a decade ago had experienced rapid growth in sales in the late 1980s, until the 1990-2 recession.

There seems little doubt that international competition in standard machine tools has pushed the British principals into a drastic overhaul of both their product range and their manufacturing methods. This competition has not simply threatened a reduction in profitablity, but the firms' very survival. Thus they have been willing to consider major changes in their behaviour. Recent redesigning of products in the British cases also has involved improving design with respect to the manufacturing process, especially the reduction in the numbers of parts and their standardization between products. This aspect has been stressed in the report by the National Economic Development Office on success factors in (mainly mechanical) engineering (1990b), discussed in chapter 3, but our study has found additionally that among the British machine tool companies, (re)design for manufacture has been linked with a wish to have components and subassemblies more suitable for putting out to subcontract.

International competition in the motor industry has been well-documented in chapter 3. However, our British motor industry manufacturer had moved to a significantly more outsourced position during the 1980s as a result of growing sales volumes. It had also engaged in considerable other measures of internal reorganization in terms of factory layout and inventory control, in order to make itself more cost-competitive, influenced by what it knew of Japanese experience. The major British components manufacturer, the second motor industry principal interviewed, commented that customers were demanding quality as never before, and this in itself was a pressure for reorganization. Both Japanese motor industry principals at the time of interview had been experiencing very rapid sales growth, including export sales.

In electronics, the major computer manufacturer interviewed in the UK, had been pushed into great reorganization by increased competition, including much increased outsourcing, but here technical change was a critical factor in competitive pressure. Competition has been intensified too by the entry of Japanese consumer electronics companies, such as Sharp, into the laptop/notebook computer market, where their established sales networks for consumer electronics give them an advantage in reaching a wide and less specialized market. However, Japanese computer companies have been rather less successful in penetrating the mainframe computer markets of the USA and continental Europe, than have Japanese companies in other industries, although this failure is now less important with the growing use and capabilities of micro computers.

8.1.3 Technical change

Mechanical engineering companies in Britain spoke of technical change as having accelerated about a decade ago, but having settled somewhat within the past five years. All the British subcontractors who were heavily using CNC equipment kept considerable conventional machining capacity for smaller jobs, and several thought many competitors had overinvested in CNC which they could not fully utilize. Several subcontractors had greatly modified and improved existing equipment, sometimes bought second-hand. For the British machine tool principals, and to some extent their subcontractors, the incorporation of electronics technology (often obtained from Japan, but not exclusively so) both into their end-products and into their own manufacturing methods has been crucial in allowing a move 'upmarket', to compete with Third World machine tool manufacturers. Japanese principals (and subcontractors) had updated at an earlier stage. For the British companies, electronics technology was less a driving force in reorganization, than a way of doing it in the face of competition. Much of this competition was perceived as coming from the Third World; it was imitative, and based on competitiveness springing from low wage, labour-intensive production methods, rather than being driven by technical change. Nevertheless, technical change emanating from Japanese engineering also has been a powerful long-run influence on the prospects for British engineering.

According to the 1981 survey by the Japan Society for Promotion of [the] Machine Industry, a combination of rapid technical change and intensified competition was forcing changes in subcontracting, although less in the amount of outsourcing than with regard to the relations between principal and subcontractor (KSK, 1982). Indeed, there were some expectations that the already high degree of subcontracting might be somewhat diminished in the process of rationalization. This expectation has been born out by data from the Japanese Small and Medium Enterprise Agency, presented in chapter 3, which show a fall in the proportion of Japanese SMEs engaging in subcontracting, and has been also noted in the Japanese view of subcontracting presented in chapter 7. The harsher attitude was stressed by one of the Japanese electronics principals, who regarded the Japanese long-term-relation type of subcontracting as pointlessly traditional (5). This firm spoke of the ever-shortening life-cycle of computer products (down to less than two years) as requiring much technical change by subcontractors. He gave contracts only for one or two years (i.e. for the product's life), and for the next product he was quite willing to change suppliers.

The major Japanese motor components principal (regarded as a principal because of its large size, independent technological capacity and own use of subcontractors) regarded the promotion of technical change as a key part of its competitive stategy, and spent 20% of its sales receipts on new investment and R&D.

8.2 The present reasons for subcontracting

Why do principals and subcontractors feel that subcontracting increases efficiency? Among the British mechanical engineering and motor companies a strong impression came across that subcontractors had specialized expertise, often backed by specialized equipment. The expertise factor was very strong in electronics too. Also, because of lower overheads, the subcontractors' costs, as expressed for example in terms of hourly rates for machining, were substantially lower than the principals' in-house costs. These factors also characterize Japan, but in Japan there is the additional dimension that wages were said by the companies to be lower in subcontractors who were smaller than the principals. This is the segmented labour market thesis discussed in chapter 2 (6). However, subcontractors in Japan are required to keep abreast of technical change, especially changes associated with the introduction of new products, if they are to retain their principals' business. This requirement came across most strongly in Japanese electronics, as has been noted above, where technical change has occured more rapidly and over a wider field than in the auto industry or in machinery production.

As reported in chapter 2, the University of East Anglia survey (see Lyons and Bailey, 1991) found that special expertise and technology received the largest number of mentions when British subcontractors were asked what they considered to be the major sources of their competitive advantage over in-house production by principals. Only a third of British subcontractors thought they had access to cheaper labour (with reasons equally split between a lower degree of unionization,lower overheads, and being in a geographically low-wage area). None of the subcontractors thought low-cost labour was their most important advantage.

In the motor industry, and mechanical engineering, both British principals spoke of buying-in items such as castings, which are subject to large economies of scale, and whose suppliers can sell to a wide range of customers - a very standard reason for subcontracting. British principals spoke of limited capital funds, which made them search for suppliers who had specialized equipment which the principal would not wish to buy, as also did the Japanese motor manufacturer.

In electronics, the smaller British computer firms routinely bought-in metal fabrication and plastic mouldings, which they regarded outside their expertise, and printed circuit boards, which were subject to very large economies of scale in manufacture. The metal items and mouldings were usually highly specific to the principal's requirements, and where tooling was required it tended to be supplied by the principal, who knew it would have little alternative use.

Among the Japanese electronics principals, the largest said it kept in-house those processes subject to large economies of scale, and subcontracted more specialized and variegated items; but when a product was coming towards the end of its life, it would then be subcontracted. It manufactured a range of electronics products and wished to manufacture itself those suitable for mass production. In contrast, the major Japanese motor industry component supplier (whose products incorporate much electronics) outsourced at an earlier stage of the product cycle; it said it only kept in-house newish items where it wished to preserve secrecy, and subcontracted everything with a mature technology. This company had built its reputation by being at the forefront of technology, and being able to initiate the supply of new and advanced components to motor manufacturers both in Japan and overseas. Such components would also be more profitable than mature ones.

8.3 The economic basis of increased subcontracting

Although increased market volatility, increased international competition and technical change create pressures on firms to react, they do not necessarily provide opportunities for reorganization in general or increased use of subcontractors in particular. For example, the increased international competition from labour-abundant countries exporting labour-intensive machine tools suggests that Western producers should move upmarket in their products as the Japanese have done. This does not necessarily imply reorganization or more outsourcing, although when taken together with changes in technology and consumer markets it may do so (7).

The economic theory of transactions costs introduced in chapter 1 explains the efficient vertical boundary of the firm (perceived by businessmen as the make/buy decision) in terms of the specificity of capital assets required to produce particular inputs, and the economies of scale in production of those inputs (8). This is in the context of opportunism being expected on the part of other parties, and monitoring being hampered by limited information - which leads to decisions being taken on the basis of 'bounded rationality'. In these circumstances suppliers may be unwilling to invest in assets to supply a particular customer which have little or no alternative use (9), and principals may fear to become dependent on outside supply for crucial components. However, in-house production may fail to utilize potential economies of scale, unless the principal can enter the market as a component supplier -in which case the asset could not have been totally specific to her (10) own needs anyway. Thus outsourcing is likely to be low if very specific assets are required, and higher if suppliers can achieve economies of scale by supplying a range of customers.

Therefore one might suppose that outsourcing would only increase with a changed external environment if those outside pressures reduced the degree of required asset specificity or increased the economies of scale (given the context of bounded rationality and expected opportunism). In mechanical engineering, technical change in the form of flexible, computer-numerically-controlled equipment has reduced asset specificity to some extent, as well as allowing firms to cope more easily with a demand for frequent product changes and more differentiated products. Also, the more expensive CNC equipment may generate economies of scale which are unusable by smaller principals. In electronics, the development of surface-mount technology in printed-circuit-board assembly is a clear case of the underlying transactions cost determinants changing. Here, the change has greatly increased economies of scale and greatly increased outsourcing, but the economies of scale are so large that the suppliers are themselves quite large firms, rather than the small and medium enterprises often associated with subcontracting. These larger assemblers tend to work mainly for larger electronics manufacturers.

In the motor industry it has been argued that technical change in the form of more flexible manufacturing systems has made for smaller scale units (Bessant et al, 1984), though the principal effect of this appears to give medium size producers like Rover a better chance of competitive survival. However, many aspects of motor manufacture are subject to very large economies of scale still, and these include engines and gearboxes, which are generally regarded as core items.

Differences between motor manufacturers in the UK with regard to the amount they subcontract, and between them and motor manufacturers overseas, suggest that outsourcing decisions are not straightforwardly determined. A major dilemma about outsourcing is that some items can be obtained more cheaply from external sources, yet a firm may wish to keep them production in-house because innovation in these items contributes to its core skills. Thus, as noted above, castings often are subject to large economies of scale and could be outsourced more cheaply (11), but the motor manufacturers regard aluminium cylinder head manufacture, for example, as crucial to maintaining their in-house design capability to generate technical progress in making engines (DTI, 1990b). Engine manufacture though usually seen as an in-house activity, is not always so. Also, motor manufacturers have been willing to enter the market as component suppliers, such as Volkswagen's sales of gearboxes to Rover (Bessant et al, 1984,p.25)), or Ford and GM's sale of automatic transmissions to Rolls Royce (Rhys,in Bhaskar, 1979, p.314). On engine manufacture, motor manufacturers sometimes collaborate in order to share development costs, and smaller manufacturers may buy-in some engines while producing others in-house (e.g. Volvo from Volkswagen - see Bessant et al, 1984, p.25). Similar dilemmas arise in electronics, where major companies, both the British and Japanese interviewees, have substantial in-house production of integrated circuits. Interestingly, the smaller Japanese computer manufacturer spoke of keeping about half its PCB [printed circuit board] assembly in-house, using a very advanced form of surface-mount technology. The consumer electronics principal of one of the Japanese subcontractors kept some complex PCB assembly in-house too, even though it subcontracted most of it, in order (the subcontractor thought) to keep abreast of the technology and to have its own information on costs.

Recent British experience suggests, however, that, beyond any changes in asset specificity and economies of scale, a reappraisal based on observation of Japanese practice has taken place. This includes that of Japanese foreign investors in Britain (Trevor and Christie, 1988). Outsourcing has increased, based on a belief that the transactions cost of using subcontractors can be reduced by appropriate supply chain management, including better use of contracts and conscious effort to build supplier trust. This implies that **there were (and still are) unexploited oppportunities for efficient subcontracting, previously constrained in Britain by expected transactions costs,** and survey evidence has been put forward in chapter 2 to support this. This change in attitude has come to the attention of public agencies in Britain, who are now (in the early 1990s) trying to reinforce it, in the expectation that better subcontracting arrangements would improve competitiveness. For example, the Confederation of British Industry's Partnership Sourcing Initiative, financed by the Department of Trade and Industry. As of 1991, many of the firms interviewed had yet to hear of the work of the CBI and DTI in this area, and had come to their own realization of the need to outsource more.

8.4 Supply chain management

The context in which issues concerning the selection, development and monitoring of subcontractors by principals arise, and comparisons between the UK and Japan, vary between the three industries in which firms have been interviewed in this study. In mechanical engineering, the British machine tool companies are moving from a quite a high degree of vertical integration towards greater use of subcontractors. By starting from scratch they in principle could avoid some of the difficulties of the motor industry, already highly outsourced in the UK, and where there is a long history of bad relations between motor manufacturers and suppliers. Motor industry principals are more interested in improving the organization of their existing supply chains rather than in the widespread selection and development of new suppliers. Electronics in the UK represents an intermediate position, where IBM, the largest company interviewed, has greatly increased its outsourcing, but where the other interviewees outsourced only to a moderate degree. In the case of all three industries in Japan, subcontracting was already substantial, though the organization of subcontractors was not static - it was evolving, subject to pressures for change, as we have seen, from technical advances and the high Yen.

Among the large Japanese principals with elaborate organization of suppliers, the large motor manufacturer would review existing suppliers at the start of each new model, which was about every two years. It was less willing than previously to select on the basis of a past relation, and stressed the need for subcontractors to keep up to date technically. As chapter 3 has shown, this is to some extent a general tendency in Japanese manufacturing, and it was found to the greatest extent in the attitude of the smaller of the two major computer manufacturers interviewed in Japan. All the larger Japanese principals had formal associations of suppliers, and a firm could move up (or down) in the hierarchy as its technological capabilities and general performance improved (or worsened) overtime. Dropping a subcontractor in Japan would be a very gradual process, with plenty of warning. IBM in the UK would behave similarly. The largest Japanese electronics principal explained how it sought high technological capabilities in suppliers - and suppliers without these would be likely only to get orders for old products with low profit margins.

In general, Japanese principals were interested in suppliers' innovative capacity, and looked towards joint innovation, although there were clearly defined core items which were continued in-house to preserve the principal's own innovative capabilities. In electronics especially, the cost of R&D was becoming so high that cooperation was needed not only between principals and suppliers, but increasingly between principals. Thus IBM has announced cooperation with Apple in the USA, and with major rivals like Toshiba (on flat colour screens for portable computers), and with Siemens on chip development. Similar cooperations are found the motor industry, as we have seen. Within Japan itself, however, such cooperation between large companies normally is only seen when organized and financed through the Ministry of International Trade and Industry.

A striking feature of the Japanese subcontracting scene, in all three industries, is its organization into **layers**. In mechanical engineering,

133

with the high degree of divisibility of components and scope for verticaly disintegrated production, sub-subcontracting in Japan may go down as far as five layers below the principal. In mechanical engineering, each layer is responsible for the work of the layer below. In the motor industry and in electronics, much of the supply chain management is devolved onto large first tier suppliers, sometimes too large and technologically independent to be called subcontractors, who have their own organizations of subcontractors, though usually in fewer layers than machinery production. In the motor industry the large motor manufacturer, however, did take an interest not only in the first but in the second layer too (where products covered by safety legislation were concerned). The importance of these large first-tier suppliers is illustrated by the fact that the largest supplier of the largest Japanese electronics principal went in advance to an Asian country where the principal was planning a foreign investment, to organize a local network of suppliers. Similar services were to be performed by one of the large suppliers of the Japanese motor manufacturer interviewed; this supplier was going to follow the principal to another Asian country, where the principal already had invested, in order to improve the local subcontracting network. Interestingly, large suppliers in the Japanese system were expected to anticipate their principal's wishes in these regards, rather than waiting to be asked!

Of course, the existence of several levels of suppliers is not unknown in the UK. The structure of the British motor industry, with its large first tier suppliers, already has been mentioned in chapter 3, as also has been the history of bad relations between them and the motor manufacturers. The major British component manufacturer spoke wistfully of his envy of the Japanese layering of suppliers - he had to adjudicate, for example, in disputes between foundries and machine shops, and dealt with both directly, whereas in Japan one supplier would have handled the other in a fairly clearly defined hierarchy, with obvious savings in transactions costs.

In the UK, in both the motor industry and electronics, and to some extent among the mechanical engineering companies which are already substantially outsourced, there was much talk of rationalizing supply chains, reducing the supplier base to a smaller number of better, more reliable companies, with whom there would be more cooperative relations. For example, in the UK the Anglo-American motor companies are reducing their direct relations from 1200-1500 suppliers down to under 700. This contrasts to Nissan's declared intention to have only 120 main suppliers and Toyota's to have 300 local (UK and European) suppliers (DTI, 1990b, p.33). Quality is still perceived as a serious problem (e.g. by Ford), and incoming Japanese foreign investors are recorded as making strenuous effort at supplier development to overcome this (NEDC, 1991a, p.8). Reductions in the size of the supplier base can also be used as an opportunity to create more 'layering'. This would appear to be what the Japanese principals had already achieved by the end of the 1960s.

A study by the UK National Economic Development Council (NEDC, 1990a) of supply chain management in UK engineering provides a useful standard of comparison for some of our findings. The NEDC study involved interviews with six principals and six suppliers nominated by those principals, probably in mechanical engineering (though the branches of engineering covered are not stated). It discovered wide variations in experience in most aspects of the subcontracting experience. With regard to the principals' requirements, NEDC found:

-price determination: this was sometimes based on competition between suppliers, and sometimes on close involvement with them to ensure cost-effectiveness. Among our British interviewees, very close involvement on pricing was rare in any of the three industries, and few subcontractors had experienced it, even in the context of good relationships - though several subcontractors felt their better customers were willing to pay reasonable prices for good quality and reliable delivery. In the Japanese sample, pricing was much more a two-way process, with prices often suggested by principals as a starting point.

-quality and delivery: NEDC found great variability. In our interviews, the British machine tool principals were at, or moving towards, a system of minimal use of inward inspection, and they strongly stressed reliablity in delivery as something they had found in their key suppliers. This was an aim expressed by many other British principals. The reliable delivery of minimal-defect components was a near universal feature of the Japanese sample.

-design capacity on the part of suppliers: NEDC stressed the desire of many principals to devolve design down the supply chain. In our interviews, Japanese subcontractors spoke of their need to invest to keep abreast of technological change, and principals stressed their insistence that subcontractors had suitable equipment. Japanese principals and subcontractors worked closely on technological matters. This was also a feature of the British interviewees, where there was considerable technical interchange as reported by principals in their main long term relations, although several British subcontractors felt considerably less 'nurtured' than did the Japanese ones.

-relationships were found by the NEDC to vary from highly cooperative to highly arms-length and adversarial. Among our British mechanical engineering companies, all the principals spoke of the need for cooperation, and were moving towards it. There was acknowledgement that some past relations had been unsatisfactory - good suppliers dropped because of shortage of orders for example. This was also true in the motor industry, where the large British components manufacturer observed that, despite his apparent good intentions, many suppliers were extremely suspicious of closer relations. How far optimism is justified that past poor relations can be reversed is uncertain. There was a feeling on the part of some principals that there was no shortage of prospective new suppliers, with whom a good relation could be established, though this scarcely would enhance their relations with existing suppliers! Nevertheless, all the British principals could point to major suppliers with whom long, close, and cooperative relations had been established. The experience of the British subcontractors was more variable!

The NEDC (1990b, p.9) report, on 'success factors in engineering', has suggested that in the UK, supply chain management differs somewhat between smaller and larger principals, and that: 'In smaller firms, relations were informal, personal and long-standing, with frequent long-term contracts (sic). There was also considerable trust.' Larger firms, it suggests, had more formal supply chain management policies. Large firms, it suggested, also did more in-house (12). The British mechanical engineering principals interviewed in the present research are more like the smaller type of company in the NEDC survey, and confirm the view, at first sight contradictory, that 'informal' and 'long-standing' relations with 'considerable trust' are associated with long-term contracts. This is the case with the other two industries too, with some exceptions -

that where principals want to develop better relations (especially in the context of a rationalized supplier base) they offer contracts. Whereas long-term relations seem to exist in Japan with only the non-specific framework of a basic contract [except for secrecy of technology provisions, which are backed by further contractual provisions - see chapter 7], in Britain a contract of one or two years, specifying either forecasted volumes or a percentage of business at specified prices, is seen as a sign of goodwill both when offered by principals and sought by subcontractors (13). In the British sample of mechanical engineering companies, the one relation which had relied the most explicitly on trust, in the context of an apparently Japanese style 'relationship', was the only glaring case of opportunism by a principal in that industry. The Japanese principals did fear the possibility of opportunism with regard to the secrecy of their technology.

It already has been shown that there are layers of subcontractors in the British motor industry. However, although our interviews have found a general, but limited use of sub-subcontractors overall in the British sample, this is generally only for very specialized work (and rarely for overflow). This use of sub-subcontractors in Britain is confirmed by the UEA survey of (about nearly 100) subcontractors, to the extent that 68% of subcontractors themselves subcontracted further (though no further details were obtained).

British principals seem somewhat wary of sub-subcontracting, when asked directly, fearing it involved a loss of control. On the other hand, principals in all three industries spoke of a desire to buy in sub-asemblies rather than components to assemble in-house, which may well involve sub-subcontracting!

In Japanese engineering, the firms interviewed viewed sub-subcontracting as a common practice, with each tier being responsible for the one below. In the KSK survey of engineering, broadly defined, 45% of subcontractors surveyed, themselves used 10 or more subcontractors, and only 7.3% used none (KSK,1982,p.18).

8.5 Subcontractors' experiences - dependence and opportunism?

Among the British companies interviewed, both principals and subcontractors were against excessive subcontractor dependence. Desired shares of 25-30% of sales going to the main customer were typical, and rarely exceeded in practice. That this is a general trend is confirmed by the UEA survey, where the median dependence was found to be 30%, and where firms previously more heavily dependent on single customers had reduced their dependence in the last five years (Lyons and Bailey, 1991).

The Japanese subcontractors and principals interviewed were somewhat less worried about subcontractor dependence, but the dependence in most cases was not greatly above the British level, with subcontractors liking a diversified customer base. In the 1981 KSK survey, no average figure of dependence was given, though it was noted that a third of subcontractors wanted to decrease dependence on one principal, while over half wanted to retain the current level (KSK,1982,p.14). There was a widespread tendency among Japanese principals to wish to limit subcontractor dependence - the motor manufacturer thought subcontractors should have at least three customers, at least one of which was outside the motor industry. Japanese principals wished to avoid having to take responsibility for subcontractors in difficulties, a social obligation stronger in Japan than the UK if the principal obviously is to blame for a subcontractor's difficulties. IBM in the UK would ask a supplier to take action to reduce its share of sales going to IBM if that share rose much above 30%.

The countervailing power structure of the motor manufacturers and the first tier suppliers, and changes in their relative position over time in Britain was noted in chapter 3. Bessant et al (1984) estimate that Rover's first tier suppliers are dependent on the group for about a third of their sales, and the second tier suppliers each sell about 15% of their turnover on average to first tier components suppliers. The bad relations between suppliers and assemblers (including willingness to exploit competitive advantage) appear to have no overt counterpart in Japan, at least in recent years. They have led British component manufacturers to seek a more diversified base, and motor manufacturers to become more willing to source globally.

No cases of obviously opportunistic behaviour by principal to subcontractor were found among the Japanese companies interviewed. Opportunism, however, is alive and well in British industry, and two cases of extreme bad treatment, and obvious abuse of trust, were found in the British interviews. Many British subcontractors spoke of improvements in treatment over the 1980s, with a possible return to harsher treatment in the current (1990-2) recession. Principals saying they wanted better, closer, and longer term relations were sometimes treated with suspicion, sometimes justifiably so.

Many British subcontractors complained of not being 'nurtured' by their customers. For many too the deliberate delaying of payment by principals, and the lack of British legislation to prevent it, was a serious source of worry, as was the lack of understanding by high-street banks of their problems.

Technical advance among small and medium firms in Japan, as argued in chapter 7, has led to a greater degree of independence for them, with some sales of their own products to consumers. In consequence, the importance of subcontracting for Japanese small and medium firms has fallen somewhat over the past decade. Some British subcontractors are moving towards selling their own final products too, even though subcontracting in British engineering appears overall to be on the increase.

8.6 Conclusion: how can British subcontracting be improved in the light of Japanese experience?

We have seen that both in Britain and Japan subcontracting tends to be most intense in the same industries - engineering, broadly defined, and also textiles and clothing - which suggests there is some degree of technological determinism, such as the divisibility into many components of much machinery production. Yet in general (with the partial exception of motor vehicles) Japanese firms subcontract in these industries to a greater extent than their British counterparts. It seems that interfirm relations can be handled more effectively in Japan in a climate of greater trust and less naked opportunism. Given that many British firms are aware of the need for better relations with their suppliers, and wish to increase their outsourcing and improve the way it is organized, how can they go about it, and how can the government help?

Many Japanese companies see good long term interfirm relations as a setting in which continuous innovation can take place, with an efficient division of labour between principal and highly specialist suppliers who achieve economies of scale in production and highly focused R&D activities. If such relations are to grow in the UK, there needs to be more realization among British firm that not only is subcontracting a way of cutting present-day costs, but that it also is a vehicle for continuous improvement in performance.

This is not to say that the division of labour in the Japanese subcontracting system is static - suppliers change their position in their principals' hierarchies, and the hierarchies themselves evolve (14). Chapter 7 has shown that networks of small and medium firms have evolved in Japan, so that relations are not always simply vertical either. Japanese principals invest much time and effort in subcontractor selection and development. They are as interested in a subcontractor's potential as much as in its actual performance at the start of the relationship. Nevertheless the relation, though mutually supportive, is not cosy. Suppliers in the Japanese motor industry, for example, may be required to achieve progressive price reductions. Suppliers constantly are evaluated, and that evaluation is made public within the hierarchy as a spur to performance. Dropping an unsatisfactory subcontractor is not done lightly or arbitrarily; it is a gradual process, but it can happen. In the 1960s Japanese principals behaved with great ruthlessness, and this has reemerged to some extent following the high Yen crisis, and the acceleration of technical change. As a result, the continuity of relationships has become less important, and there is a somewhat greater use of time-limited contracts.

British industry has been moving towards greater use of subcontracting as much under extreme competitive pressure as because the underlying transactions-cost determinants have changed. Using opportunities for cost-reducing outsourcing, which were previously underutilized because of mutual fear of opportunism by principals and prospective subcontractors, calls for a better handling of inter-firm relations. To achieve this there needs too to be more protection against opportunism, especially by principals. Many large British companies have adopted the rhetoric of long term cooperation, but have stooped to opportunistic behaviour on occasion towards subcontractors who genuinely were trying to cooperate. Reputation effects seem more important in Japan as a guard against opportunism, and more public resistance by subcontractors who have been badly treated might be a useful step. Most of the small British firms interviewed felt the single most useful measure the government could take would be to enact legislation to enforce payment by customer firms to their suppliers, as in Japan and many European countries. Certain large British companies have been notorious for exploiting their suppliers by the deliberate delaying of payment, or the use of delay as a threat to change contract conditions. Although some of our principals have been sensitive to their suppliers' position, other principals have used payment delays to shift the burden of recession onto small firms. Prosecution, or civil law suits against the violation of payments standards, might be a credible deterrent. Opportunistic behaviour is not unknown among subcontractors either. Some Japanese inward investors in the UK have been surprised by the lack of loyalty on the part of suppliers to whom they have transferred technology and given advice, and who have then offered their new skills to other customers. If the British subcontracting climate begins to move towards more cooperation, reputution effects may begin to work here too.

It seems unlikely that the Japanese system of relations based on trust, with largely ritualistic contracts, can easily be transferred.

Firms in the UK do not seem at a stage yet where trust can substitute for contract. Indeed, many British companies appear to see contracts, which are normally time-limited, as expressions of trust rather than as a (albeit partial) substitute for it (15). Large British firms wishing to rationalize their supply chains and improve their relations with suppliers generally have expected to make greater use of contracts, while expecting better supplier performance in terms of quality and just-in-time delivery. Good relations in these areas probably must precede a better division of labour with regard to innovation between principal and subcontractor. Some British principals however, especially in electronics, still fear transferring technology to subcontractors (both in Britain and overseas) lest those subcontractors subsequently set up as rivals; sometimes those fears have been justified.

Although it seems that the offering of longer term contracts, by generating goodwill, can be a more effective way of initiating more cooperative relationships than is the rhetoric of partnership, the initiatives of the DTI and the CBI on encouraging partnership sourcing are still useful. Their value lies particularly in offering periodic forums in which firms can meet together and exchange experiences. In 1991 only a minority of the British firms interviewed had heard of these initiatives, and the initiatives could have benefitted from larger budgets in order to widen their publicity, and perhaps to lower the cost of their seminars to make them more attractive to small businesses.

The layering of suppliers in an elaborate hierarchy results in great savings in transactions cost in the Japanese system. It allows principals to make use of very large numbers of firms, ranging from the quite large to the tiny, while devolving much of the supply chain management onto the larger suppliers, who in turn devolve to the next layer down. Moves towards the use of this system, by buying-in subassemblies rather than components to assemble in-house, is one of the most important lessons from Japan, and it can be carried out along with increased outsourcing. British firms, while improving relations with their suppliers, should specifically aim at getting existing smaller subcontractors to change to dealing with first tier suppliers where appropriate, and so on down the chain. Reform here may well be easier for sectors such as machine tools, which are to some extent developing outsourcing from afresh, than in already highly outsourced industries like motor vehicles.

To achieve the reorganization necessary to compete internationally, many British firms, especially the mechanical engineering principals, felt there could usefully be more state aid for restructuring, as in agriculture. There was also a widespread view among British subcontractors that the banking system did little to help their activities. Although British banks have had problems of their own in the 1980s and early 1990s, they do seem particularly insensitive and ill-informed about the needs of subcontractors, and a process of self-education on the part of the banks would be welcomed by small firms.

Ultimately, most of the changes required in British subcontracting suggest the need for a change in the attitude of firms away from the short-termism implicit in the willingness to renege on a partner for immediate gain at the expense of the long-term benefits of cooperation. Although the current (1990-2) recession in the UK has made some interfirm relations more cutthroat, it has also brought a realization to some British companies and their suppliers that their interest in survival is a mutual one, which can be ensured better by cooperation than conflict (16).

NOTES

1. See in particular Atkinson and Meager (1986)

2. See chapter 2 (section 2.1).

3. As part of the present research some UK textile companies were interviewed (see chapter 3, note 5). These were mainly in the manufacture, dyeing and finishing of knitted cloth, and were producing for the ladies fashion garment trade. This is an area where British firms have been able to hold their own against import competition by being highly responsive to fashion changes. Also, shakeouts of unsuccessful firms during the recessions have meant that those that remain have been able to make profits. Although some other firms in the textile industry are more vertically integrated, the present interviewees saw compelling reasons for the organization of the different production stages to be in different firms. Knitters argued that integrating forward into dyeing would mean carrying much larger stocks (i.e. in many colours) and mean the employment of sales and design staff. At present an intermediary known as a merchant converter would buy grey cloth from the knitter and get it dyed on a commission basis. The dyer-finisher would then deliver directly to the garment manufacturer. Knitters felt they would alienate the merchant converters if they tried to forward integrate. Also, it was argued by dyers, that minimum efficient size was larger in dyeing than in knitting, so dyers would work for several knitters. All stressed the 'flexible specialization' notion (though not using that terminology) that much coordination was needed to achieve the speed of response necessary for the fashion trade, and they stressed the closeness of relations with trusted customers and suppliers. Nevertheless, one dyer spoke of there being considerable opportunism in the textile trade (though he certainly trusted the main knitting company with which he dealt, which was interviewed also), and he had various devices to keep himself informed of rivals' activities. The one Japanese company interviewed was in a different branch of textiles, with a different organization of production. The impression was gained that the organization of production, and the underlying economic determinants, differ considerably from branch to branch of the textile trade, and wider research would be necessary before sensible conclusions could be drawn about subcontracting behaviour.

4. However, note that imports from Taiwan in 1990 were only 2.2% of total British imports in SITC division 73, metal working machinery. In contrast, imports from Japan were 14.8%, and from (West) Germany 32.0%. The Taiwanese share was larger than that of India, South Korea, Hong Kong, Singapore and China, combined, however. (CSO, 1990b).

5. Note that this company, which is 'ELEC-J-P2' in chapter 6, has not been included in the set of companies discussed by Makoto Takashima in chapter 7, as it was not one of his interviewees. The companies of chapter 7 already have appeared in chapters 4, 5 and

6, but, in the interests of preserving companies' anonymity, no explicit cross-referencing has been done company by company.

6. This impression is reinforced for engineering, broadly defined, by the KSK data (KSK,1986, p.20), where cash payroll costs per employee in engineering companies employing 10-99 workers were 77% of those in companies of 300-999, while very small firms (4-9) workers had cash payroll costs per employee of 57% of those in companies over 1000. To a some extent, though, this reflects a higher proportion of female workers, who receive lower wages in smaller companies; and of older workers, for whom differentials are greater between small and large companies than is the case with younger workers (Chalmers, 1989, ch.2). [see also section 2 of chapter 2, and note 3 of ch.4]

7. Milgrom and Roberts (1990) have argued that the variety of continual changes in the firm's external environment which have led firms towards 'flexible specialization', have done so by requiring 'substantial and closely coordinated changes in the whole range of a firm's activities' (p.513). Increased competitive pressure, specifically, might also involve a firm's moving offshore, as Japan has done in the case of many labour-intensive industries (Steven, 1990, ch.3), and as German companies have done in mechanical engineering (Frobel et al, 1980). Piore and Sabel (1984, ch.8) have argued strongly that moves offshore may be forestalled by reorganization, however (see also Kaplinsky, 1991).

8. Of course, this abstracts from other reasons for outsourcing, especially segmentation in the labour market which allows principals to tap into low-cost (e.g.non-unionized) labour, and the fact that even activities not subject to significant economies of scale may sometimes be outside of what the principal regards as its expertise.

9. With regard to specific assets, the University of East Anglia survey found such under-investment to exist quite widely, but Lyons' (1991a) econometric study could not find a significant relation between this underinvestment and the variables reflecting the degree of trust in the principal.

10. In the interests of gender equality, this book has made use of both female and male pronouns and possessives when referring to people running companies. Unhappily, every interviewee - British and Japanese, principal and subcontractor - was in fact male!

11. But note that, according to Bessant et al (1984,pp.70-71), technical change in casting, by making for a less labour-intensive operation and allowing for better integration with assembly operations, could lead to some casting work being taken back in-house in future.

12. However, in a large econometric study covering much of the American engineering industry, Kelly and Harrison (1990, pp.1282-3) found that the larger the principal, the _more_ use was made of subcontracting.

13. See Lyons (1991a) for an econometric study based on the UEA survey data set, which relates the extent of the use of contracts to variables reflecting technology, vulnerability, information, trust, and firm size. The mean length of relation of subcontractors with their principals was over 11 years; but only 23% of subcontractors had a formal contract with their most important principal.

14. The term hierarchy is used here for convenience to stress the layering aspect of Japanese buyer-supplier relations. Note that Aoki (e.g.1988) has stressed that in important respects Japanese corporations do not function as top-down hierarchies, and he emphasizes the exchange of information at all levels.

15. In this sense contracts are not only a means of economizing on trust (Gambetta, 1988, pp. 220, 229-30), but also of generating the climate of goodwill in which trust may flourish in the future.

16. Taking the low-trust adversarial outcome which is the traditional British solution to buyer-supplier relations, and the Japanese high-trust cooperative solution, as alternatives, it may be difficult for any two players (i.e principal and subcontractor) to move in the UK from the former to the latter. This is so because either party gains from reneging if the other shows trust, even though the cooperative solution gives bigger payoffs to both players (in the form of higher profits from enhanced international competitiveness) than if they both behave with opportunism. This is the well-known Prisoner's Dilemma of game theory. Hargreaves Heap (1991,1992), as part of an analysis of the role of culture in the choice of equilibria in economics, argues that the inertia associated with the inferior institutional arrangement in such cases may need to be broken by government or collective action. This appears to be precisely what the Department of Trade and Industry and the CBI are attempting (as of 1991-2) in their efforts to promote partnership sourcing in British industry.
We have seen, though, that sheer competitive pressure on British industry is also breaking the inertia. It is difficult to put this change towards cooperation into the context of orthodox game theory, at least in one-off Prisoner's Dilemma games. This is because the intensified competition is equivalent to changing the payoffs in Prisoner's Dilemma, and this does not change the outcome so long as we stay within the Prisoner's Dilemma framework. However, if games can be repeated (and if there is some possibility of further repetition) a cooperative solution possibly could prevail, for example through the introduction of reputation effects. Thus a principal who behaves well to a subcontractor may thereby encourage other subcontractors in the future to believe she will behave well. Another possibility, though, is that the strength of international competitition changes the game payoffs over a period of time to such an extent that we move from a Prisoner's Dilemma game (where one party gains more from reneging than from cooperating when the other cooperates) to an 'assurance' game, where the gains to one party from cooperating are larger to her than from reneging, provided the other party cooperates. Here, not only the non-cooperative outcome (i.e. where neither party cooperates) but also the mutual cooperation outcome are Nash

142

equilibria (in the sense of being the best each party can achieve given what the other is doing), and cooperation, though not certain, would not be a surprising outcome. In practice, this situation could arise if in the short term one firm, say a principal, could gain from reneging on a contract with a subcontractor more than he could gain from harmoniously fulfilling the current contract; but would go out of business in the longer term unless he induces the subcontractor to undertake cooperative innovation to combat an overseas competitor who is gradually improving product quality and price competitiveness. This is the case in the UK machine tool industry in face of Taiwanese and Korean import competition, for example. [For a discussion of game theory, see Hargreaves Heap et al (1992, ch 7)]

References

Allen,J. (1988) "Fragmented Firms, Disorganised Labour," in J. Allen and D. Massey (eds), Restructuring Britain: The Economy in Question, Sage Publications for Open University, London.

Amsden, A.H. (1977), "The Division of Labour is Limited by the Extent of the Market: the Case of the Taiwanese Machine Tool Industry", World Development, No.3

Aoki, M. (ed) (1984), The Economic Analysis of the Japanese Firm, North Holland, Amsterdam

Aoki, M. (1987), "The Japanese Firm in Transition", in Yamamura and Yasuda (eds) (1987)

Aoki, M.(1988), Information, Incentives and Bargaining in the Japanese Economy, Cambridge University Press, Cambridge

Aoki, M. (1990), "Towards an Economic Model of the Japanese Firm", Journal of Economic Literature, March

Aoki, M., B. Gustafsson and O.E. Williamson (ed) (1990), The Firm as a Nexus of Treaties, Sage Publications, London.

Asanuma, B. (1985), "The Organization of Parts Purchases in the Japanese Automotive Industry", Japanese Economic Studies, summer

Asanuma, B. (1989a), "Manufacturer-Supplier Relations in Japan and the Concept of Relation-specific Skill", Journal of Japanese and International Economics, 3

Asanuma, B. (1989b), "Nihon ni okeru mehkah to sapuraiyah tono kankei" (Relations between manufacturers and suppliers in Japan), in M. Tsuchiya and Y. Miwa (eds), Nihon no chuushou kigyou, Toukyou daigaku shuppan kai

ACeM (1991) [Association of Contract Electronics Manufacturers], ACeM - Profile, London

Atkinson, J., and N. Meager (1986), Changing Working Patterns. How Companies Achieve Flexibility to Meet New Needs, National Economic Development Office, London

Bessant, J., D.T. Jones, R. Lamming and A. Pollard (1984), The West Midlands Automobile Components Industry: Recent Changes and Future Prospects, a report for the West Midlands Country Council Economic Development Unit, Birmingham

Bhaskar, K. (with contributions by G.Rhys) (1979), The Future of the UK

Motor Industry. An Economic and Financial Analysis of the UK Motor Industry against a rapidly changing background for European and Worldwide Motor Manufacturers, Kogan Paul, London

Bollard, A. (1983), "Technology, Economic Change, and Small Firms", Lloyds Bank Review, January

Bosanquet, N., and P.B. Doeringer (1973), "Is there a Dual Labour Market in Great Britain?", Economic Journal, June

Broadbridge, S.A. (1966), Industrial Dualism in Japan. A Problem of Economic Growth and Structural Change, Cass, London

Carr, C. (1990), Britain's Competitiveness. The Management of the Vehicle Components Industry, Routledge, London

CSO (annual:a) [Central Statistical Office], Report on the Census of Production, Her Majesty's Stationary Office, London

CSO (annual:b) [Central Statistical Office], Overseas Trade Statistics of the United Kingdom, Business Monitor MA20, Her Majesty's Stationary Office, London

CSO (annual:c) [Central Statistical Office], United Kingdom National Accounts Blue Book, Her Majesty's Stationary Office, London

Chalmers, N.J. (1987), Industrial Relations in Japan: the Peripheral Workforce, Routledge, London

Cheung, S.N.S., (1983) "The Contractual Nature of the Firm," Journal of Law and Economics, April, Vol XXVI.

Chudnovsky, D., M. Nagao, and S. Jacobsson (1983), Capital Goods Production in the Third World. An Economic Study of Technology Acquisition, Pinter, London

Clark, R. (1979), The Japanese Company, Yale University Press [page numbers refer to Tuttle edition, Tokyo, 1987]

Coase, R.H. (1937), "The Nature of the Firm", Economica, 4

CBI (1991) [Confederation of British Industry], Partnership Sourcing, London

Cross, M. (1991), "Flexible Manufacturing: Made to Order", Japan Update, Spring

Crum, R., and S. Davies (1991), Studies in the UK Economy: Multinationals, Heinemann, Oxford

Davies, S.W., and C. Morris (1991), "A New Index of Vertical Integration: Some Estimates for UK Manufacturing", Economics Research Centre Discussion Paper No. 9120, University of East Anglia, Norwich

DE (monthly) [Department of Employment], Employment Gazette, Her Majesty's Stationary Office, London

DTI (1990a) [Department of Trade and Industry], An Overview of European Users' Purchasing Practices, in "Electronic Components. A Decade of Change" series, London

DTI (1990b) [Department of Trade and Industry], Automotive Castings, a study by Wolverhampton Polytechnic Enterprise Studies Unit, commissioned by the DTI's Industrial Materials Market Division, London

DTI (1990c) [Department of Trade and Industry], The European Market to 1995, in "Electronic Components. A Decade of Change" series, London

DTI (1991a) [Department of Trade and Industry], Market Opportunities for Electronic Component Manufacturers. A Study of Demand Created by Japanese Electronic Equipment Manufacturers in the UK, London

DTI (1991b) [Department of Trade and Industry], Power in Partnership. Building Business with Japanese Electronics Manufacturers, London

Dore, R.(1983) "Goodwill and the Spirit of Market Capitalism," British Journal of Sociology, December, 34, IV, reprinted in Dore (1987), to which page numbers refer.

Dore, R.(1987), Taking Japan Seriously. A Confucian Perspective on

Leading Economic Issues, Athlone Press, London.
FEER (various issues) [Far Eastern Economic Review], weekly, Hong Kong
FT (various issues) [The Financial Times], weekday daily, London
Freeman, C.(ed) (1985), Technological Trends and Employment. 4: Engineering and Vehicles, Gower, Aldershot
Friedman, D. (1988), The Misunderstood Miracle. Industrial Development and Political Change in Japan, Cornell University Press, Ithaca, NY
Fröbel, F., J. Heinrichs, and O. Kreye (1980), The New International Division of Labour. Structural Unemployment in Industrialized Countries and Industrialization in Developing Countries, Cambridge University Press, Cambridge (originally published in German by Rowohlt, Hamburg, 1977)
Galbraith, J.K. (1977), Economics and the Public Purpose, Penguin, London [first published in the USA in 1973]
Gambetta, D. (1988), "Can We Trust Trust?", in D. Gambetta (ed), Trust: Making and Breaking Cooperative Relations, Basil Blackwell, Oxford.
GATT (1990) [General Agreement on Tariffs and Trade], International Trade, 1989-90, Geneva (in two volumes)
Germidis, D. (ed) (1980), International Subcontracting: A New Form of Investment, Organization for Economic Cooperation and Development, Paris
Geroski, P.A. (1992), "Vertical Relations between Firms and Industrial Policy", Economic Journal, January
Glasmeier, A., and N. Sugiura (1991), "Japan's Manufacturing System: Small Business, Subcontracting and Regional Complex Formation", International Journal of Urban and Regional Research, September
Greenaway, D.(1988), "Effective Tariff Protection in the United Kingdom", Oxford Bulletin of Economics and Statistics, August
Gregory, G. (1982), "Asia's Electronics Revolution," Euro-Asia Business Review, Vol.1 No. 1.
Hargreaves Heap, S. (1991), "Culture and Competitiveness", mimeo, University of East Anglia, Norwich
Hargreaves Heap, S. (1992), "Entrepreneurship, Enterprise and Information in Economics", in A. Ross and S. Hargreaves Heap (eds), Understanding the Enterprise Culture: Themes in the Work of Mary Douglas, Edinburgh University Press, Edinburgh
Hargreaves Heap, S., M. Hollis, B. Lyons, R. Sugden, and A. Weale (1992), The Theory of Choice. A Critical Guide, Blackwell, Oxford
Hirst, P. and J. Zeitlin (eds) (1989), Reversing Industrial Decline? Industrial Structure and Policy in Britain and her Competitors, Berg, Oxford.
Hirst, P. and J. Zeitlin (1991) "Flexible Specialization vs. post-Fordism: theory, evidence and policy implications," Economy and Society, February, Vol. 20, No. 1.
Holmes, J. (1986), "The Organization and Locational Structure of Production Subcontracting", in Scott and Storper (1986)
Horsley, W., and R. Buckley (1990), Nippon, New Superpower: Japan since 1945, BBC, London
HoC (1987) [House of Commons], The UK Components Industry. Third Report from the Trade and Industry Committee Session 1986-7. Report, Proceedings of the Committee, Minutes of Evidence and Appendices, London
Ide, S., A. Takaeuchi and H. Sawada (1977), Keizei chiiki no kenkyuu - Keihin chiiki no kougyou to nougyou (An economic area study - industry and agriculture in Keihin), Bunka shobou hakubun sha
Ikeda, M. (1979), "The Subcontracting System in the Japanese Electronics

Industry", Engineering Industries of Japan, no.19

Imai, K. (1983), Nohon no sangyou shakai - shinka to henkaku no doutei (Japan's industrial society - the process of progress and change), Chikuma shobou

Imai, K. (1984), Jouhou nettowaaku shakai (Information network society), Iwanami shoten

Imai, K. and I. Kaneko (1988), Nettowaaku soshiki ron (An essay on network organisation), Iwanami shoten

Imrie, R.F. (1986), "Work Decentralization from Large to Small Firms: a Preliminary Analysis of Subcontracting," Environment and Planning, Vol. 18, pp 949-965.

Joselyn, L. (1991), "Procurement Task Requires a New Way of Thinking [for IBM, UK]", New Electronics, January

Kaplinsky, R. (1991) "Direct Foreign Investment in Third World Manufacturing: Is the Future an Extension of the Past" Institute of Development Studies Bulletin (University of Sussex), April.

Kawasaki, S., and J. McMillan (1987), "The Design of Contracts: Evidence from Japanese Subcontracting", Journal of the Japanese and International Economies, 1

Katz, J.M. (ed) (1987), Technology Generation in Latin American Manufacturing: Theory and Case Studies Concerning its Nature, Magnitude and Consequences , Macmillan, London

Kelley, M.R. and B. Harrison (1990), "The Subcontracting Behaviour of Single vs. Multiplant Enterprises in US Manufacturing: Implications for Economic Development, World Development, September, Vol. 18, No. 9.

Klein, B, R.G. Crawford and A.A. Alchian (1978), "Vertical Integration, Appropriable Rents, and the Competitive Contracting Process, Journal of Law and Economics, Vol. 21, part 2.

Koshiro, K. (1990), "Japan", in Sengenberger et al (eds) (1990)

KSK (1982) [Japan Society for the Promotion of Machine Industry], "Progress of Technological Innovation in the Japanese Machine Industry and Subcontract Manufacturers", Engineering Industries of Japan, No.22

Leibenstein, H. (1987), Inside the Firm. The Inefficiencies of Hierarchy, Harvard University Press, Cambridge, Ma.

Leung, H.M., J. T. Thoburn, E. Chau, and S.H. Tang (1991), "Contractual Relations, Foreign Investment, and Technology Transfer: The Case of China", Journal of International Development, June

Levy, B. (1991) "Transactions Costs, the Size of Firms and Industrial Policy. Lessons from a Comparative Study of the Footwear Industry in Korea and Taiwan," Journal of Development Economics, 34.

Lewis, T.R., and D.E.M. Sappington (1991), "Technological Change and the Boundaries of the Firm", American Economic Review, September

Lloyd, C. (1988), "Restructuring in the West Midlands Clothing Industry", New Technology, Work and Employment

Lorenz, E.H. (1989), "The Search for Flexibility: Subcontracting Networks in British and French Engineering," in Hirst and Zeitlin (eds) (1989), pp 122-132

Lyons, B.R. (1991a), "Contractability and Underinvestment by Subcontractors: A Transactions Cost Approach", University of East Anglia, Norwich, mimeo

Lyons, B.R. (1991b), "Specialized Technology, Economies of Scale, and the Make-Buy Decision: Evidence from UK Engineering", University of East Anglia, Norwich, mimeo

Lyons, B.R., and S. Bailey (1991), "Small Subcontractors in UK

Engineering: Competitiveness, Dependence and Problems", University of East Anglia, Norwich, mimeo

Marsden, D. (1990), "United Kingdom", in Sennenberger et al (eds) (1990)

Mason, C.M. (1987), "The Small Firm Sector", in W.F. Lever (ed), Industrial Change in the United Kingdom, Longman, Harlow

Matsui, T. (1989), "Motokata fukusuuka dankai no shitaukesei to shitaukesei riron no tayouka - shitaukesei no henka to shitaukesei riron no saikouchiku" (The Subcontracting system at the stage of multiple parent companies, and the development of new theories on the subcontracting system), Kikan Keizai Kenkyuu (Economic Studies Quarterly) (Institute of Economics, Osaka City University), Vol. 11, No. 4

McCormick, K. (1988) "Small Firms, New Technology and the Division of Labour in Japan," New Technology, Work and Employment, Vol. 3, No. 2.

McMillan, J. (1990), "Managing Suppliers: Incentive Systems in the U.S. and Japan, California Management Review, Summer.

McNabb, R., and P. Ryan (1990), " Segmented Labour Markets", in D. Sapsford and Z. Tzannatos, Current Issues in Labour Economics, Macmillan, London

Meegan, R. (1988), "A Crisis of Mass Production," in J. Allen and D. Massey (eds), Restructuring Britain: The Economy in Question, Sage Publications for Open University, London

Milgrom, P., and J. Roberts (1990), "The Economics of Modern Manufacturing: Technology, Strategy and Organization", American Economic Review, June

Minato, T. (1988), "Sentan gijutsu kaihatsu to nihon-gata shitauke seisan shisutemu" (Development of high technology and Japanese-style subcontracting production system), in K. Takizawa and E. Ogawa (ed), High Technology and Medium and Small Enterprises, Yuuhi kaku

MITI (1990) [Ministry of International Trade and Industry, Japan], Statistics of Japanese Industries, Tokyo

Mitter, S. (1986), "Industrial Restructuring and Manufacturing Homework: Immigrant Women in the UK Clothing Industry", Capital and Class, winter

Morgan K. and A. Sayer (1988) Micro-Circuits of Capital: 'Sunrise' Industry and Uneven Development, Polity Press, Cambridge.

MVMA (1989) [Motor Vehicle Manufacturers Association of the United States], World Motor Vehicle Data, 1989, Detroit

Murray, R. (1985), "Benetton Britain. The New Economic Order", Marxism Today, November

NEDC (1986) [National Economic Development Council], Financial Aspects of Restructuring, London

NEDC (1987) [National Economic Development Council], Dynamic Response. How Retailers, Knitwear Manufacturers, Spinners and Dyers Can Together Improve their Response to Consumer Demand, London

NEDC (1988) [National Economic Development Council],Performance and Competitive Success. Strengthening Competitiveness in UK Electronics, (the McKinsey Report), London

NEDC (1990a) [National Economic Development Council], Developing Suppliers in Engineering, London.

NEDC (1990b) [National Economic Development Council], Success Factors in Engineering, London

NEDC (1990c) [National Economic Development Council], The Performance and Position of the UK Engineering Industry, London

NEDC (1991a) [National Economic Development Council], The Experience of Nissan Suppliers - Lessons for the United Kingdom Engineering

Industry, London.

NEDC (1991b) [National Economic Development Council], Winning Together in UK Electronics. Collaborative Sourcing in Practice, London

Nelson, R.R., and S.G. Winter (1982), An Evolutionary Theory of Economic Change , Harvard University Press, Cambridge, Ma.

Nihon kaihatsu ginkou, Setsubi toushi kenkyuu sho (Institute of Investment of Plant and Equipment, Japan Development Bank) (1978), Oota-ku niokeru kogyou ritchi no doukou - toshi niokeru seizougyou no seiritsu kiban to tokusei (Trends in industries located in Ohta ward - the basis of existence, and characteristics of, manufacturing industry in urban areas)

Odagiri, H. (1992), Growth through Competition, Competition through Growth. Strategic Management and the Economy in Japan, Clarendon Press, Oxford

Odaka, K., K. Ono, and F. Adachi (1988), The Automobile Industry in Japan: a Study of Ancillary Firm Development, Oxford University Press/Kinokuniya, Tokyo

OECD (1985) [Organization for Economic Cooperation and Development], The Semi-Conductor Industry: Trade Related Issues, Paris.

Oota-ku (1986), Nashonaru tekunoporisu Oota-ku niokeru koudo kougyou shuuseki no kadai (Problems of high industrial integration in Ohta ward, a technological city of national interest)

Oota-ku (1989), Oota-ku kougyou no kouzou henka to shourai tenbou (Structural change and perspectives on industry in Ohta-ward)

Orru, M., G.G. Hamilton, and M. Suzuki (1989),"Patterns of Inter-firm Control in Japanese Business", Organization Studies, 10/4

Pack, H. (1981), "Fostering the Capital Goods Sector in LDCs", World Development, March

Paine, S. (1971), "Lessons for LDCs from Japan's Experience with Labour Commitment and Subcontracting in the Manufacturing Sector", Bulletin of the Oxford University Institute of Economics and Statistics, May

Parkinson, S.T. (1984), New Product Development in Engineering. A Comparison of the British and West German Machine Tool Industries, Cambridge University Press, Cambridge

Phillimore, A.J. (1988) "Flexible Specialization, Work Organization and Skills: Approaching the 'Second Industrial Divide,' New Technology, Work, and Employment.

Pinch, S.C., Maron and S. Witt (1991), "Flexible Employment Strategies in British Industry: Evidence from the UK 'Sunbelt,' Regional Studies, June.

Piore, M.J., and C.F. Sabel (1984), The Second Industrial Divide: Possibilities of Prosperity, Basic Books, New York

Porter, M.E. (1990), The Competitive Advantage of Nations, Macmillan, London

Portes, A.M., Castells, and L.A. Benton (eds) (1989), The Informal Economy. Studies in Advanced and Less Developed Countries, John Hopkins University Press, Baltimore.

Rainnie, A.F. (1984), "Combined and Uneven Development in the Clothing Industry: the Effects of Competition on Accumulations," Capital and Class, Spring, No. 22.

Reischauer, E.O. (1988), The Japanese Today, Harvard University Press, Cambridge, Ma.

Reve, T. (1990), "The Firm as a Nexus of Internal and External Contracts," in Aoki, Gustafsson and Williamson (eds) (1990).

Richardson, G.B. (1972), "The Organization of Industry", Economic Journal, September

Rosenberg, N. (1982), _Inside the Black Box: Technology and Economics_, Cambridge University Press, Cambridge

Sako, M. (1988), "Partnership between small and large Firms: The case of Japan," in _Partnership between Small and Large Firms_, Proceedings of the conference held in Brussels, 13-14 June 1988, edited by D.G. XXIII-Directorate for Enterprise - of the Commission of the European Communities and European Association for the Transfer of Technologies Innovation and Industrial Information, Graham and Trotman, London.

Sako (1990), "Buyer-Supplier Relationships and Economic Performance: Evidence from Britain and Japan", University of London Ph.D. thesis

Sako, M. (1991), "The Role of Trust in Japanese Buyer-Supplier Relationships," forthcoming in special issue of Richerche Economiche "Current Topics on the Japanese Economy," edited by M. Aoki and G. Brunells.

Sako, M. (1992), _Prices, Quality and Trust: How Japanese and British Companies Manage Buyer-Supplier Relations_, Cambridge University Press, Cambridge, forthcoming.

Sato, Y. (1984), "Nihon chuushou kigyou mondai no toutatsuten to kenkyuukadai' (Research themes on the problem of small and medium enterprises in Japan), in Nihon chuushou kigyou gakkai (Japan medium and small business society) (ed), _Medium and small enterprises problems - understanding of their present state and view point - Collected papers of Japan medium and small enterprises society, No. 3)_, Douyuukan

Sato, Y. (1985), "Shitaukesi mondai no henbou to shitauke chuushou kigyou taisaku" (Changes in the problems of the subcontracting system and measures for medium and small firms which subcontract), in Kikai shinkou kyoukai (Machinery Industry Promoting Association), _Nihon no kikai sangyou no kouzou henka to shitauke bungyou kouzou_ (Structural change in Japan's machinery industry and subcontracting division-of-work structure)

Sayer, A. (1989), "Post-Fordism in Question", _International Journal of Urban and Regional Research_, 13(4)

Schmitz, H. (1989), "Flexible Specialization - a New Paradigm of Small-scale Industrialization?", Institute of Development Studies Discussion Paper No.261, Sussex

Scott, A.J., and M. Storper (eds) (1986), _Production, Work and Territory_, Allen and Unwin, London

Sengenberger, W., G.W. Loveman, and M. Piore (1990), _The Re-emergence of Small Enterprises: Industrial Restructuring in Industrialised Countries_, International Labour Organisation (International Institute for Labour Studies), Geneva

Shimokawa, K.(1986), "Product and Labour Strategies in [the Automobile Industry] in Japan", in Tolliday and Zeitlin (eds) (1986)

Shoukou kumiai chuuou kinko chousabu (Research department, Central Bank of the Association of Commerce and Industry) (1977), _Shitauke chuushou kigyou no genkyou - antei seichou keizai ka ni ikiru michi_ (Present state of medium and small firms which subcontract - a means of living under a stable growth economy), Yaesu shoukou

(Small and Medium Enterprises Agency) (ed) (1991), _(White paper on medium and small enterprises - 1991 edition)_,

SMEA (1978a,1989a,1990a, 1991a) [Chuushou Kigyou Chou (Small and Medium Enterprise Agency)] _Heisei # Nen Ban, Chuusjou Kigyou Hakusho_ (White Paper on Small and Medium Enterprises in Japan), Ookurashou insatsukyoku (Printing Bureau, Ministry of Finance), Tokyo (annual)

SMEA (1989b and 1990b) [Small and Medium Enterprise Agency], _Small_

Business in Japan (English translation of shortened version of SMEA, 1989a and 1990a), Ministry of International Trade and Industry, Tokyo (annual)

Soete, L.(ed) (1985), Technological Trends and Employment. 3: Electronics and Communications, Gower, Aldershot

Steven, R. (1990), Japan's New Imperialism, Macmillan, London

Stigler, G.J. (1951), "The Division of Labor is Limited by the Extent of the Market", Journal of Political Economy, June

Szarka, J. (1990), "Networking and Small Firms," International Small Business Journal, January - March, Vol.8, No.2.

Takeuchi, A. (1978), Kougyou chiiki kouzou ron (An essay on the structure of industrial areas), Taimei dou

Takeuchi, A. (1980), "Daitoshi reisai kougyou no genjou to mondai ten" (Present state and problems of small workshops based in large cities), Kokumin kinyuu kouko (People's Finance Corporation), Cousa geppou (Monthly Bulletin of Research), January

Tatsumi, N. (1979), "Sangyou kouzou no henka niyoru shitaukesei kougyou no tenkai to tokuchou" (Development and characteristics of industries using subcontracting in changing industrial structures), in T. Kimura and H. Yamazaki (eds), Sangyou kouzou no tenkan to nihon keizai (Transformation of industrial structure and the Japanese economy), Toukyou daigaku shuppan kai

Tatsumi, N. (1986), "Shitaukesei nikansuru ichi kousatsu (A consideration of the subcontracting system), Osaka keidai ronshuu (Bulletin of Osaka College of Economics), No. 174

Tatsumi, N. (1987), "Shitaukesei kougyou no henka to mondai ten" (Changes and problems of industries using subcontracting), Kikan keizai keikyuu (Institute of Economics, Osaka City University), Vol. 9, No. 4

Thoburn, J.T. (1973), "Exports and the Malaysian Engineering Industry: A Case Study of Backward Linkage", Oxford Bulletin of Economics and Statistics, May

Thoburn, J.T., H.M. Leung, E.Chau and S.H. Tang (1990), Foreign Investment in China under the Open Policy: the Experience of Hong Kong Companies, Avebury/Gower, Aldershot

Thoburn, J.T., H.M. Leung, E. Chau and S.H. Tang (1991), "Investment in China by Hong Kong Companies", Institute of Development Studies Bulletin, Sussex, April

Trevor, M., and I. Christie, (1988), Manufacturers and Suppliers in Britain and Japan. Competitiveness and the Growth of Small Firms, Policy Studies Institute, London.

Tse, K.K (1985), Marks and Spencer, Anatomy of Britain's Most Efficiently Managed Company, Pergamon Press, Oxford.

Tolliday, S., and J. Zeitlin (eds.) (1986), The Automobile Industry and its Workers. Between Fordism and Flexibility, Polity Press, Cambridge

Turner, G. (1964), The Car Makers, Penguin, London

UNCTC (1981) [United Nations Centre on Transnational Corporations], Transnational Corporation Linkages in Developing Countries: the Case of Backward Linkages via Subcontracting. A Technical Paper, New York, ST/CTC/17.

UNIDO (1974) [United Nations Industrial Development Organization], Subcontracting for Modernizing Economies, Vienna, E.74.II.B.12

Vogel, E.F. (1980), Japan as Number One: Lessons for America, Tuttle, Tokyo

Walker, G., and D. Weber (1984), "A Transaction Cost Approach to Make-or-Buy Decisions", Administrative Science Quarterly, September

Walker, R. (ed) (1985), _Applied Qualitative Research_, Gower, Aldershot

Watanabe, S. (1970), "Entrepreneurship in Small Enterprises in Japanese Manufacturing", _International Labour Review_, No.6

Watanabe, Y. (1983-84), "Shitauke kigyou no kyousou to sonritsu keitai - "Jiritsu" - teki shitauke kankei no keisei wo megutte - (Jou) (chuu) (ge) (Competition and the state of subcontracting firms - the formation of 'independent' subcontracting relationships - (1st) (2nd) (3rd))", _Mita Gakkai Zasshi_ (Bulletin of Mita Academic Society), Vol. 76, No. 2, 3; Vol. 77, No. 3

Watanabe, Y. (1989), "Nihon kikai kougyou no shakaiteki bungyou kouzou - shitaukesei kenkyuu no aratana shiza o motomete - (jou) (ge)" (Social division-of-work structure of Japan's machinery industry - seeking a new view of studies on the subcontracting system - (1st) (2nd)), _Mita Gakkai Zasshi_ (Bulletin of Mita Academic Society), Vol. 82, No. 3, 4

Williamson, O.E. (1975), _Markets and Hierarchies: Analysis and Antitrust Implications. A Study in the Economics of Internal Organization_, Free Press, New York

Williamson, O.E. (1985), _The Economic Institutions of Capitalism: Firms, Markets, Relational Contracting_, Free Press, New York

Woronoff, J. (1990), _Japan as - anything but - Number One_, Yohan, Tokyo

Yamamura, K., and Y. Yasuda (1987), _The Political Economy of Japan_, Vol.1, _The Domestic Economy_, Stanford University Press